F

Incident at Eagle Ranch

Donald G. Schueler

Incident at Eagle Ranch

Man and Predator in the American West

SIERRA CLUB BOOKS   SAN FRANCISCO

THE SIERRA CLUB,
founded in 1892 by John Muir, has devoted itself
to the study and protection of the earth's scenic
and ecological resources—mountains, wetlands,
woodlands, wild shores and rivers, deserts and
plains. The publishing program of the Sierra Club
offers books to the public as a nonprofit
educational service in the hope that they may
enlarge the public's understanding of the Club's
basic concerns. The point of view expressed in
each book, however, does not necessarily
represent that of the Club. The Sierra Club has
some fifty chapters coast to coast, in Canada,
Hawaii, and Alaska. For information about how
you may participate in its programs to preserve
wilderness and the quality of life, please address
inquiries to Sierra Club, 530 Bush Street,
San Francisco, CA 94108.

Portions of this book were previously published in
Audubon magazine.

LIBRARY OF CONGRESS CATALOGING IN
PUBLICATION DATA
Schueler, Donald G
Incident at Eagle Ranch.
Bibliography: p. 285
Includes index.
1. Poaching—Texas—Real County. 2. Golden
eagle. 3. Birds, protection of—Law and
legislation—United States. 4. Eagle Ranch,
Tex. I. Title.
SK36.7.S36   333.95'8   80-13588
ISBN 87156-230-8

Jacket design by Paul Bacon
Book design by Jon Goodchild
Printed in the United States of America
10 9 8 7 6 5 4 3 2 1

TO
WILLIE FARRELL BROWN, JR.

Contents

Acknowledgements

I AM INDEBTED to each of the hundreds of people who helped me while I was collecting information for this book. I would especially like to thank Les Line and Roxanna Sayre for the assignment that started all of this, Dede Armentrout for her invaluable assistance during my investigation of the eagle case, Betty Wisdom for the splendid job of indexing, Don Balsar for the important research information he provided, Bill Nelson for opening doors to the operations of the U.S. Fish and Wildlife Service in the Southwest, Bill Sims for helping me meet representatives of the ranching community, Roy McBride for the memorable days in the rimrock country, and Joe Matlock and Jim Stinebaugh for their patience in answering my countless questions.

Incident at
Eagle Ranch

Introduction

THE GOLDEN EAGLE, the coyote, the bobcat, and the mountain lion are notoriously inconvenient creatures; ever since the conquest of the West began, the prevalent attitude towards them has ranged rather narrowly between moderate loathing and hatred. Until recently. In the last fifteen or twenty years, during which the West has been rewon by a new, more numerous breed of more-or-less urbanized humanity, growing numbers of people have come to regard the erstwhile varmints as more beautiful than bothersome—or, even more appealingly, as the wildlife equivalent of an oppressed minority. Most important of all, they have become the focus, the *cause celebre,* for an evolving perception of all wildlife, in which esthetic, philosophic, and humane values are regarded as more significant than most utilitarian considerations.

A major consequence of this developing public attitude is an ongoing, no-holds-barred struggle between the new breed of environmentalists who are determined to promote these predators as respectable, even glamorous members of the wildlife community, and the traditional western groups, notably the ranchers and some grassroots factions in the hunting fraternity, who are determined to keep them on the Wanted List. Pro and con, passionate argument abounds. The traditionalists bitterly point out that in Washington, where the laws are made, the predator lovers win most of the rounds. The environmentalists angrily insist that out on the range, where no one can see, the varmint haters have it all their own way. On both sides there are a great many made-up minds. Bits and pieces of evidence are cited for and against. Yet, amazingly, neither side has constructed the kind of case that would stand up in a court of law.

Given that view, it is ironic that my own active involvement in the predator controversy began in a courtroom. In December 1977, Audubon magazine assigned me to cover the San Antonio trial of two ranchers and a government trapper who had been charged with conspiring to kill and/or actually killing a number of golden eagles in the nearby Texas hill country.

The eagle case, which is where this book begins, is also where I began a search for as much of the objective truth of the predator question as I could find. I knew that I had not discovered much of it at the San Antonio trial; indeed, the case was a perfect microcosm of all the tensions and contradictions that promote misunderstanding and inaccuracy in the larger controversy. I soon learned that truth was not easily come by in the available literature, either. Popular books and articles were almost invariably biased and selective in their evidence. More disturbing, when I turned to the scientists, I found that I was not much better off. Quite a bit was known about the ecology of some predators, notably the coyote, but hard data about the influence of predation on livestock and wildlife were not only conflicting but dismayingly scant. After reading widely in the professional publications, I concluded that the truth, at least a lot of it, was still out there on the range where no one could see.

During the two years since the eagle trial in San Antonio, I have traveled thousands of miles of western roads, interviewing and occasionally living with a wondrous assortment of people—trappers, biologists, enforcement agents, wildlife management officials, environmentalists, and scores of ranchers. I was lucky enough to spend considerable time in a West that I had never visited before—an immense rangeland world of rimrock and scrub, usually off-limits to outsiders, where I could observe coyotes, eagles, sheep, and ranchers being themselves in their natural habitat.

It was a powerful experience. What I learned is what this book is ambitiously about. By the last page the reader is meant to know most of what there is to know about the current uneasy relationship between predator and man in the American West. He may even know a little more than he did about the West itself. Most important, he should be able to reach some rational conclusions about the predator controversy. My temperamental bias, which I have not tried to conceal, is towards the environmental view of this angry issue. However, when I began this inquiry, I promised myself—the reader will judge to what effect—that I would not permit subjective feeling to traduce objective fact in any way, a resolution that has more than once led me out by a different door than I came in. This is not to say that I have assumed the objective pose of a scientific researcher or a reporter. I have done my best to give everyone a chance to have a say: myself included. I have felt free to comment on inconsistencies and misleading statements as well as on candor and sincere feeling wherever I met with them. And, in the later chapters, I have urged my own solutions to the controversy, solutions that I immodestly believe make better sense than some of those now supported variously by ranchers, environmentalists, and government officials.

One thing is certain: rational solutions must soon be found to the real and imagined problems that predators generate just by being themselves. To varying degrees, depending on the species, their fate is in the balance. On occasion, so is the livelihood of decent, hard-working people. Perhaps even more important, the management decisions now being made concerning predators will inevitably lead to a larger conservation ethic in which either the utilitarian or the intangible values of wildlife predominate. And those decisions will influence the fate of the West itself.

Part One

Incident at Eagle Ranch

1. The Predator Club

LATE IN THE AFTERNOON of December 10, 1975, Alfred Zimmerman and his eighteen-year-old son, Cecil, were working at the lodge of Eagle Ranch, a 6000 acre tract west of San Antonio, Texas, in the hill country of Real County. The place had recently been converted into a game preserve; whitetail and axis deer, aoudads, and Indian black buck browsed the rocky pastures where sheep and cattle had formerly grazed. Zimmerman managed the ranch for a wealthy businessman in Houston, supervising the help, making sure the plush living quarters for conventioneers and hunter guests were properly kept up, and guiding the latter to the more or less docile trophies they had come to shoot.

At about 4:15 P.M., Zimmerman and his son emerged from the lodge in time to hear the distinctive sound of an approaching helicopter, still about a mile away but well within the boundaries of the ranch. Zimmerman never doubted whose machine it was. Just a week earlier a chopper had put down next to the ranch headquarters and he had exchanged a few words with its owner-pilot, a man named Al Barnes who said he was hunting coyotes. A month before that Zimmerman had reluctantly joined a "predator club," composed of local ranchers, that had hired a helicopter company to hunt predators in the area. Zimmerman had disliked the whole idea—predators were not a problem at Eagle Ranch—but his employer had instructed him to cooperate; Real County's sheep raisers claimed, with some justice, that game

Incident at Eagle Ranch

ranches served as breeding grounds for coyotes, so it would be good public relations to go along with this effort to control them. Zimmerman obeyed, but he had reason to suspect that coyotes, never common in the hill country, were not the helicopter's only target.

The sound of the helicopter was getting closer. After a second's hesitation, Zimmerman decided to investigate. He and his son jumped into a pickup and headed towards a high bluff from which the racket seemed to come. The road led through wintry thickets of shinnery oaks, past scattering herds of dappled axis deer, over two shallow crossings of the Nueces River, and finally out onto a boulder-strewn slope overlooked by a steep red bluff.

A golden eagle, one of several that frequented the place during the winter months, swept out into the sky above the Zimmermans. Directly behind it, at a slightly higher elevation, the helicopter was in close pursuit. The bird knew it was in trouble and feinted first toward then away from the cliff; but the pilot was evidently familiar with such tactics; he steadily maneuvered the helicopter into a position from which its quarry would present an easy target. The eagle, as Cecil Zimmerman would later testify, never had a chance. Cecil's father furiously blinked the lights of the truck; he could see the gunner turning his head to look down at them. But it made no difference. Three shots followed in rapid succession. The eagle's wings collapsed against its sides, then stretched out again as the bird fell towards the slope.

The Zimmermans watched the helicopter disappear into a side canyon, then headed angrily for home, where they found Zimmerman's wife, Alyn, impatient to know what was going on. She had heard the helicopter and the shots; and when she learned the reason for them she joined her husband and son in their outraged mood.

The Zimmermans were not an introspective family. During an interview two years later, after they had ample time to examine their motives, they still found it difficult to explain why they had been so upset. When Alfred Zimmerman rather doubtfully posited the explanation that he wanted to uphold the law against killing eagles, his son Cecil had scornfully cut him short. "We like 'em, that's why. . . . We always been that way. Hell, we got this one poor old fellah—he might even have been shot—anyways, he's got a broke foot that just hangs down when he goes to flying. He stays up and down the river. But he makes it, y'know. He somehow makes it." Listening to his son, it had occurred to Mr. Zimmerman that he also liked this eagle:"We see him light down by the river on the rocks. I believe he's looking for fish." At this remark Mrs. Zimmerman's face had lit up in mock surprise. "Now you mention it, I wonder if that's the son of a bitch that's been getting my ducks!" Her husband and son had whooped mockingly at this. Not at all put out, Mrs. Zimmerman added,"I just don't know why we like them. The funny thing is, we're all hunters." "Yeah," Cecil had cut in, "but I don't just go banging away at everything I see. There's a line somewheres. Maybe if there was a lot more eagles and there was a season on them, I don't know, I might even shoot one if I could think of something to do with it. . . But even a dove, you know, I'll shoot him, but it bothers me if he's not dead. I believe I feel sorry for the old boy."

"Now I shoot doves," Mrs. Zimmerman had explained, "but I won't shoot quails. I love my quails! That quail, he's mine; he's here all the time. But those doves'll be in Mexico, and somebody is going to kill them anyway." "Ah hell," Cecil had snorted, "You don't shoot the eagles, do you? And they're gonna be gone in a few months' time." "Well then," Mrs. Zimmerman said, giving up, "I just don't know why we like them."

Mrs. Zimmerman might have difficulty explaining why she liked eagles, but she had no trouble deciding what should now be done: her husband must call Grover Grant, the local game warden, at once. Her son agreed. Mr. Zimmerman, the least impetuous of the three, hesitated. As manager of the ranch, he was supposed to stay on the good side of the neighbors. He had done his best, assuming a folksy heartiness in his dealings with them; but without any notable success. His family had never bothered to try. They knew they were outsiders, temperamentally as well as literally, and did not seem to mind. They were all outspoken and hot-headed, more apt to show anger than affection even among themselves. And Alyn Zimmerman was angry now. She told her husband that if he didn't call the game warden, she would. Zimmerman shrugged and picked up the phone. After all, he was aggravated too. When he told Grant what had happened, the warden said he would do what he could, but he reminded Zimmerman that in Texas only federal law, not state law, protected golden eagles. He also asked if the eagle's carcass had been recovered. Without that, there would be no case at all.

As soon as he hung up, Zimmerman and his son returned to the bluff. A chilling winter dark was moving in and the wind sighed along

Incident at Eagle Ranch

the limestone slope. The two men searched the stony pasture in the vicinity of a deer stand where they were both sure the eagle had come down, but found nothing. As they headed home again, Cecil suggested that maybe the bird had escaped after all. Later events would prove this hopeful surmise wrong. While the Zimmermans were phoning the game warden, the helicopter had returned. Its occupants, seeing the eagle's body lying in plain view among the rocks, had landed, picked up the incriminating trophy, and carried it away with them.

Both the eagle killers and the Zimmermans assumed that nothing further would come of the incident at Eagle Ranch. In fact, one of the most dramatic and important chapters in the annals of conservation law had only just begun.

Almost a month later, on January 7, 1976, Jim Stinebaugh, an investigative agent for U.S. Fish and Wildlife Service, received a call at his Laredo office from a Texas Parks and Wildlife supervisor stationed in Kerrville. The supervisor told him that one of his wardens, Grover Grant, had reported a possible violation of Title 16, Section 668, of the federal Bald Eagle Protection Act (which also prohibits the killing of golden eagles). Perhaps Stinebaugh might want to check it out?

Next day, January 8th, Stinebaugh visited the Eagle Ranch and heard the Zimmermans' story. Alfred Zimmerman assured him the helicopter involved was one hired by the local ranchers' recently formed predator club. At his employer's insistence, Zimmerman had attended the first meeting of the club, held the previous October at a crossroads community center about twenty miles southeast of Eagle Ranch. He recalled that some of the assembled ranchers had talked of killing eagles—a predator considered a more serious threat than coyotes to the area's sheep. And he remembered that the club's chairman, Judge W. B. Sansom, who also happened to be the long-time political master of Real County, had declared that no one in his county would be prosecuted for killing eagles as long as he was in office. Then, to Stinebaugh's surprise, Zimmerman remarked: "Some of your own people were there too."

Zimmerman was not referring to Stinebaugh's Enforcement Division, but to another agency of U.S. Fish and Wildlife, The Division of Animal Damage Control, which concerned itself with suppressing coyotes and other predators throughout the western ranching country. Apparently the local district supervisor of ADC, accompanied by one of his trappers, had handed out aerial permit forms for the ranchers to sign at the meeting and had listened to the talk of eagle killing with no visible concern.

Stinebaugh asked Zimmerman if he had signed an agreement permitting the helicopter to hunt Eagle Ranch. He said he had not. In that case, Stinebaugh realized, the pilot was violating state law, which required any aircraft service engaged in aerial predator hunting to have both a state license for that activity and a signed agreement permit for every ranch over which it flew. Zimmerman distinctly recalled that when the helicopter had landed at the lodge a few days before the eagle shooting incident, its pilot-owner had remarked that he had been hunting the Eagle Ranch—for coyotes; but no permit had been mentioned.

Alyn Zimmerman had an anecdote to add to her husband's story. The day after the shooting she had stopped at Garvin's Store, at the same crossroads where the predator club had convened months earlier. A helicopter was parked near the building, refueling. She never doubted that this was the same machine her husband and son had seen. How many choppers could be whirring around Real County in less than 24 hours? She had advanced on the three men standing next to it, none of whom she knew, and, in her usual forthright way, had "cussed them out." According to her, they smirked, looked uncomfortable, and claimed not to know what she was talking about. When she turned away she announced over her shoulder that from then on it would be "open season on all helicopters" at the Eagle Ranch.

Stinebaugh was not sure whether he had the makings of a case or not. When he visited the bluff with Alfred Zimmerman, they had no luck discovering the missing *corpus delecti;* and neither Zimmerman nor his son had thought to note the helicopter's number though it must have been plainly visible from the ground. Still, the story intrigued him, especially when he visited a couple of nearby ranches that same afternoon. From their owners he learned that Zimmerman's call to the game warden was already common knowledge, and that some Animal Damage Control people had indeed been present at the meeting of the predator club. One rancher also admitted that the helicopter had hunted his land without a signed permit. But for the most part the neighbors seemed uneasy and uncommunicative, as though they knew more than they wished to tell.

Stinebaugh decided to pursue the matter. If Zimmerman was to be believed, Real County ranchers and the helicopter people they had hired

Incident at Eagle Ranch

were not adverse to shooting eagles; and the helicopter company was certainly guilty of violating the state's permit law. Most troubling of all, there was the possibility that "federal people" were in some way suspect. He called his supervisor, Gust Nun, at Fish and Wildlife's regional office in Albuquerque, New Mexico, and briefed him on what he had thus far learned. Nun told him he would discuss the matter with Bill Nelson, the regional director of Fish and Wildlife. Next day, he called Stinebaugh back. He was to go ahead with the investigation even if Fish and Wildlife people were involved. Nelson had said—and Nun quoted—"let the chips fall where they may."

It is one of the curiosities of the eagle case that the main characters were so representative of the various, usually contentious, forces involved, that within the intense context of the investigation, their comments and actions, even their personalities, assumed an almost archetypal rigidity. There was nothing half-way about them. They became The Conspirator(s); The Informer; The Meddler; The Loyal Friend; The Behind-The-Scenes Bigshot.

And, of course, the Young Hero: Jim Stinebaugh was the law enforcement agent incarnate. He showed every sign of genuinely believing in the laws he had sworn to uphold, and he could be downright relentless in pursuing people who broke them. He grew up not far south of Real County in a very small town with the Oz-sounding name of Crystal City, the son of a postal employee father and a strong-minded mother, neither of whom believed in overindulging children. He worked on ranches during the summer months, went hunting with his friends on winter weekends, and watched westerns at the local movie house, learning there, as well as at home, that Texans should "walk tall." Physically on the short side, he carried himself ramrod straight and, like all males west of San Antonio, wore cowboy boots and hat so that he seemed taller than he was. Also like the other males of the region, he could cuss and drink when the occasion required, but he didn't do it routinely. He believed unashamedly in the Boy Scout virtues and tried to keep his life as upright as his posture. In Crystal City, such ideals were not considered aberrant.

He always had a generalized interest in the out-of-doors. During a stint in the Marine Corps he was deputized as a game warden at the California base where he was stationed. He took an instant liking to the work and decided he would make a career for himself in the wildlife

8   field. A year at Texas A & M convinced him he didn't want to be a wild-life biologist, so he passed a qualifying examination and became a state game warden instead. He was assigned to Duval County in south Texas, and there began a career remarkable for the controversy it has generated. Typically, Stinebaugh described his first assignment in positivist terms: "If you were going to pick a place to start out as a game warden, you couldn't do better than Duval County. Lots of wildlife, and all the illegal hunters you could ask for. I wouldn't take anything for that experience." Understandably, Duval County's illegal hunters did not share the young warden's enthusiasm about becoming learning experiences, expecially after Stinebaugh had rounded up a good many of them.

Stinebaugh had not been on the job long before he learned that the most compulsive poacher in the county was also its leading citizen, George Parr, otherwise known as the "Duke of Duval." Parr's title had no official sanction but it described exactly the measure of his power. Although in his later years he disdained official positions and did not even own much property in his own name, he controlled immense land holdings through relatives and sycophants, and doled out every political and patronage job in the county. His influence reached far beyond the county's frontiers, never more so than when he arranged the notorious "Ballot Box 13 incident," the apparently rigged election at Alice, Texas, which launched Lyndon Johnson on his political career. The large Mexican-American population in south Texas, accustomed to the *patron* system, approved Parr's high-handedness; and the Anglos, most of them, did too. In contrast to power brokers in other states, who tend to be discreet, Parr, like many other influential Texans, subscribed frankly to the dictum that the only point in having power was being able to flaunt it.

The "Duke" possessed a collection of whitetailed deer heads large enough to fill the Smithsonian (where some of them ended up). All of these trophies were equipped with heavy antlers except one small buck. Parr would point to this diminutive specimen and explain that it was the only legal deer he had ever shot. Most of his constituents considered the remark the very pinnacle of wit, but Stinebaugh, when he heard of it, was not amused. He decided he would "get" George Parr.

Parr was particularly noted for shooting deer from a helicopter and Stinebaugh on several occasions tried unsuccessfully to catch him in the act. The confrontation finally came one night when Parr and a bodyguard were more conventionally jack-lighting deer—a practice that allows a poacher an easy shot while the deer is immobilized by a blinding beam of light. As soon as the young warden accosted them, the Duke and his henchman took off, and a wild chase ensued through the Texas night at speeds sometimes in excess of 100 m.p.h., with Parr drawing a bead on Stinebaugh everytime he pulled up alongside. The pursuit went on until state troopers finally intercepted the speeding cars. The troopers, expecting to arrest a teenager or a drunken cowpoke, were understandably dismayed when they discovered who they had caught. Parr was promptly released; but the old man was a tartar, notorious for his rages, and he swore both in English and Spanish that he would have Stinebaugh's hide for this indignity. His frame of mind was not improved when the news media, amused by the David and Goliath aspect of the story, played it up.

Some nights later, a trap was set for Stinebaugh, a staged jacklighting that would lure him to an isolated spot where several of Parr's henchmen lay in wait for him. The agent obligingly drove right into the planned ambush, but luckily his supervisor was accompanying him on his rounds that night; the plotters canceled their plan. The next day a state senator belatedly warned Stinebaugh's supervisor that his warden's life was in real danger; and the senator proceeded to describe in some detail the plot that had just miscarried. For Stinebaugh and his wife, Virginia, whom he had only recently married, the next forty-eight hours were bizarre and incomprehensible. A state conservation officer abruptly escorted her from the sixth grade class she was teaching and sequestered her at the home of a rancher friend—none too securely it turned out; an unidentified helicopter circled the house during the several hours of her stay. Meanwhile, the protesting Stinebaugh was being told by his superiors to move himself and his wife at once to a district far removed from the angry Parr; their belongings, he was assured, would be sent after them. A long day's drive later, the exhausted couple arrived in the town of San Saba, in central Texas, with nothing but their dog and the contents of a couple of suitcases to remind them of the life they had lived in Duval County.

Stinebaugh still refuses to believe that Parr would have gone through with the plan to have him killed. "He wanted to show everybody he could run me off," he says bitterly, "and that's exactly what he did. I had the naive idea that this was a case of the state versus George Parr, but of course it wasn't that at all." Political pressure, some said, was brought to bear by Senator Wayne Connally (brother of the ex-governor) on Texas Parks and Wildlife in an effort to get Stinebaugh fired; if this occurred, the agency resisted. Nevertheless, Stinebaugh was "pretty disenchanted" with the way matters had worked out and a few months later he quit his job.

For two years he was employed by the U.S. Border Patrol, coralling "wetbacks" and smugglers; but he sorely missed working in the wildlife field. When he was eventually offered a position with the U.S. Fish and Wildlife Service's Enforcement Division, he jumped at the chance. The federal government, he felt sure, would be immune to the influence of privileged and arrogant men. He resolved that he would never again be "run-off" by anyone.

During the late seventies, he was stationed in Laredo, not far from George Parr's home county. By this time the old man was besieged by illness, family problems, and the IRS, and his feud with the smart-aleck young game warden no longer seemed to matter. The "Duke of Duval" killed himself not long before the incident at Eagle Ranch occurred.

With his supervisor's permission, Stinebaugh asked an old friend, Joe Matlock, to help with the eagle case. Matlock, the senior resident agent for the Houston subdistrict, was then almost sixty and soon to retire. He was a sociable but crusty man, with a piercing blue stare, a salty vocabulary, a taste for red rum, and a habit of talking out of the corner of his mouth. His round, choleric face and veteran's mien were a perfect match for Stinebaugh's Clark Kent good looks and crisp professional style. During the months to follow, the friendship between the two would steadily deepen. Matlock would later remark that if he had a son—he had lost his own—he would want him to be "just like Jim."

Their first step was to interview Jim Beavers, the U.S. Animal Damage Control supervisor for the Uvalde–Real County district, who had taken part in organizing the Real County predator club. On January 19, 1976, they went to Uvalde. Beavers, a gentle but fidgety man, was visibly unnerved by their visit, particularly when Stinebaugh, as a matter of form, read him his rights. To the agents' astonishment, the supervisor took the fifth amendment soon after they began to ask him questions about the meeting at Garvin's Store community center. After a few minutes, he did calm down enough to admit that he had been present, but only to discuss complaints about coyotes in the hill country; he had heard no talk of killing eagles. He also volunteered that he had been accompanied by one of his trappers, a man named Andrew Allen, and by Al Barnes, the co-owner of South Texas Helicopter Service which was headquartered in Uvalde. He had brought them along because Allen was his most experienced aerial gunner and Barnes' helicopter company was the closest one available to Real County. Also, it was under contract with ADC to do aerial control work in the district (although in the case of the Real County hunt no ADC funds had been requested).

Stinebaugh asked Beavers to show him the records, required by law, of any aerial hunts in Real County in which Allen or Barnes had been involved, particularly those for December 10th, 1976, when Alfred and Cecil Zimmerman had witnessed the shooting at the bluff, and December 11th, when Alyn Zimmerman had seen a helicopter parked at Garvin's store. At this request, the already nervous supervisor began to panic. According to Matlock, "He like to had a heart attack." He told the agents that if they wanted to see his records they would have to get clearance from his boss, Milton Caroline, the head of U.S. Animal Damage Control in Texas. In the meantime, he would tell them nothing more.

First thing next morning, Stinebaugh and Matlock invited Andrew Allen to have coffee with them at Uvalde's Ramada Inn. The ADC trapper was a small wiry man with a large drooping moustache. He was not at all surprised by this invitation, and in dealing with the agents he was a striking contrast to Beavers; "cool and flip," in Stinebaugh's words. When he was asked whether he had killed, or tried to kill, an eagle on December 10th, he cheerfully answered, "Keep shooting, boys, you ain't hitting nothing yet." He acknowledged that he "rode shotgun" that day for the Real County ranchers' club, but insisted that coyotes and bobcats were the only targets. He also identified the pilot as a man who worked for Barnes, Jerry Heintzelman; but when asked who else might have been involved in the aerial hunt, he became vague. As though to redirect the line of questioning, he made a sudden, unexpected confession: "If you boys want to get my job," Matlock remembers him saying, "you got it, because the records'll show I was somewhere else."

Allen had already been warned of the agents' interest in Beavers' records by the supervisor himself, and had decided to admit to a forgery which he assumed they would eventually discover anyway. He told them that he had doctored his reports and travel vouchers for three days— December 10–12—when he was aerial gunning in Real County; the

The Predator Club

12   forms would wrongly indicate that he had spent the interval in Uvalde County, running a trap line, and had claimed 200 miles in auto mileage. Yet in spite of this admission, he maintained an almost jaunty, by no means repentant air. He had helped the Real County ranchers "out of the goodness of my heart," and had forged the travel vouchers so he could get some compensation for the time he had volunteered. He assured the agents that neither the government, the ranchers, nor Al Barnes had paid him anything for his efforts.

After Allen's departure, Stinebaugh and Matlock headed for South Texas Helicopter Service's office at the Uvalde airport, where they met Al Barnes, a burly, red-faced man wearing a stained white cowboy hat. He was polite enough on this occasion but made it clear that he had nothing to say. He referred them to Alvin Connell, his business partner, for records of company activities; his own memory for such details was very poor. The agents, of course, had no legal right to press him further. However, as they were about to walk away, Stinebaugh, acting on a hunch, asked if he would tell them where he had flown that very morning; surely he could at least remember that? After an instant's hesitation, Barnes gave them the name of a rancher, Dick Herndon, on whose ranch he and his partner, Connell, had been hunting coyotes.

Back in town, the agents contacted a friend of theirs, Raymond Custer, a Texas state game warden for the Uvalde area, and asked him to drive out to the Herndon ranch to see what might be learned. Meantime they returned to Beaver's office to check Allen's forged records. The place was locked, and when they showed up at the supervisor's home, his wife told them he was too ill to speak to anyone.

Later that day, Stinebaugh and Matlock met with their warden friend, Custer. He had some news for them, he said, that would "blow your skirt up." While driving out to the Herndon ranch, he had picked up a conversation on his CB between an unidentified person and Herndon himself, in which the shooting of eagles was being discussed. Unfortunately, Custer had caught only a fragment of the exchange, with no times or places mentioned. When he later confronted Herndon, asking him if he knew anything about an eagle killing, the rancher looked startled but denied any such knowledge. He did say that Barnes and Connell had hunted coyotes on his place and he had paid them for it; he also admitted they had not asked him to sign an agreement form—still another instance in which the helicopter company had violated the state's

Incident at Eagle Ranch

regulations on aerial hunting. Armed with this information, Stinebaugh called Al Springs, the appropriate official at Texas Parks and Wildlife, and told him what he had learned thus far. Springs thanked him and said he would look into the matter himself.

The next day the agents contacted Milton Caroline, the ADC Director in Texas, and tried to persuade him to meet them in Uvalde to help examine Beavers' records. They had contacted him before this but he had been "too busy" to leave San Antonio. Judging from his complaints to the Albuquerque office, Caroline felt that the agents had not sufficiently respected the bureaucratic chain of command; in other words, they had begun their investigation without consulting him. Even now when he knew about Allen's forged expense accounts, he agreed to come only as far as Hondo, a town just halfway between Uvalde and San Antonio.

The meeting was not exactly successful from the agents' point of view. Caroline was a commanding sort of person with a pedagogical style, who made it clear that he was more accustomed to asking questions than answering them. He assured Stinebaugh and Matlock that if there was any wrongdoing in the Uvalde office he could handle it himself. In fact, he would not tolerate even the suspicion of guilt. If Allen merely *seemed* guilty, Caroline would fire him. As for Beavers, he had talked to the man and it was clear that he was on the verge of a nervous breakdown; the agents should leave him alone. Stinebaugh and Matlock had protested desperately at this: if Beavers was too sick to be interviewed further, and Allen was dismissed—and thereby removed from their inter-agency jurisdiction—the investigation would be seriously hampered. Caroline was unmoved. He advised them, somewhat loftily, that he would get in touch with Allen and do whatever was necessary.

That night, when the agents returned to Uvalde, Allen called them at their motel. He cheerfully announced that Caroline had just fired him, that he was no longer subject to their questioning, and he had nothing further to say.

The following Monday, January 26, Stinebaugh and Matlock presented themselves at the expensive-looking suburban residence of Alvin Connell, vice-president of South Texas Helicopter Service and operator of several large west Texas ranches. He was extravagantly

The Predator Club

friendly, assured the agents of his wish to cooperate, and even allowed them to briefly thumb through some of the records he had on hand. He told them that although ranchers and county governments often paid the helicopter service out of their own pockets for control work, a large percentage of the company's revenues derived from ADC contracts for aerial predator hunts, and company officials would be very foolish to jeopardize that income by shooting eagles. He was sure that all the records were in order, and if they came to the office tomorrow they could make copies of whatever they wanted.

Next day, however, the office was locked. At the airport, they did find Jerry Heintzelman, the pilot who had flown Allen on his Real County hunting spree, but the young man had obviously been warned to expect them. He cut their questions short and walked away.

The agents were in their motel room that evening, debating their next move, when the telephone rang. It was Alvin Connell, apologizing for missing them at his office, and inviting them instead to come next day to the office of the company's attorney, Jack Ware. They could talk further then.

Though the agents could not know it at the time, the group gathered in the ante-room of Ware's office next morning included most of the major participants in the case that would develop. Besides Alvin Connell and the attorney, Jack Ware, there were half a dozen men sitting or standing in the crowded room: Andrew Allen; Al Barnes; Jerry Heintzelman; and three others whom the agents had not thus far met: Lanny Leinweber, a sheep rancher and Real County commissioner; Clay Hunt, a multi-millionaire and self-described silent partner in the helicopter service who remained quietly on the sidelines during the ensuing scene; and Judge W. B. Sansom, the old-line politician and friend of Texas governors who was reputed to run Real County as he pleased.

Judge Sansom was seated at the secretary's desk. Pounding his fist, he demanded to know what crime Stinebaugh and Matlock were investigating and what evidence they had found. When Stinebaugh answered that they were checking out a reported violation of the Bald Eagle Act, the attorney, Ware, snorted angrily that there were no bald eagles in south Texas. The Judge, after unsuccessfully trying to learn just why the agents had been questioning some of the people in the room, accused them of getting "this fine boy Andy Allen" fired from his job with Animal Damage Control. Allen grinned. Still pounding his fist, Sansom declared that "if any of my people have done anything wrong, I've got a right to know." Ware, cursing heartily, warned the investigators that they had better not harass his clients further. Al Barnes joined in, demanding angrily that the agents should arrest him if they had anything on him, or else leave him the hell alone.

Stinebaugh and Matlock waited through about fifteen minutes of this curious and noisy proceeding, Stinebaugh's mouth getting thinner, Matlock's face redder, all the while. Finally Stinebaugh, deciding enough was enough, announced that he and Matlock were leaving; but they would be glad to talk individually to any of those present if they had anything more to say. At this point, Jack Ware abruptly volunteered that if they wished to question Jerry Heintzelman they could do so now in his private office, with himself as Heintzelman's attorney. The agents agreed. The pilot was calm during the subsequent interview, denying any knowledge of eagle killings. He explained that he was a native Pennsylvanian, new to the area, and that he flew wherever the gunners wanted him to go. He had been up in Real County with Allen last December, but they were shooting coyotes, not eagles; and he had no idea what ranches they had hunted. While he talked, Ware sat nearby, intent and, for a change, silent.

Stinebaugh and Matlock returned to their motel room to discuss this unexpected encounter. The fact that Barnes, Connell, et al., had recruited Ware and Judge Sansom to try to browbeat the agents suggested more than a shared sense of righteous indignation. Obviously, they were worried. Sansom's involvement was particularly interesting. Notwithstanding his concern for "my people," almost everyone the agents had interviewed was from Uvalde County, not Real. Then there was Lanny Leinweber, the Real County supervisor and rancher; he, at any rate, was one of Sansom's "people"—but he had not figured in the case until now, although Zimmerman had mentioned him as one of the ranchers who attended the meeting at Garvin's Store. And there was the pilot, Heintzelman. The fact that Ware had arranged to have him interviewed in his office suggested that this young outsider was perhaps considered a frail reed by his cohorts.

Added together, these implications confirmed Stinebaugh's and Matlock's strong suspicion that the case involved quite a bit more than just that "fine boy Andy Allen's" expense account, or even a single impul-

The Predator Club

sive attempt to shoot an eagle. "We knew it was a conspiracy," says Stinebaugh, "and we knew it involved all these people, ranchers, some ADC
people, Barnes and his crew; but we didn't know how they all fit in."

A conspiracy, of course, required something to conspire about, and
the agents were pretty sure they had the answer to that, too: an attempt
was under way to resurrect the custom of killing large numbers of eagles
in the Texas hill country with the aid of aircraft. This practice had once
been common throughout west Texas and other sheep raising areas of
the West, and had been used with telling effect. In Texas alone, several
hundred migrant eagles were slain each winter, and the resident population had been almost wholly annihilated. The inclusion of the golden
eagle in the Bald Eagle Protection Act in 1962 had been meant to put a
stop to this wholesale killing, but sheepmen, especially in Texas, had
protested furiously, and there was some question whether the law could
be enforced. In May, 1963, a year after the act was passed, a U.S. Fish
and Wildlife Enforcement supervisor in Texas, Kenard Baer, wrote the
Regional Director in Albuquerque: "We found several indications that
there was some airplane hunting going on . . . Evidence is very difficult
to obtain and our feeling is that even in the unlikely event we could make
an apprehension with good evidence, a successful prosecution in the
study area would be *impossible.* An undercover operation is a must if
unauthorized airplane hunting becomes a serious problem." During that
year and the next, researchers and wardens in the hill country noted,
and sometimes photographed, the bodies of numerous eagles defiantly
displayed on ranchers' fences, along with the usual lineup of coyote,
hawk, and bobcat carcasses. Then, in the late sixties, a case in Wyoming
attracted national attention. A wealthy and influential rancher was
charged with a slaughter of hundreds of eagles, many of the bodies
found rotting in a pit. Before the man could be brought to trial, however,
he was killed in an auto accident. There had been almost universal
agreement at the time that even if he had been found guilty, the sentence
would have been the rock-bottom minimum allowed by law. ·

Stinebaugh and Matlock had little cause to feel confident about
their investigation's prospects. It was anything but an undercover operation, evidence was as difficult as ever to obtain, and there was no reason
to suppose that the chances of a "successful prosecution in the study
area" were any better than they had ever been.

But even without these unpromising considerations, the two men
had enough to brood about. The session in Ware's office had shaken

them more than they cared to admit. Much later, the mere thought of that day would set Matlock pacing the floor of his living room, nipping his red rum. "You should have heard them," he would growl, "even though they weren't entitled to know a damn thing about that investigation! They were trying to put us on trial." Later still, Stinebaugh would remark, "I felt like I'd been there before. I was getting a little tired of folks who were too used to having their own way."

A week later, on February 3, 1976, Stinebaugh and Matlock's complaints to the Albuquerque office finally had the desired effect: Milton Caroline came to Uvalde. In his presence, the two men were allowed to open the file cabinet in Beavers' office—the supervisor himself was still in hiding—only to discover that the records they contained were worthless.

U.S. Fish and Wildlife regulations require that ADC trappers must fill out travel vouchers, rancher agreement permits, and weekly itineraries whenever they run a trap line or take part in an aerial hunt. In the case of aerial hunts, the names of the aircraft company and pilot as well as the number of predators taken are supposed to be filled in. District supervisors like Beavers are expected to examine these reports, approve them, and send them on to Caroline's federal office for review. From there copies go to Texas A & M and then the state treasurer's office, being checked along the way. That is the theoretical procedure. In practise—well, there was no practise, as the agents quickly learned. Almost all of the required information was missing; and even in the generally poor showing, Andrew Allen's records were remarkable for the blank spaces they contained. During the three days in December when he claimed he was running a trap line in Uvalde while actually aerial gunning in Real, his reports indicated nothing except the falsified expenses and the county: Uvalde. For December 12, the report was totally blank except for Allen's name. As Matlock would observe, "It was like he didn't care a damn if he was caught. Either that, or he knew for certain he wasn't going to be checked."

Caroline accounted for these procedural deviations by insisting again that Beavers was not a well man, and that he, Caroline, was investigating the matter now. When Stinebaugh asked him about the hundreds of hours of aerial gunning in which Beavers' ADC district and South Texas Helicopter were involved together, Caroline explained that ADC in all the western states had recently received an extra appropriation, more than a million dollars, for aerial predator control, and Texas had been allocated its fair share. It was generally assumed that President

The Predator Club

Ford had arranged for this largesse to keep the ranchers happy during the upcoming election year. South Texas Helicopter Service had, of course, benefited too.

While Stinebaugh and Caroline were talking, Matlock prowled about the office. When he glanced at an expense account lying in plain view on Beavers' desk, the signature leaped out at him. It proved to be a voucher filled out a day or two earlier by Andrew Allen. Yet Allen was still telling everyone in Uvalde that he had been fired. And Caroline himself had not said otherwise. Matlock angrily waved the document at the ADC director. If Allen was fired, why the hell was he still filling out expense account forms? Caroline, who until that moment had maintained a rather haughty, if not actually martyred, demeanor in the presence of the agents, was clearly discomfited. He first insisted that Allen had indeed been fired and that the voucher must be a mistake. When pressed, however, he explained that he had not meant to say the trapper was "fired," only suspended. He went on to explain that the suspension had never gone into effect. Caroline had talked the matter over with his regional supervisor in Albuquerque and it had been agreed that Allen would be more useful to the investigation if he remained on the payroll. Stinebaugh and Matlock pointed out that they had several times mentioned the trapper's name that morning, but Caroline had neglected to tell them of this decision; and even more mysteriously, Allen was still giving it out that he was fired even as he signed expense vouchers and went about his job. But the Director, who had recovered his composure, made it clear that he had explained the matter to his own satisfaction, if not theirs.

In questioning Caroline further, the agents also learned that Beavers, despite his supposed illness, was not on sick leave. They demanded that Caroline let them interview both men again. When the Director resisted the idea, Stinebaugh called the Albuquerque office and succeeded in getting the needed clearance.

The interviews took place the next day, but with a minimum of privacy. Caroline brought his San Antonio office manager, Thomas Fowler, to Uvalde as a witness; and Allen and Beavers were accompanied by the cantankerous Jack Ware. Stinebaugh wondered silently what Ware was doing there. "He was the helicopter company's attorney, so why was he representing Beavers and Allen?"

Allen repeated his earlier admission about the forged expense account. Asked why he had not filled in his reports, he tapped his forehead and replied, "It's all up here." He evaded further questions about his whereabouts on December 10–12 by saying he couldn't remember anything. Beavers' memory was equally deficient, but his manner was less composed. Questioned about the trappers' records he was supposed to check, he cried, "I can't take any more of this. I'm an old man!" and when Stinebaugh asked him whether Allen, or anyone connected with South Texas Helicopter Service, might have been killing eagles, he shouted, "I don't blame them if they was. If those things was on my land, I'd kill them too!"

"He said that," Matlock recalls, "right in front of Caroline. Here was a man working for the king's shilling, and he could say a thing like that! And when you'd ask him why the records were in bad shape, or where he'd been, his memory would fail him just like his health. The best you could say for him was that he was inefficient as a pissant; although that's unfair to pissants. A hard working pissant would have been a model he could follow."

However, inefficiency is not a crime. During the next several days, the agents interviewed various ranchers whom they suspected of being connected with the case. Always they had the sense of people knowing more than they would tell; but because of Beavers' worthless reports, and the unavailability of the helicopter company's records, they were unable to pin down the activities of Allen, Barnes, Heintzelman, and the others to specific times and places. It was thankless work; the ranchers and their wives did not conceal their resentment at being questioned.

Then, on February 9, the case took a different turn. The Real County game warden, Grover Grant, advised Stinebaugh that two brothers, Rex and Steve Davenport, had been inquiring in Leakey, the county seat, about where they might find a taxidermist who would mount an eagle. According to rumor, one of the brothers had said the bird was shot from a helicopter. On hearing this, Stinebaugh took off for Real County almost before Grant had a chance to hang up. That evening, when Rex Davenport left his job at a Leakey cedar mill, the agent was waiting for him. Davenport, flustered by this display of federal interest, told what he knew: a few nights earlier, he and his brother, Steve, had been jacklighting ringtailed cats, raccoons, and other "varmints" (a legal practise in Texas) on the Prade, a game ranch north of Leakey managed by their cousin, Dennis Davenport. Their spotlights had picked out a large bird that was "acting kind of sick." Steve Davenport delivered the *coup de grace* with his .22. (He would later claim that he realized he had killed a golden eagle only after recovering its body.) The bird had indeed been sick; there was a large, festering wound in its wing. Since Steve had recently noticed a helicopter "working" the canyons of the Prade, he had simply assumed that it was responsible for the eagle's injury.

Rex Davenport acknowledged that the eagle cadaver still reposed in a freezer at the Prade. Stinebaugh, accompanied by the reluctant young mill worker, drove to the ranch that evening and, after identifying himself to Dennis Davenport, the manager, confiscated the body of an immature golden eagle, wrapped in a plastic shroud, in the name of the U.S. Government. Greatly excited by this new find, he drove back to Uvalde and called Matlock, who had returned to his post in Victoria a few days earlier. The two men took the body to a local veterinarian to be x-rayed. Matlock recalls that two or three ranchers who were at the animal hospital on other business were much agog at these proceedings. The veterinarian, pointing first to the place where Davenport's .22 had penetrated the eagle's chest cavity, then to the much larger wing area darkened by a shotgun pattern, drily observed that the agents could "rule out pneumonia as the cause of death."

The agents returned to the Prade ranch, this time accompanied by Rex's brother, Steve, who led them to the steep, rock strewn bluff where he had put an end to the eagle's misery. Stinebaugh promptly waded the icy, shallow stream at the base of the escarpment, and began exploring the juniper studded scree on the other side. A few minutes later he returned, grim and triumphant, holding in his arms the desiccated body of yet another golden eagle.

When they returned to Prade Ranch headquarters and questioned the foreman, Dennis Davenport, they turned up one additional clue: at about the time his cousin Steve had noticed a helicopter working the ranch, Dennis had received a call from his neighbor, Buddy Pape, the manager of the Dan Auld ranch—a sheep and goat operation—which adjoined the Prade to the north. Pape had explained that a helicopter, hired by Real County sheep ranchers, was hunting predators on the Auld ranch. If it chased a coyote onto the Prade, was it all right to come after it? Davenport had readily given his permission; like Zimmerman's boss, he wanted to stay on the right side of his sheep raising neighbors.

Joe Matlock listened to this information with particular interest. He had worked as an agent in Real County many years ago and knew the Dan Auld ranch; its owner had been an old-timer even then, strong-willed, rich, and leather-tough. Matlock dimly recalled that Auld had travelled all the way to Washington in 1962 to testify in opposition to the bill that would include the golden eagle in the Bald Eagle Protection Act.

The agents stopped by Pape's home, but he wasn't there and his wife did not know when he would return. The two men drove back to Uvalde in moody silence. They had been so preoccupied with questioning the Davenports, finding the eagles' bodies, checking dates, that it had just now struck them that these killings must have occurred sometime between the day Grover Grant had notified his supervisor of Alfred Zimmerman's complaint, and the day four weeks later when the supervisor finally contacted Stinebaugh.

In mid-February, Stinebaugh and Matlock brought their findings to the attention of Wayne Speck, Chief of the U.S. District Attorney's Criminal Division in San Antonio. Speck was interested, but with no one except Zimmerman, who could not identify anyone, as a witness, indictments were out of the question. As for the helicopter company's permit violations, that was a state affair, as was Allen's forged expense account. Besides, such offenses had no "sex appeal." The attorney decided they had better go for an investigative grand jury instead.

Andrew Allen, Al Barnes, and Jim Beavers appeared before the grand jury on February 24, 1976. This was an investigative proceeding, not designed to produce indictments; but it had three significant consequences: One of these was that the subpoenaed men were required to swear under oath that they had not, as Allen put it, killed "eagles or any other type of buzzard." In the heirarchy of judicial sins, killing an eagle was a misdemeanor, but lying before a grand jury was a felony. Thus, if any of these men were later convicted of the misdemeanor, they would also be subject to prosecution for the felony.

Second, since records of the South Texas Helicopter Service had been subpoenaed, they were now available to Matlock and Stinebaugh, who had them copied.

The third result was that Texas Parks and Wildlife revoked the helicopter service's aerial hunting permit a day or two before the grand jury was to meet. Until now, the man in charge of issuing the permits, Al Springs, had not shown much interest in the violations uncovered by Stinebaugh and Matlock, but the prospect of a federal grand jury hearing had apparently spurred him to take action.

These developments, though promising to begin with, would come to nothing, at least in the short term. After giving their testimony, the subpoenaed men went home, convinced that the grand jury had more or

The Predator Club

less cleared them. As for the helicopter company records, there was abundant evidence that they had been fabricated, and none too carefully. Barnes, for example, often reported that he had herded sheep or cattle by air for certain ranches; but the ranchers themselves unwittingly contradicted Barnes's reports by saying they had paid him to hunt predators—coyotes, of course—on the days in question. Unfortunately, these discrepancies, while adding to the company's list of state violations, brought Stinebaugh and Matlock no closer to a resolution of the eagle case, and the ranchers now greeted the agents with frank hostility. "Out in this country," Matlock rumbles, "it's like a slap in the face not to offer someone a cup of coffee. Or not to walk him to the door when you're done talking. But we got used to finding the door for ourselves." Stinebaugh remembers visiting the Silver Lake Ranch, a site of some importance in the case, as subsequent events would prove. The manager, a man named Ballew, was on horseback when the agent walked up and introduced himself. "In ranch country," Stinebaugh explains, "it's unheard of to stay mounted while a man is trying to talk to you. But Ballew just sat up there, looking down at me, letting his horse stamp back and forth. I told myself right then that if I ever had a chance to bring him down off that saddle, I would surely do it."

The ranchers' ill-feeling did not always end at their thresholds. An influential state senator, Lloyd Bentsen, persuaded by one of his wealthy constituents, demanded an investigation of Stinebaugh and Matlock's activities, in an unsuccessful attempt to prove they were "harassing" those they questioned. Matlock snorts, "We were being polite as hell. They were the ones harassing us."

The most interesting non-result of the grand jury hearing concerned the revocation of the helicopter service's permit. Jack Ware, the company's hot tempered and influential attorney, wasted no time in requesting Texas Parks and Wildlife to review Al Springs' decision. Stinebaugh provided the state's attorney with evidence of some thirty violations, including falsified company records and the names of people who could testify, including Al Zimmerman, Matlock and himself. From these, the lawyer for Texas Parks and Wildlife chose a single violation (Al Barnes' failure to obtain a permit before hunting the Eagle Ranch), assuring the agent that one would suffice. At the ensuing hearing, however, Stinebaugh claims he was not permitted to produce witnesses or enter other evidence. Even the cancelled checks made out to Al Barnes for his services were not considered sufficient proof that he had hunted the ranch in question without a permit. Since the state made no effort to pursue other allegations or conduct its own investigation, the company's license was quickly restored.

The reasons for this "farce," as Matlock calls it, have been variously explained. Veteran Parks and Wildlife officials in the field detect the influence of then-Governor Dolph Briscoe. He is a native of Uvalde and reputedly the largest individual landowner in the state, with extensive holdings in the town's vicinity. His views on predators, particularly eagles, had been much publicized the previous year, when he unsuccessfully petitioned the U.S. Department of Interior to open the western third of the state to uncontrolled eagle hunting. He was also a friend of Auld, Sansom, and various people connected with South Texas Helicopter. The company had hunted predators on his ranches; and at least one ADC trapper was kept busy full-time running traplines on his land.

But there is no evidence connecting Briscoe with Texas Parks and Wildlife's decision to restore the helicopter service's license, and there are those who feel his direct intervention was not necessary. Texas Parks and Wildlife officials had their own reasons for acting as they did. The later statements of some of the agency's officials clearly indicate that they resented the federal investigation, partly because they detested federal meddling on principle, partly because it called into question the state's ability to police its own aerial hunting permit system. Whatever the reason, South Texas Helicopter Service was back in business again. At the ADC office in San Antonio, Milton Caroline noted the outcome of the state hearing. During the next year and a half, he saw to it that ADC's already generous contracts with the company were substantially increased. Beavers and Allen remained on his payroll.

The investigation had now lost all momentum. Stinebaugh and Matlock realized that as far as the eagle killings were concerned, they did not have a case; at least not until they found an eye-witness willing to testify. They were disappointed about this, but what really embittered them was the failure in cooperation at the state and federal level. "It was too bad things didn't work out better," Stinebaugh says. "We had great cooperation from our regional law enforcement office; and a lot of Texas wardens helped us out. But in the places we needed it most we got the rug pulled out. ADC and Texas Parks and Wildlife had all our stuff. They knew those helicopter people were doing wrong. If Parks and

Wildlife hadn't reinstated Barnes' license, the cracks in his outfit would have started to show a lot sooner than they did. Same thing with Caroline. If he had stopped funding the company—he was under no obligation to go on doing that—or if he had put pressure on Beavers and Allen instead of protecting them. . . . As it was, all those people thought they were in the clear now. They could go on doing anything they liked. A lot more eagles had to die because of that."

Stinebaugh and Matlock could no longer justify spending time on an investigation that had come to a dead end. Their respective offices in Laredo and Houston were swamped with cases needing their attention. "The eagle thing just went into limbo," Stinebaugh remarks, "but I kept thinking about it, off and on. I knew it was important. It just kept sort of ticking away in a corner of my mind."

If Stinebaugh was downcast by the apparent outcome of the investigation, his wife was not. "The Redhead" was Stinebaugh's cowboy-sounding nickname for his wife, Virginia, who for two and a half months had scarcely seen her husband. She had missed him; but it was more than just that: she still remembered the Duval County episode all too vividly. She asked herself how her husband could ever get anywhere if he was always getting himself embroiled in controversy, making powerful people angry with him. During their years together, Stinebaugh's enthusiasm for wild animals had communicated itself to her; she worried about what would happen to the eagles too. But whenever she remembered being pulled out of that Duval County classroom and ending up in a strange town next day, she was glad the eagle case had been dropped.

For more than a year, Barnes, Heintzelman, and the other people at South Texas Helicopter Service went about their business, herding cattle and gunning for coyotes and bobcats. And, as events would prove, killing large numbers of eagles on the side. Beavers and Allen, still unrebuked, continued to work for the U.S. Animal Damage Control. The ranchers in Real County raised and sold their annual crop of wool, mohair, and baby lambs, delighted that market prices were on the rise after a long depression in their industry, but grumbling that they would have done even better if it were not for the varmints, especially eagles. Zimmerman and his family endured the overt hostility of their neighbors. Matlock was in the Houston area preparing for retirement, only a year away. Stinebaugh was laterally transferred to the regional office at Albuquerque. The move was meant to widen his professional experience, so he could hardly complain; but like most exiled Texans he and his wife missed their native state and wondered if they would ever be able to return to it. The Redhead, in particular, felt homesick. Most of the time, Stinebaugh was too busy guarding migrant whooping cranes or rounding up illegal fur dealers to think about such things.

Until July, 1977. Stinebaugh and his family were on vacation. They had been camping for a week in the mountains near Albuquerque and had returned to the city for a couple of days before taking off on another camping trip in a different range. While they were home Gust Nun, Stinebaugh's supervisor, called with some interesting news: he had just been contacted by C. R. McCallum, the senior Fish and Wildlife agent in Corpus Christi. According to McCallum, a helicopter pilot named Jerry Heintzelman, lately employed by South Texas Helicopter Service, was trying to get in touch with Stinebaugh.

Stinebaugh reacted like a prizefighter when the bell sounds. He had been waiting for this news for a long time, without quite knowing he was waiting. He cancelled the rest of his vacation, to the Redhead's chagrin, and headed for Laredo, where Heintzelman was now working for another helicopter company, piloting Texas patrolmen back and forth along the Rio Grande.

2. The Witness

JERRY HEINTZELMAN was thirty years old. He had a pleasant, rather narrow face and high forehead, and a trim, light build. He was about the same height as Stinebaugh and resembled the agent in a superficial way: his face had a similar intense, concentrating look, and he had the same stiff way of walking, although in his case it was more practiced, something he had picked up in recent years. He was a native Pennsylvanian, and came by his real, if reckless, skill as a helicopter pilot naturally enough: his father owned a small helicopter company and for a time father and son had been partners. They had quarreled, however, and young Heintzelman had drifted south, eventually winding up in Laredo where his divorced mother lived. At first he had no luck getting a job as a pilot because he was 50 hours short of the 500 required by insurance companies in Texas. Then he met Al Barnes in October, 1975, and went to work for him in Uvalde. Later, with Barnes' tacit consent, he falsified his air time to get federal clearance to fly predator hunts sponsored by the U.S. Animal Damage Control.

Heintzelman's relationship with Barnes, more than any other factor, would determine the outcome of the eagle case. It began agreeably enough, with Heintzelman being accepted, according to his account, "almost like a member of Barnes' family." He responded eagerly to the rough and ready openness of south Texas hospitality; it may be that he mistook the generalized friendliness of his new associates for genuine

Incident at Eagle Ranch

liking and acceptance. By his own report he had always been a loner, with no strong attachment to anyone or any place, and no strong interests apart from flying. But in Uvalde he began to feel at home. Barnes encouraged him to wear cowboy hats and boots. Allen, the federal trapper, often flew with him as gunner and taught him to "ride herd" on coyotes and bobcats. And Alvin Connell, always easy to get along with, eventually provided him with a home of sorts, a trailer deposited forty miles from Uvalde on one of the ranches belonging to the company's "silent-partner," Clay Hunt. For a while, Heintzelman was pleased with having his own place; but that did not last long.

Stinebaugh, who came to know this ill-fated young man well, would later say, "Jerry had a lot of potential, but he just didn't seem to know how to get himself together." He was easily bored, living in his isolated trailer with a TV set that did not work very well. He took to travelling into Uvalde at night, drinking more beer at the local joints than he could handle, then driving home drunk. On three occasions during 1976 he was arrested and convicted for driving while intoxicated—experiences which somewhat darkened his view of Texas hospitality: "The very judges who try you are the biggest drunks themselves, only they don't get caught. The city police know who they're going to arrest and who they're not. I was easy pickings. If my daddy were a rich rancher I could probably have got away with murder. That's what I mean by politics down there. Basically, I'm a law abiding person. If I'm speeding down the highway I'll get caught. But if I'm being treated unjustly, and I get arrested and somebody who lives there doesn't, that doesn't sit too well."

By late spring of 1976, not long after Stinebaugh and Matlock had temporarily abandoned their investigation, Al Barnes was not sitting too well with Heintzelman either. The Texan's attitude, which had begun by seeming paternal, seemed exploitive now. The pilot felt, with some justice, he was being underpaid; and as though to add insult to injury, Barnes sometimes borrowed money from him and was not always in a hurry to pay it back. "When Barnes started owing me money," Heintzelman would later complain, "things changed. I was the outsider, looking in." In spite of these "cracks" in their relationship, the two men teamed up in a business partnership during the summer of 1976—a scheme to supply film cassettes of ranch properties to real estate brokers and ranchette promoters, who could then screen them for clients. Somehow it ended up with Barnes owing Heintzelman more than two thousand dollars which he never paid back.

The Witness

By the fall of that year, Heintzelman had entered into a common-law marriage with a Uvalde woman whom he had met on the night of his third DWI arrest. She already had one child, and another was soon on the way. He attributes his eventual decision to "go to the feds" to his new status as a family man: "I didn't want this [the investigation] hanging over me . . . I wasn't going to protect Al Barnes' butt anymore." Early in 1977, after brooding for months about the wrongs Barnes had done him, he either quit the company or was fired, depending on whose account one believes. By this time his affection for Uvalde and its citizens had faded too. "They're warm people, but they still won't let you in."

In April, Heintzelman tried, in effect, to pressure Barnes and his partner, Clay Hunt (Alvin Connell had by this time sold his interest in the company): if Barnes did not make good his debt, the pilot would inform the Federal Aviation Administration that the helicopter service's maintenance on its aircraft was dangerously inadequate. Barnes and Hunt reacted, according to Heintzelman, with more murderous threats of their own. From that moment, Heintzelman said later, "closing down the company was the one thing I wanted to do. They all wanted to be above the law, to make me look bad. After that going to the feds seemed the shortest route."

Even so, it was not until July, almost three months later, that he met Stinebaugh at a Holiday Inn in Laredo and the real story of the "eagle conspiracy" began to unfold. During the interval, Heintzelman must have weighed his festering desire for revenge against a genuine fear that he might be putting his life in jeopardy. He sincerely believed that in south Texas influential people could get away with murder. He had himself listened-in on discussions in the coffee shop at Uvalde's Kincaid Hotel during which plans were made to "get even" with Alfred Zimmerman. In the end, however, his own desire to "get even" won out.

During his first talk with Stinebaugh, Heintzelman maintained a rather cocky tune; but he insisted that in exchange for his testimony he would receive not only immunity but protection during and after the trial. Stinebaugh, after checking with the U.S. Attorney's office in San Antonio, assured him these conditions would be met. The two men travelled at once to San Antonio where the pilot gave a sworn deposition in the presence of Stinebaugh and a court recorder. At first he was reluctant to implicate people like Connell and Andrew Allen, against whom he had no grudge, but the U.S. Attorney's office refused to guarantee anyone's immunity except his own.

Incident at Eagle Ranch

The story Heintzelman told then, augmented with further details later on, and subsequently swore to on the witness stand, began on December 10, 1975, the day the Zimmermans witnessed the shooting of an eagle. That morning, Barnes had informed Heintzelman that he would be hunting in Real County, and that eagles, not coyotes or bobcats, would be the target species. Apparently speaking from experience, he briefed the pilot on how such hunting was done—the correct speed, distance, and angle from which a flying eagle should be approached.

Heintzelman rendezvoused with Andrew Allen, the government trapper who would be his gunner that day, and the two men hauled the helicopter by trailer up to Real County. At Leakey, the county seat, they met briefly with Judge Sansom and the county commissioner, Lanny Leinweber, both of whom had used their influence to obtain county funds to help pay for the forthcoming hunt. While Heintzelman half-listened, Allen, Sansom, and Leinweber discussed over coffee the ranches on which the hunts would be conducted. Then the Judge absented himself and the others headed north to the Bill Diedert ranch about ten miles east of Rock Springs. This became the base of operations for several of that day's flights. People would "just show up" when Heintzelman landed to refuel, including the company's then vice president, Alvin Connell. At each take-off, a different passenger would occupy the gunner's seat. Eagles were flushed frequently among the neighboring bluffs and canyons, and although Leinweber had no luck, Allen and Connell each bagged several. About a dozen of the birds were shot that day, plus a "falcon" killed by Allen, who insisted that even the smaller raptors preyed on sheep.

Allen was an aerial marksman of the first order. Heintzelman would later exclaim admiringly, "I've seen Andy do impossible things. We'd overtake a coyote, for instance, and he'd hang out of the 'copter, holding the shotgun in one hand, and blow it right into the ground." But late in that afternoon, on his last turn, Allen began to miss his shots. He became angry, and when he and Heintzelman routed an eagle from the bluff at Eagle Ranch he was determined not to let it go—even when the Zimmermans' pickup hove into view, lights blinking an angry warning.

After recovering and hiding the dead eagle while Zimmerman made his phone call, Heintzelman and Allen spent the night at a hunting lodge on Lanny Leinweber's ranch. Next morning, December 11th, they moved their operations to Dan Auld's hilly 14,000 acre ranch, locally renowned for its concentration of wintering eagles. On that day and the next, the ranch foreman, Buddy Pape, accompanied Heintzelman in the gunner's seat. According to the pilot, his score was impressive: about fifteen eagles killed on the 11th, somewhat fewer on the 12th. All told, the tally for the three–day hunt was at least thirty-five birds. On January 6th, Barnes again sent Heintzelman to the Auld ranch to meet Pape and kill eagles. About twenty-five eagles were dispatched that day.

During the same winter, Heintzelman flew Alvin Connell on two or three occasions over the rough country between Brackettville and Camp Wood, where Connell owned or leased thousands of acres of ranchland, in search of eagles. Connell, like Allen, was "a crack shot," and several birds were killed. During this same period he also obliged a wealthy rancher named Bill Morriss by enabling him to shoot an eagle. The grateful Morriss rewarded him with a one hundred dollar tip. But by far the most notable hunt to which Heintzelman was assigned during these months occurred on the Silver Lake Ranch. On this occasion, the foreman, Jim Ballew (who would not dismount when Stinebaugh later tried to talk to him), his son, Connell, and several other people were gathered for a day's sport. Most of them had no personal vendetta against eagles. They were on hand, as Matlock would sourly observe, "because this kind of thing was a big fun deal down there." Most of the gunners Heintzelman took up that day were amateurs; he was angered because some of them came close to shooting through the rotor blades when he banked the machine in pursuit of an escaping eagle. Even so, more than a dozen birds were taken. At least one was a bald eagle, shot by Ballew's son. The young man had himself photographed holding the lifeless bird, perhaps as a way of commemorating the nation's bicentennial year.

By March, the hill country's surviving eagles headed for their unknown nesting territories further north. When they came back the following fall they were let-off for a while, at least as far as Heintzelman's assignments were concerned, except for one incidental episode in which he and a Comstock rancher, while searching for a pack of sheep-killing dogs, pursued and killed a golden eagle as it was trying to catch a jackrabbit. But South Texas Helicopter Service had too many commissions to kill coyotes for the ADC and to herd cattle for the ranchers to bother much with eagles for the time being. Even so, the company's operations were not always legitimate: Heintzelman would reluctantly admit to Stinebaugh that he and Andrew Allen, while under contract with U.S. Animal Damage Control to shoot coyotes in the vicinity of

Highway 90, would fly to the cattle country further south. Their aim was to shoot bobcats—not as a control measure (bobcats cause only minor trouble in sheep pastures and none at all on cattle range), but to collect their skins, which had lately begun to escalate in value. Sometimes the two men would kill a dozen of the animals on a single flight. The pelts were then sold, *sub rosa,* to a fur dealer recommended by Barnes. (Stinebaugh would later check out this admission, as well as most else in Heintzelman's account, and find it to be true. The fur dealer would confirm the transactions, while denying any knowledge that the hides were sold to him illegally.)

Early in 1977, the eagle hunting resumed. On January 19th, Barnes once again scheduled Heintzelman to fly the Auld ranch. Pape's wife, Reba, had set a generous table for lunch that day, and Dan Auld, the ranch's elderly owner, presided at the table. While they ate, the group discussed the risks of another illegal foray. Although it was generally assumed that the federal investigation had come to nothing, Reba was worried on her husband's account and became upset when Heintzelman and Pape teased her. Heintzelman himself was a bit uneasy. His relationship with Barnes was by now very strained, and he bitterly resented an assignment that required him to break the law without even the incentive of a special bonus. Nevertheless, the air-time supplement to his salary would come in handy. With Auld advising caution, it was decided that the hunt was on. On this occasion, Heintzelman kept a coded record in his personal notebook: The exact score that day was nineteen eagles, several of them bald eagles.

One other major hunt occurred before Heintzelman left the company. In February, while he and a rancher named Neal Jernigan were flying the hill country, they came upon a remarkable concentration of eagles, "not less than twenty," gathered at an earthen water tank. "It was a field day. Before it was over we ran out of shells. We definitely got twelve. Some, you'd knock the flip out of them the first shot. Others would need more." It must be said of Heintzelman that, in describing the havoc he had wrought among the area's wintering eagles, he did not pretend to a belatedly awakened ecological conscience. When he was interviewed two years later it is true that he claimed he was troubled, when he first worked for Barnes, at the thought of killing helpless animals from the air. But his own narrative, and the testimony of others, provide convincing evidence that he soon learned to enjoy his work.

The Witness

Heintzelman's confession was submitted to a relentless scrutiny by Stinebaugh and Matlock. His claims were cross-checked with other evidence—the locations where bodies of eagles had been found, the testimony of the Davenports and the Zimmermans, the records of the helicopter service. They invariably checked out. Equally convincing, he was quick to say when he could not remember exact places, names, or numbers; he had, after all, no grudge against the men most obviously implicated by his testimony. Ironically, Barnes, with whom he had a score to settle, was the one principal he could not implicate as an eagle killer; since both men were pilots, they had always flown separately. Heintzelman's hearsay evidence about Barnes' own eagle hunts, if it could have been substantiated, would have increased the total number of eagles destroyed considerably; but even without this increment, the score was impressive: Heintzelman's activities alone had brought about the deaths of more than one hundred bald and golden eagles during the winter seasons of 1975–76 and 1976–77.

Stinebaugh and Matlock reviewed the pilot's testimony with their supervisor, Gust Nun, and the regional director of the U.S. Fish and Wildlife Service, Bill Nelson. It was decided that a task force of nine men—most of the available agents in the southwestern division—would question the people Heintzelman implicated, in the hope that some of them would confess or produce conflicting testimony. On August 11, 1977, the agents, working in pairs, set out to question Andrew Allen, Lanny Leinweber, Buddy Pape, Bill Morriss, and Neal Jernigan. Pape and Leinweber denied everything. Morriss was away from home for several days at a racetrack in New Mexico; when he returned, he promptly confessed to the single eagle-killing incident in which he was involved. As for Jernigan, when two of the agents approached him, his wife threw a round of ammunition into a rifle and would have handed it to him if the investigators had not uncovered their own weapons. The rancher angrily insisted on his innocence; but some months later, faced with the likelihood of being indicted if he did not testify against Al Barnes, he reluctantly admitted his part in the eagle killings.

Stinebaugh and Matlock reserved Andrew Allen for themselves. When they arrived at his Uvalde home, the trapper told them he would not answer any questions. They advised him that they were not going to ask any; they merely wanted him to listen to a tape they had brought

along. The tape, of course, was of Heintzelman's voice describing
Allen's involvement. According to Matlock, when Allen had listened for
a few minutes, he "hung his head like you'd hit him between the eyes
with a baseball bat.""You got me," the trapper said,"but if I go to jail, I'm
not taking those other good people with me." He refused to say more until the agents were about to leave. Then he remarked, bitterly,"It's no different than it's always been; you get the little guys, but the big ones
always get away. When this is over, whether I go to jail or don't, then I'll
tell you some things that'll really surprise you." Stinebaugh and Matlock
urged him to surprise them now, but he declined.

On October 11th, after considerable debate in the U.S. District Attorney's office about which specific charges of eagle killing would stand
up in court, and which of the suspects were most susceptible to the available evidence, Buddy Pape, Lanny Leinweber, and Andrew Allen were
charged with conspiring to violate Title 16, Section 668 of the federal
Bald Eagle Protection Act, as well as the Airborne Hunting Act, which
forbids aerial hunting of most wildlife species. Allen and Pape were ad-
ditionally charged with several counts of actually killing eagles with the
aid of a helicopter. Allen was separately charged with perjuring himself
before a grand jury and was scheduled to stand trial on that count later
on. Pending the trials, Bill Nelson, the regional director of U.S. Fish and
Wildlife Service, directed Milton Caroline to suspend Allen and his
supervisor, Beavers. He also ordered a hiatus on all federally sponsored
aerial predator hunts in Texas.

As soon as the indictments were returned, Matlock, accompanied
by a U.S. Deputy Marshall, went to Uvalde to arrest Allen. Stinebaugh,
paired with another deputy, headed for Real County to pick up Leinweber and Pape. They were met at a Leakey cafe by the county sheriff,
John Elliott, who offered to accompany them when they arrested Lanny
Leinweber. Ordinarily, a county sheriff would be the last person to vol-
untarily participate in the federal arrest of a county commissioner, but
Elliott had his reasons. First Leinweber was taken from his home, with
Elliott looking on, and then Pape. Both men were handcuffed and
driven to San Antonio to be charged, after which they were released pending trial. This matter of handcuffing, although a fairly standard procedure even in misdemeanor cases, profoundly shocked the families and
neighbors of the accused. To them it signified the implacable vindictive-
ness of federal power in general, and of its instrument, Jim Stinebaugh,

in particular. Moreover, they construed the gratuitous presence of Sheriff Elliott at Leinweber's arrest as evidence of an "eagle conspiracy" quite unlike the one that Stinebaugh and Matlock were concerned about.

The case was assigned to an Assistant U.S. District Attorney named Ray Jahn—a choice that would subsequently gladden the hearts of everyone on the prosecution's side. Jahn was a brilliant, grinningly energetic lawyer who bore a startling likeness, both in looks and style, to the young Teddy Roosevelt. Although only misdemeanors were involved, he understood the importance of the case and prepared it with the attention he would have given to a felony charge. He would end by being wryly impressed that this case, of all the major ones he had prosecuted, should be the first to receive national news coverage; for that matter, the first to pack the courtroom.

Stinebaugh and Matlock wanted Jahn to "see Real County for himself, so he could tell the jury how all this had happened." The attorney willingly agreed, and in mid-November he and Stinebaugh arrived by helicopter at Garvin's Store, where they were met by Matlock and Sheriff Elliott. The latter has some news for them: he had come by a rumor that a U.S. Border Patrol agent had seen Judge Sansom, no less, with a dead eagle in his possession. Elliott did not know the agent's name; but he was stationed in Uvalde and ought to be easy to find. Jahn made a note of this information, after which the group went to the Prade Ranch, where the attorney questioned the reluctant witness, Dennis Davenport, and visited the bluff under which Stinebaugh had found a dead eagle. The winter migration was under way, and Jahn was "thrilled" to see several of the majestic birds very much alive and soaring overhead. It had never occurred to him that live, wild eagles could be observed within a hundred miles of San Antonio. He remarked that when the trial was over, win or lose, he would bring his son out to Real County one day so he would have a chance to see, and remember, this spectacle.

The trial was to begin on December 5th, 1977, a few days short of two years since the incident at Eagle Ranch. In the interim, Stinebaugh spent much time with the prosecution's chief witnesses, Zimmerman and Heintzelman. Both men were nervous and looked to the agent for reassurance. Zimmerman's life had been threatened, and he and his family had been subjected to considerable harassment. Moreover, his domestic life had become increasingly unstable, and he confided to

Stinebaugh that he was thinking of a divorce. This, plus the prospect of the trial and his neighbors' increasing hostility, had made a tangle of his life, and there were moments when Stinebaugh feared that he might refuse to testify. Matlock is convinced that the unhappy man would have bolted if, notwithstanding the marital breach, his wife's strong will had not kept him in line. As for Heintzelman, he and his family were now living incognito at a trailer park on the outskirts of San Antonio, existing on a modest government allowance and part time work. He was troubled that his former friends and associates now pronounced his name as a curse; and he brooded because his enemy, Al Barnes, had not been charged with Allen and the others, all of whom he rather liked. On the other hand, he sometimes told Stinebaugh how relieved he was to have made a clean breast of it; even his complexion was clearing up. He collected clippings about the upcoming trial from newspapers all over the country and, later on, he even considered buying the huge transcript of the trial. Whenever he and his wife quarreled, she accused him of enjoying the publicity. He denied this; but it is possible that he was sincere and his wife was right. After all, the young outsider whom no one would listen to—not his father, not Al Barnes, not the Uvalde judges—was finding that a lot of people listened to him now.

Especially Stinebaugh. The young agent felt oddly protective of his restless, moody charge. But he also felt restless and moody on his own account. For the first time, the Eagle Act was being put to the test. Throughout the West, the ranching community was rallying to the defense as to a crusade, contributing large sums to a fund set up by the Texas Sheep and Goat Raisers Association. Stinebaugh feared that if Allen and the others were declared innocent, it would be the equivalent of declaring open season on that other community, of eagles, which he wanted very much to protect. And in the more general controversy concerning a redefinition of man's relation to predators, the ranchers would have won an important round.

As the date of the trial approached, there were moments when Stinebaugh could hardly bear the suspense. The Redhead waited suspensefully too. Ever since Heintzelman had come forward with his testimony her husband had spent most of his time in Uvalde and Real counties; but on one of his visits home she had conceived their third child. Even before it was born, the couple had begun to refer to it as the "eagle baby."

The trial was held at the San Antonio federal courthouse and lasted five days. The defense team was led by Will Morriss, a craggy faced old gentleman with a personal interest in the case: it was his nephew, Bill Morriss, who had tipped Heintzelman so generously for helping him to kill an eagle. Morriss decided that the defendants would plead not guilty. He would build his case on the uprightness of his clients' characters.

In the prosecution's opening statement, Ray Jahn told the jury that the U.S. Congress, responding to the wishes of the American people, had decreed that the golden eagle "had a right to live," and that the only issue in the trial was whether or not the accused had violated that right. Morriss, when his turn came, stressed the wholesomeness, civic virtue, and innate law-abidingness of the defendants, and expressed his confidence that the jury would find them innocent of all charges. This tactic was a surprise to Jahn. He had expected Morriss to base his defense on arguments of "confession and avoidance"—that is, a plea of self-protection and protection of property: since eagles were killing the defendants' sheep and goats, the defendants had the right to kill eagles. He was prepared to rebut such arguments with the testimony of scientists who had studied eagle predation. Now, however, he would have to readjust his strategy to deal with the character witnesses whom the defense would call.

After the prosecution's witnesses—Zimmerman, his son, Cecil, Stinebaugh, Heintzelman, and others—had given their testimony, and Morriss, during cross-examination, had made much of the government's financial aid to Heintzelman (a total of about three thousand dollars), the defense produced the promised character witnesses, a group of Real County's most prominent citizens, all of whom vouchsafed the moral integrity of the defendants. In a surprising move, virtually all of them also testified that they did not believe eagles were a problem in Real County, despite the fact that some of them had publicly proclaimed their strong views to the contrary in the weeks before the trial. The intent was to eliminate the defendants' motive for killing the birds. During cross-examination, Jahn repeatedly challenged the credibility of these witnesses. He made clear that some of them like Auld and Sansom were allegedly implicated in the case; he forced others to admit that they were the recipients of Leinweber's and Sansom's political patronage; still others were made to contradict their own testimony.

Jahn's handling of Sansom was particularly interesting. The wily old Judge had been subpoenaed as a defense witness, but his doctor had announced that he was ill and could not appear in court. Rather than lose his testimony, both the defense and prosecuting attorneys visited

Incident at Eagle Ranch

him at his Leakey home and obtained his sworn deposition. The transcript was introduced at the trial, with stand-ins reading Sansom's answers to the attorneys' questions as though the man himself were there. From the defense's point of view, his read-out responses to Jahn's questions left a lot to be desired. For example, the Judge said that he had heard that Alfred Zimmerman was not a man of good character. Pressed about his source, Sansom produced the name of a south Texas businessman. Later, when rebuttal witnesses were called, Jahn presented the businessman himself, who declared under oath that he could not have talked about Zimmerman because he did not know him.

At another point, Jahn had asked the Judge if he had ever possessed an eagle. Indeed he had not. Was he positive of that? Certainly. A few minutes later, however, Sansom had uneasily changed his mind. His wife had reminded him that, yes, he had once found a dead eagle on the road. He had given it to his hired hand, "my Mexican," to burn because he suspected it might be "rabid." Jahn had gently inquired whether the Judge had shown the bird to anyone else. Definitely not; only the Mexican had seen it. There the matter rested for the moment. But again, on rebuttal, Jahn produced an unexpected witness—the Border Patrolman whom Sheriff Elliott had mentioned—who now swore that he had observed Sansom, outside a Leakey cafe, proudly telling his acquaintances to look in the opened trunk of his car—where a dead eagle was on display.

A San Antonio attorney who watched part of the trial was later moved to observe that, "in Real County, perjury must be a way of life." The jury, after several hours of debate, must have come to the same conclusion. On Friday, December 9, 1977, they returned a verdict that found all three defendants guilty on all counts. The stunned silence that followed—most of the audience in the packed courtroom was composed of friends and families of the accused men—was broken by the weeping of Lanny Leinweber's daughter.[1]

Part Two

The
Ranchers

3. Real County

THE MENGER HOTEL is something of a San Antonio landmark. It is next-door to that most sacred of Texas shrines, the Alamo, and its own venerable walls have contained a fair share of Texas history; Teddy Roosevelt recruited Rough Riders in the barroom. It is the right place for an old-line rancher like Bill Sims to register when he comes into town on business or to observe what he regards as the unjust persecution of friends and fellow ranchers. It is the right sort of place to meet such a man for lunch. Sims proved to be a pleasant-looking, pleasant-acting man, attired in the inevitable cowboy boots and hat. As well as being a dedicated sheepman, he is the executive secretary of the Texas Sheep and Goat Raisers Association, an organization which, despite its modest membership, is a potent force in Texas and national politics when its own interests are at stake.

We met on December 6, 1977, the second day of the eagle trial. I was covering it on assignment and had already become as interested in the testimony outside the courtroom as that within. Both the environmentalists and the ranching community saw the case as a focal point in the long standing predator controversy and felt that their opposing views on the subject were as much on trial as the three defendants. The environmentalists feared that not only the Eagle Act but the eagle itself, and by extension, all predators in the American West, would suffer a serious setback if the accused were let-off. The ranchers and their wives,

Incident at Eagle Ranch

who came in droves from Real County and beyond, were even more intensely engaged. When I spoke with them during intermissions, their remarks sometimes suggested that their livelihoods and life-style, as well as their attitudes toward predators, were in the dock awaiting the verdict of the outside world. All of them assumed that the defendants were involved in a slaughter of eagles, but most were pretty certain that the jury would find them not guilty. They saw the Eagle Act not only as an unjust law, but the symbolic expression of all federal meddling in their lives, and they believed the jury would see it that way too.

For myself, I discovered how little I knew about eagles or ranchers or the troubles they were having with each other. How little I knew, in fact, about the whole emotionally charged issue of predators and their status in the West. I had read this and that, here and there, but nothing that was of much use now. I was certainly biased: I did not want the eagle and its supporters to lose. But the more time I spent outside the courtroom, the more I was impressed by the ranchers' passionate sense of injury, their sometimes lurid accounts of disemboweled or eyeless lambs, their statistics of economic loss. I began to wonder whether they did not, after all, have a right to feel angry and frustrated. I decided to learn more than the trial itself could teach me. The meeting with Bill Sims seemed as good a place as any to begin.

Right off, Sims acknowledged that the Sheep and Goat Raisers Association had set up a trust fund to pay for the defendants' legal fees, although he was less forthcoming about the amount of money involved. Nor did he mention the fact that the association expected future breaches of the law. As its own press release put it, "The fund . . . will outlive the present case and offer a certain measure of security in possible future instances where ranchers are attacked for protecting livestock." Perhaps understandably, he did not volunteer the fact that one of the accused, Lanny Leinweber, was also one of the more active members of the association's board of directors.

On the whole, however, Sims was plain-speaking and more than willing to exchange views. He felt powerfully about the injustice of the trial and saw the defendants as victims of an environmentalists' conspiracy—"Defenders of Wildlife and the Audubon Society are the worst"—to destroy ranching as a way of life. When I asked whether he thought the accused were actually guilty of killing eagles, his usually steady gaze glanced off his spoon, a neighboring table, and a pot of

42 ferns. "Well," he said, "if Lanny Leinweber says he didn't do it, then I have no reason to disbelieve him."

He conceded that in his own area there were no great problems with eagles or any other predators, "but a lot of good people say they do have trouble, and I have faith in them." He mentioned several studies, including one of his favorites, a survey done in 1967 which indicated that 17 percent of the total mortality among lambs was due to eagles. But he admitted the survey depended solely on the testimony of the ranchers themselves. Another study in the late sixties, conducted by Texas Tech and financed by both the National Audubon Society and the National Woolgrowers Association, concluded that there was little evidence that eagles were a serious problem. Sims scoffed at these findings: "Problem was they had people who didn't know what an eagle looked like. They started their research way too late in the lambing season, they used graduate students, and the man who conducted the whole thing was a *duck* man!" He was much more enthusiastic about the 1975–77 study sponsored by the federal government at the Joe Helle ranch in Montana, and he could cite its findings chapter and verse. This now well-known case documented an unusual concentration of eagles on Helle's ranch and verified the fact that heavy predation on lambs did in fact occur. Although Sims admitted this type of incident was unusual and localized, he still felt strongly that an across-the-board reduction in eagle populations was the only solution.

Sims clearly disliked environmental organizations because, as he put it, they exploited partial truths about endangered species to increase their membership. But he did believe that a dialogue between "protectionists" and livestock interests could somehow be maintained. "If we could resolve two things, coyotes and eagles, we'd have more in common than we have differences. The rancher is doing a lot more for wildlife than all the environmentalists put together. We don't have to allow deer to live on our property. Hell, when I cleared my land I left a couple hundred acres of brush for the deer and turkey to hide in. My neighbor now, he loved his wild turkeys. But then he took all his brush off and he lost them."

A question about mismanagement of rangeland, particularly overgrazing, was also dealt with firmly: "My grandfather and people like that, they didn't know any better, so of course they overgrazed. In this dry country it takes a while for land to recover from something like that, but it is improving. Ranchers are more enlightened now."

Incident at Eagle Ranch

After lunch, as we were returning to the courthouse, I suggested there were legal remedies if a sheepman were losing stock to eagles; that ranchers in Real County ought to demand that the government investigate their claims instead of killing the birds themselves. "Would you want the federal government coming on your place?" Sims asked. "Would you want them investigating you? I'll tell you something: I did have the most positive attitude in the world until I heard about the grand jury indicting these people. After this trial there's no way in the world I'm going to ask any rancher to do anything. This trial will lock the gate, damn right it will. *My* gate is locked, I can tell you."

Might anything happen to open the gate again? "You tell your people that if they'll come up with a program that'll stop eagles from killing lambs, we'll cooperate. But you better understand that you're going to have to kill some eagles." He tapped at my lapel. "Are you going to be ready to do that?"

We were now at the courthouse steps. As we shook hands, Sims said, "You don't have to believe what I'm telling you about eagles. Go on up to Real County and see for yourself."

Kerrville, Texas, is a boom town perched on the edge of the Edwards Plateau. Houses climb steadily higher on the slopes of surrounding hills and cling to miles of rocky ledge along the south fork of the Guadalupe River. It is not uncommon to see herds of deer, no longer sure of where they are supposed to be, wandering across parking lots between supermarkets and neon-lit motels.

Dan Auld's office is on the second floor of a new office building. His secretary, an implacably smiling woman he referred to as Miss Agnes, showed me in. Auld was sitting behind his wide empty desk, eyeing me severely. Our meeting had been arranged beforehand, but Auld now seemed to feel he had made a rare mistake. He threw up his hands, palms out: "I have nothing to say to you. I don't have any respect for you. You don't want to hear my side."

Two weeks earlier, I had watched Auld testifying for the defense. At the time he seemed hard of hearing and somewhat confused. It had been difficult to relate that impression to the comments various ranchers had made about him—that he was a great character, tough, patriarchal, representative of those laissez faire values that west Texans most admire. The man I bearded in his lair, however, was better matched to the stories.

At eighty-one, Auld was physically frail, but not just from age. Twenty-five years ago, while galloping along a Montana mountainside in pursuit of a grizzly, his horse took a spill and almost killed him. He retains a crippled shoulder as a souvenir. Five years ago, he sustained a broken back and shattered jaw in a jeep accident. However, there was nothing frail about his thoughts or feelings.

Auld was not indicted in the eagle case, despite Heintzelman's assertion that he was present at the home of his foreman, Buddy Pape, when eagle killing was discussed. But apart from the fact that Pape killed more of the birds than anyone else and that much of the hunting took place on his ranch, Auld has made an avocation of disliking eagles. In 1962, when hearings were being held in Washington, D.C., on the proposed law to protect golden eagles, he led rancher opposition, and made two trips to the capital to testify against the bill. In 1964 he told a federal official that he was "definitely going to quit the sheep business" the next year because of eagles. He will never forgive Secretary of the Interior Stewart L. Udall for not listening to him. "The Department of Agriculture subsidizes us to grow more wool and lamb," he growled, "and then Udall turns around and makes it against the law to destroy what's destroyin' your lamb crop. They want to make it against the law to make an honest livin' on your own property."

Though still glowering, Auld finally decided he would talk to me. I asked him why eagles seemed to be such a problem in the hill country. "Roosevelt gave us subsidies to take the brush off," he replied. "That had a lot to do with it. Open land makes it easier for 'em to get at the lambs." When I inquired whether it might not be more profitable to let the brush return, Auld cuffed the air impatiently. "Damn sure wouldn't. We have a hell of a lot of good ranch land now where we used to have brush. We can run four times the stuff we used to. Why should we go back?" Nevertheless, Auld professed not to like subsidies: "We don't ask for subsidies: they just give 'em to us. I don't believe in 'em myself." Then he paused, shifting agitatedly in his chair. "On the other hand," he added, "every little bit helps. What's goin' out in one way we're glad to get back in another."

What is going out, he made clear, is the lamb crop, and to his mind, eagles are the culprit. Auld's ranch is a large operation by Real County standards, where holdings are not as vast as they are farther west. Its 14,000 acres hold 2,200 yearling ewes and 400 head of purebred

Incident at Eagle Ranch

Angus, "plus a few eatin' goats." Some years back the ranch supported many more goats. But that, according to Auld, was before the bottom fell out of the mohair market. "Nowadays, a lot of people have turned entirely to cattle, but you can't make money off cattle." He paused, thinking of his Angus. "Well, you can make some, but you can't make it like you can off sheep. Why should I switch? Anyways, a lot of the ranchers raisin' cattle are these New People that have come up here; they just buy land for investment, for income tax purposes. They don't need the money."

The New People might say the same of Auld, who is a multi-millionaire, thanks to oil and the ranch, which he admitted had "a pretty good income." Yet he assured me that the eagles nevertheless were taking the very food out of his mouth. The statistics were impressive: "In one pasture last year we had 125 pregnant ewes, and we had 135 in another. When we rounded up the lambs for docking, there were just 19 left in that one pasture and 23 in the other. No, no, it's not coyotes! We have damn little problem with coyotes and bobcats. Always had worlds of bobcats, but they don't bother the sheep much. And we keep the coyotes caught. We was rid of them for a long time until the government stopped using 1080 on them and they begin comin' back. Even so, if a coyote causes trouble, he's not there a week but we latch on to him."

Could overgrazing have anything to do with the mortality of lambs? Again the air around Auld was soundly swatted. "Oh," he snorted, "that's what them Audubon people claim!" While he paused to stare balefully at me through his spectacles, Miss Agnes, who had been hovering protectively in the background, ushered forth a plaque awarded to Auld by the Soil Conservation Service for sound grazing practices on his ranch. Auld eyed it sourly. "Can't buy anything with that," he said.

Well then, if eagles are the problem, there are legal ways of getting help, aren't there? "Hell," he exclaimed, "our governor tried to get a blanket permit to kill eagles for 31 counties out here, and Interior turned him down!"

What about requests for more specific aid? The Bald Eagle Protection Act provides for federal control of eagles if a rancher can prove damages. That's what happened at the Helle ranch, isn't it? In reply, Auld growled that "the lambs would be all eat up before you'd hear from 'em. We'd get the permit next year—for this year!" He recalled that Pape once called in the area game warden, but it took two months for the man to show up. "It's the federal government and Audubon that oughta pay for our losses. If they like eagles so damn much, they ought to pay for 'em."

I remarked that if he could really prove eagles were taking that many of his lambs, I might agree with him. Auld's canny old eyes fixed on me skeptically, "Well," he said, "you'll be out at the ranch tomorrow. See for yourself!"

I got up to leave and immediately stumbled. Auld's office is a hazardous place to move about in. There were three bear hides on the floor —two grizzlies, one Alaskan brown, all enormous. The gaping jaws of one of them had caught my foot. The walls bristled with mounted heads, antlers, horns of Cape buffalo, moose, deer, and mountain sheep. Auld explained that these trophies were a mere nothing. He had 150 others displayed elsewhere, including two rare African bongo, mounted whole.

Auld's passion for hunting has taken him around the planet many times—five trips to Africa, a couple to Asia, twenty to Alaska. On the office wall facing his chair hangs an enormous moose head which gazes back almost at eye level. "You know what they're going to do in Alaska now, don't you? They're going to turn it all into national parks. No one'll be able to hunt there except the wolves. Damn wolves," he snapped. "They'll eat anything—a whole moose. Can't see why anybody would want to protect a wolf! They ought to be exterminated. They're just like those eagles that're eating us out of house and home."

It has never occurred to Auld that when it comes to predation, wolves and eagles could learn a thing or two from him. I remarked that men, especially hunters, are predators just like wolves (I dared not mention eagles), except that wolves must make a living at it. Auld responded by looking irritably at bay; this was not at all what he wanted to hear. Miss Agnes, hovering nearby, said cooly, "Mr. Auld thinks predators should be in zoos. If people want to see them, that's where they should go."

Auld stared at his moose. Judging from his expression, he did not like anyone, not even Miss Agnes, putting words in his mouth.

The next day I drove through the Texas hill country to Auld's ranch to see the first of the defendants, Buddy Pape. This is terra incognita to most travelers passing through the state. This is particularly true of the Balcones Escarpment, the broken land, "all up and down" as the locals say, out of which the uneven limestone shelf of the Edwards Plateau rises toward the much noted bigness of the Texas sky. It is a transitional zone not only geologically but scenically, falling halfway between the deadening blandness of Texas east and north and the beautiful but inhospitable starkness of Texas south and west. Some people call the area The Brakes, after the cedar brakes (actually juniper) with which many of the hillsides are densely vegetated. But it could as easily be called "the breaks," because the whole area has the broken look of an abandoned stone quarry, with slabs and shards of rock thrown about like the contents of some gargantuan Indian midden. It looks dry, although in fact it gets more rain than the plateau itself or the Trans Pecos farther west. Along with the cedar, a considerable variety of oaks flourish here: shinnery, blue, Spanish, as well as a stunted version of the live oak. The soil, what there is of it, is remarkably rich. Where it hasn't been overgrazed, every loamy spot among the rocks supports a thick cover of switch grass, bluestem, grama, Indian grass, wild rye, and buffalo grass. It is, among other things, the sort of country where eagles like to spend their winters.

But eagles are not the only visitors. There are hundreds of new vacation homes, guest lodges, and summer camps along the narrow, shallow gorge cut by the south fork of the Guadalupe River. The folksy-looking general store at Hunt has a bulletin board that attests to the presence of the new clientele: dozens of snapshots of vacationing men, women, and children posed beside slain deer, Russian "hogs," and a run-over mountain lion.

I followed the winding ranch road that links Kerrville with Leakey, nearly fifty miles away. As soon as the road left the river, the world emptied out, at least of people. For an easterner, the view that now unfolded was bound to seem extraordinary. It was evening, and on either side, rocky, high-fenced pastures faded off into cedared hills. This was the heart of sheep country, although I saw more cattle than sheep, more white-tailed deer than cattle, and, amazingly, more axis deer, or chital, and black buck than native whitetails. At times it was like traversing the hilly edge of some international veldt. But the strangest part of this spectacle was the almost eerie docility of all these animals. Half a dozen times I stopped the car. The deer, ten or twenty yards away, raised their heads to stare. When I got out, the whitetails bolted only to stop and gaze back from thirty yards away. The axis deer and black buck held

Real County

their ground. I slammed the car door. They trotted off up a hill, then turned and stared some more. I shook my head in disbelief. I was too accustomed to the vanishing flash of an eastern whitetail's rump when a car so much as slows down not to be amazed at the suicidal tranquility of these animals. Apparently the news had not registered that the hunting season was still on.

My home that night was Leakey, Real County's one and only town. At eight o'clock the next morning I left the community's only motel and drove north again through a cold winter fog. I had the road to myself. At times there were smatterings of rock on the blacktop, fallen from the overhanging limestone cliffs. Then, gradually, the mist was left behind. I was in the high country, sheep country, cleared of cedar. On the other side of the fences that accompanied the road, the earth was worn to the nub, nothing but boulders and brown sward as short as the felt on a billiard table.

My destination, Pape's house, was a modest square building with a fence a few feet in front of it to ward off livestock. Buddy Pape was outside, waiting for me next to a four-wheel-drive. In the courtroom three weeks earlier, I had watched him listen to the evidence that would convict him. His head was always tilted back, the long, rather imperious nose pointed directly at the witness box. From that angle, his face had seemed to come to a narrow point. I was surprised to discover that it is actually quite broad, almost Indian-looking. The same wind and sun that give so many ranchers' faces the texture of a crumpled paper bag had polished his, planing the surfaces smooth and taut. It is not the sort of face that gives its owner's thoughts away. Auld had asked him to show me around the ranch, so that was what he would do; but it must have seemed an imposition. Nevertheless, he invited me inside, where I met his attractive, worried-looking wife, Reba, and his young son and teenage daughter. The latter, blond like her mother, had a hard time mustering up a smile of greeting; her father's conviction was not something she could stoically accept.

Buddy Pape is a native of this hill country, unlike many Real Country residents, and he is a person of some standing in the community, a member of the school board and a model of moral rectitude in the eyes of his neighbors. Although he has ranched in the area all his life, he has never owned his own land. "A poor fella like me can't ever buy land no more. All these oil people, lawyers, doctors, and what-have-you that

Incident at Eagle Ranch

come out here to buy ranches have drove the price so high there's no chance for a poor person. It used to be that if you worked hard enough all your life you could save and buy land, but you can't hardly do that anymore." He must think back wistfully to the days of Auld's father, when an enterprising fellow could sign up for four sections under the Homestead Act, hire a Mexican to run sheep on them for four years, then come back and collect the title. As it was, he worked on a salary for Auld. Although he had nothing but high praise for his employer, it was clear he would have preferred to manage the ranch on shares: "Mr. Auld won't do that though. He told me he had a bad experience tryin' shares with some other fella before I come along, but he never would say what the bad experience was." Then, lest he seem disloyal, he assured me he admired Auld's reticence. "When he does tell you somethin', he's goin' to stand by it." One of the things Auld would stand by was his assurance that he would pay any fines Pape received, if it came to that.

Buddy Pape's is the perfect voice of this dry stony land. It registers the high plaintive, nasal twang of a banjo in need of tuning. The pronunciation is west Texas to the core: you is "yew," think is "thank," can't is "caint."

When Auld arrived for his weekly tour of his domain, he seemed tired, willing enough to let others speak. He was accompanied by a young hired hand, Billy Mogford. At the trial Mogford was summoned as a defense witness, and his testimony was the subject of some amused commentary among those who supported the prosecution. At first he claimed that no eagles were killed at Auld's ranch on December 11, that only a number of Russian "hogs" were shot. He said he had driven about in a pickup, flushing the boars out. However, under cross-examination, he admitted he inadvertently routed the hogs while feeding cattle, and, other than seeing the helicopter give chase to them had not seen what it was up to.

The conversation inevitably turned to eagles. No one present claimed to have seen an eagle kill a lamb, but Buddy and Billy had seen the birds "eatin' on them." Mogford also referred to a lamb carcass he had found a few days earlier: "The rib bones and all was completely gone. . . . There was several eagles and ravens eatin' on this one. I even saw a white-headed eagle there."

I asked Buddy if he was guilty of killing the eagles. There was an instant's silence; then he said, no, he wasn't. However, the façade of innocence had a way of slipping in forgetful moments. Even the defense attorney, after building his case on the total innocence of his clients, had described the self-confessed pilot, Heintzelman, to the jury as being "just as guilty as they are." Now Pape exclaimed, "We're not exactly, so you say, killin' those things [the eagles] because we're starvin' to death." That last point was one that Buddy Pape held dear. He genuinely felt that Texas sheep were important to the world's food supply, that the eagles were taking the food out of the mouths of needy children. He did not seem to realize that the grain needed to help carry cattle and sheep through the Texas winter would surely feed more hungry people than the same grain translated into meat—meat that really hungry people could not possibly afford.

When I asked Reba Pape what she thought about the trial and its outcome, she first gestured helplessly. But then, choosing words carefully, she tried to explain: "It's more the frustration than anything. Anything you don't understand will frustrate you, and we can't understand how they could do this to us. If we went to a grocery store to steal a piece of meat, the grocer could probably shoot us and get away with it, but these eagles are stealing our meat, and there's nothing we can do about it! I wish they could build a wall around us that don't want the eagles; that's what I wish."

Auld and Mogford had already begun their tour of the ranch in another jeep. Buddy and I passed through one enormous pasture after another, unhooking aluminum gates, following a track so lumpy with rocks that any vehicle other than a four-wheel-drive could not survive a mile without internal injury. The sky was overcast, the air cold. On either side there were frequent flocks of ewes and lambs and occasional herds of splendid-looking Angus. In most places the grass was bitten back to the quick, and the earth's limestone skeleton protruded through tattered strips of lava-black soil. When I remarked on this, Buddy pointed out small swatches of green, flat as moss, that spread under stunted oaks and along the track, wherever moisture was able to collect. He claimed that sheep, even cattle, could nibble up these tiny green blades, along with what was left of autumn grass, and he said that a few handfuls of this fare, even in winter, were worth more nutritionally than a bale of hay from less mineral-rich regions. This may be so. However, it is also true that the density of livestock on the Auld ranch, more than one sheep or cow for every five acres, is a high ratio for western rangeland that is supposed to be well managed. There was much supplemental feeding; cattle troughs filled with protein blocks were in evidence everywhere. If this operation deserved a Soil Conservation Service award, I wondered what the ones look like that got the booby prize.

We had not gone a mile before we saw our first eagles, two goldens perched atop a live oak on a distant hill. When we stopped so I could get a better look through binoculars, they lifted off and disappeared behind the ridge. It was not long, however, before another eagle came into view, this one not quite so wary. In fact, when he left his perch, he coasted along a draw that ran parallel to us. I had been told frequently that these birds were almost impossible to shoot from the ground, but this one seemed a reasonably easy target. Pape, however, assured me that if I'd care to try a shot I would soon see how difficult it was.

After this, every other draw turned up an eagle. Before long I counted eight or nine. Then another gate needed opening. When I got out and looked beyond it, I realized I had seen this place before: in the courtroom, pictured in a slide to which both the prosecution and defense had referred repeatedly. This was the great yellow bluff, perhaps 150 feet high, where, according to Heintzelman, he and Pape often killed eagles. Not far from here, the Davenport brothers, while hunting at night, had found the dying eagle which they had subsequently tried to have mounted. Near here Agent Stinebaugh had recovered the body of still another eagle from among the jumbled rocks.

Pape's voice interrupted: "There's some more of them." Four large birds were cruising back and forth in front of the cliff face. We moved closer. I took out my binoculars to focus on them, then felt my jaw sagging. These were bald eagles, four adults, sailing past each other, settling now and then on boulders at the crest of the bluff, then languidly launching into space again. The sight was so lovely, so wholly right, that for some moments I was aware of nothing else.

Then two of the birds began flying slowly toward each other from opposite ends of the bluff. I kept expecting one of them to swing aside, but both seemed intent on a midair collision. Then, at the last possible second, they undertook a heart-stopping maneuver: the eagle approaching from the left abruptly somersaulted onto its back, while the other, its enormous wings extended stiffly upward, vaulted elegantly over the first. For one instant the two birds were joined in a perfect balletic composition; then the upside-down one was right side up, and both were on their separate ways again.

"Did you see *that?*" Buddy exclaimed. His countenance was, for him, remarkably agitated. "Well, let me tell you, I enjoy seein' somethin' like that just as much as anyone! If it wasn't that they was killin' lambs . . ."

Pape then pointed to a hillside on the right of the bluff. Its cropped surface was pale green and beige, littered with stones and cedar stumps. "You see that hill? We've cleared that pasture. We've cleared over 75 percent of the ranch like that to improve it. Now to me, *that's* pretty!" He took me by the elbow and turned me around. "Now look over there," he ordered. "That's the Prade ranch." I saw a line of similar hills, rocky and abrupt, but these were densely vegetated with cedar brakes and shinnery oaks. "You see that?" Buddy demanded. "That belongs to some rich east Texas people who raise game on it for other rich people to hunt. They think *that's* pretty! They think that's beautiful! And they think that," he pointed me around to his hill again, "they think that's *ugly!*"

Pape drew his chin back against his Adam's apple, as if he had said everything he had to say.

In this morning of eagles, there was one other high point. We had seen three more goldens flying singly. Then we descended into a steep draw, its dry bouldery bottom lined by Spanish and blue oak, sycamore, an occasional beech. An orange-and-black rock squirrel scampered away from us. A fox squirrel hurried up a tree, flattening out on a bare branch in plain view of us—or any passing eagle. We spotted a couple of ravens. There were sheep everywhere.

Then, a sense of movement in the trees ahead of us, a large shadow falling on the tumbled rocks. A golden eagle, roosting in the draw, had allowed us to get unusually close before taking off. A moment later, we saw it climbing above the tree line. Three more eagles appeared over the crest of a nearby knoll. The first joined them, and all four sailed directly overhead, close enough for me to see the blotched shades of light and dark brown on some of their underwings. At least three of them were immatures. As I got them in my binoculars, Buddy spotted five others, one after another, soaring above the valley just ahead of us. While I was marveling at the sight of nine eagles in view at one time, a tenth bird emerged from behind a knoll.

This eagle parliament was a stunning spectacle, but I was beginning to register the implications of what I had seen. Listening to the testimony

Incident at Eagle Ranch

of Heintzelman at the trial, I had been made somewhat skeptical by the sheer numbers of eagles allegedly shot during just five days of aerial hunting, and I had wondered why Pape, in particular, had so much success, and why one ranch, this one, should have been the scene of so many of the killings. Now the answer was staring me in the face. I did some rough figuring. We had been traveling in a fairly narrow parabola and were beginning to head back toward Pape's house, so that some of the birds might have been repeat sightings; also, Pape had brought me through the third of the ranch where the eagles were most numerous. But I also knew that for every bird we had seen flying, a range of hills shielded one we could not see. Cut it any way I chose, there were at least 50, more likely, 80 or 90 golden and bald eagles on the Auld ranch—more that there were supposed to be on all the millions of acres of the Edwards Plateau. The incredible concentration—phenomenally rare—figured out to about one bird for every 250 or 300 acres! I had discovered an El Dorado of wintering eagles.

During the tour I had been checking out the herds of sheep we passed. On our return, I observed them more intently than ever. There were about 300 ewes and lambs in this particular draw, unconcerned, baaing and bleating in their sheepish way while ten eagles cruised directly overhead. According to Buddy, about two-thirds of the ewes had already lambed. That seemed about right, since at least two out of three sheep had babies, sometimes twins, at their sides. The lambs were anywhere from three hours to three weeks old. The ewes that hadn't lambed yet were in the last stages of pregnancy and fairly easy to spot, with their distended bellies and pink swollen vulvas. Buddy too joined in the scrutiny—rather anxiously. But even with both of us searching intently, we could discover only one lambless ewe in the entire flock that showed signs of having already given birth. Earlier in the journey, we had noted one other. Buddy was a bit troubled by the tally. "A lot of them ewes has twins," he explained. "You can't tell how many of the twins has been lost."

The sun came out as we drove along a track that followed the headwaters of the Frio River as it flowed through rocky pools below a ledge. Presently a small cabin came into view. "That's where Mr. Auld was born," Buddy explained. The structure was in an advanced state of decay; Auld is not a sentimental man. We descended from the jeep, examined the ruin for a minute, then walked around it to the stream, crossing to the other side under the cliff's overhang. Directly opposite

Real County

54 the house, a clear spring poured from the limestone sill. The water was pure enough to drink. But when I bent to catch a handful, a malodorous scent announced itself. "That water would be nice to drink," said Buddy, "if it weren't for *that*."

Just a foot away from the place where the spring joined the stream was all that was left of a lamb—hooves, hocks, some wet dirty wool, and the curved spine, all the vertebrae intact from neck to tail. No coyote, bobcat, dog, or Russian boar could have picked that backbone clean without the help of a lobster fork. I thought of all those bleating sheep among the rocks, and all those eagles coasting overhead. Before I came here I had known that eagles occasionally dine on lamb. Now I had to admit the difference between knowing something and believing it.

That afternoon I spent with Bob Ramsey and his wife at their ranch just up the road from Auld's. They were a pleasantly hospitable pair, living in a pleasant, hospitable house. Ramsey had consented to be the intermediary between me and a number of the protagonists in the eagle case and was himself an important defense witness. He takes pride in his command of wildlife lore. He has a degree in wildlife management and was an employee of Texas Parks and Wildlife before Mrs. Ramsey inherited their 5,000-acre ranch. He enjoys being described as a "rancher-biologist" and it was in this role that he was introduced as a defense witness. In his testimony he explained that golden eagles could easily be mistaken for numerous other birds—buzzards, ravens, bald eagles, falcons—the point being that Heintzelman's claims about the identity of birds shot from the helicopter could not be trusted. Unfortunately, Ramsey undermined his own status as an eagle expert under cross-examination when he conclusively identified the cadaver of an eagle as that of an adult when in fact it was an immature.

Apart from his stint as a witness, Ramsey had no known role to play either in the trial or the events that led up to it, although he was a friend of Leinweber, Pape, and Sansom, and his wife was Auld's niece. Yet, as I later discovered, he had involved himself in the drama as much as he could, not unlike a bit player in search of a leading role, and his activities significantly affected its outcome.

Ramsey was a portly man in his fifties, the features large, soft, affable. His plump cheeks had a lopsided look when a chew of tobacco was tucked in one of them. Mrs. Ramsey was a short woman with upswept graying hair who frequently suggested that I ought to have a bite to eat, or at least another cup of coffee. Both liked company. One sensed they might be a little lonely in their large house, since their only child, a daughter, was married and lived in Kerrville. Or perhaps the emptiness seemed acute when I visited them because their grandchildren had been vacationing with them before Christmas.

But both Ramsey and his wife kept themselves occupied. Mrs. Ramsey was ladylike and had artistic tastes, which were reflected in the wildlife portraits she paints on slabs of rock. Her husband constructed scarecrows and bedecked his pastures with them. He claimed they have been effective in keeping eagles away from his stock. He was also well read in Indian lore, and he not only collected arrowheads, but had even taught himself to chip his own. One avocation he did not dwell on was bounty hunting. His specialty was hunting Russian boars—another of the county's introduced species and an unpopular one with ranchers, since they have a reputation for eating kids and lambs. Real is one of a number of counties in Texas that still sponsors a bounty system with county funds. Ramsey was said to collect more of the $25 bounties on "hogs" than anyone else.

Both of the Ramseys struck familiar conversational themes: the predator problem was worse than ever; a man had an inalienable right to defend his land against them. The "New People," by buying up land and turning it into hunting preserves or ranchettes, were creating reservoirs of predators; the old-line ranchers, "100 percent of them," have sold out "because of predators, not overgrazing or mismanagement as some people think"; and the trial was "a great miscarriage of justice," especially if "those boys go to prison."

Ramsey had strong views about eagles. He had been quoted as saying they "might kill four or five lambs in a day," that they would not eat carrion when fresh meat was available, that in spite of their incredible eyesight they could not spot rabbits in brushy country, and that he himself was losing up to 20 percent of his kids and lambs to the birds every year. When I asked is he could document this loss, he allowed that it would be "very difficult" to do. Nevertheless, he rummaged through his notebooks and allowed me to look at them. They were, in fact, not record books at all but rough-and-ready diaries with notes apparently jotted down at random. I could not read them, but he could. After a bit of figuring, he estimated that whereas he had 282 kid-producing nannies

Real County

in 1976, a mere 39 kids survived until August when they were rounded up. In 1977 the survival rate was better but still remarkably low, with 286 nannies producing only 81 kids that were still alive that summer.

I was bemused by this information. For one thing, Ramsey had volunteered earlier that he ran nearly 600 goats on his property, along with an equal number of sheep and 200 cattle. With the revival of the mohair market, he was building up the goat herd through replacements, a feat hardly possible if he was losing anything like the number of kids he claimed he was losing. Secondly, the enormous loss of kids was even greater than the 10 to 20 percent he had earlier claimed for both lambs and kids. Thirdly, he had mentioned that his goats, unlike sheep, produced their young in April. This was indeed puzzling, since one of the few things everyone seemed to agree about was that all the eagles left the hill country by the end of March. I decided not to press him on the matter, however, except to wonder aloud how those scarecrows he had mentioned could have been doing the job he claimed for them.

Ramsey hemmed and hawed. "Your scarecrow is effective only if eagles can see a great distance. They might come into a pasture and make a kill when fog is obliterating the view."

I remarked that if an eagle could see a kid or lamb well enough to kill it, it could surely see a scarecrow too—even in a fog.

Ramsey considered this, then shook his head. "I'm at a loss. I don't see why the kill would be that great with scarecrows all over. But it did happen!"

I asked him how, under the circumstances, he could be in the goat business at all. "That's what people wonder about ranchers in general," he said. "We got our backs against the wall. Without the scarecrows no one would believe what our losses would have been. You are talking to people who are trying to make a living out of a harsh land!"

The harshness of the land was real enough. But the Ramseys' home did not look like it belonged to people who had their backs against the wall. Although it was time to look at part of the ranch, I was reluctant to leave the luxuriously comfortable living room, a recent addition to an already spacious house. The original living room that adjoined it was filled with Victorian furniture and seemed little used now. The new room was about the size of an Anglo-Saxon mead hall. Mounted heads of mule and fallow deer, javelina, and black buck gazed down from above the enormous hearth. A wondrous chandelier made of an antique bear trap hung overhead. The walls were covered with bookshelves, Mrs. Ramsey's pictographs, glass cases containing arrowheads, guns, and knives, and, in one corner, the stretched skin of an eight-foot rattlesnake on a red velvet board.

Leaving the house, I asked Ramsey if we could see the dead lambs. Bill Sims had recently notified members of the Texas Sheep and Goat Raisers Association that they should collect and freeze all lamb and kid carcasses they suspected had been killed by eagles. These were to be sent to a professor at the University of Montana who was involved in the study at the Helle ranch. Ramsey had mentioned that he had a few specimens in one of his freezers. (His presumably were among those later analyzed by the professor, who found that, of 55 carcasses sent to him, only 15 could be considered to be definite or highly probable eagle kills.)

We proceeded to a shed, where Ramsey produced a lamb's carcass from a heavy paper bag in the freezer. The body had been partly eaten; the pelvic area and lower spine were exposed and intact, suggesting that eagles or ravens had been feeding on it. Wanting to be helpful, I reached into the freezer, hauled out another bag, and dumped its contents on the floor: another lamb, smaller than the first. The only damage I could find consisted of several punctures along the back, each marked by a touch of dried blood. Ramsey seemed oddly fidgety as I examined the animal. When I asked where it came from, he drew my attention back to the one he was holding. A few minutes later we left.

Ramsey then took me to one of his nearby sheep pastures, exceptionally flat by the standards of this country but typically strewn with limestone rubble and grazed to the ground. There was a scarecrow in the middle of it. When my host scattered range cubes—a food supplement —from the back of the pickup, large numbers of ewes and lambs hungrily assembled, as well as a tame axis buck. Almost all the ewes had lambed, and again I searched—vainly—for a glimpse of even one of them that might have lost a lamb.

After a few minutes of supplemental feeding—it was hard to see how the sheep could survive without it—we proceeded to a much more vegetated tract. Here, where a shallow ravine divided a dense stand of shinnery oaks, Ramsey made the first of several stops to examine the bobcat traps he had set out. He had already caught three of a "family" of four that frequented the area. At this time, all the traps were empty. The first one, however, had recently dispatched a roadrunner—a useful, not very common bird in Real County—and its feathers were scattered about.

Real County

Ramsey explained he had discovered the bird on his previous round, and had used its body to bait one of the traps. As for bobcats, he admitted they were not a serious problem with lambs and goats, but he pointed out they do take fawns and showed me the remains of one to prove it. Presumably he not only got a considerable sum for the popular bobcat fur, but also collected a bounty from the county. Ramsey was not a cruel man, however; the death of the unfortunate roadrunner made him "feel bad," and he admitted that "I'm probably a little hard on my bobcats."

As we drove back through the shinnery thickets, a whitetail doe suddenly appeared and ran along beside us. She was a pet, Ramsey explained. When we pulled up at a small pen, and Ramsey scattered corn inside it, she leaped in at once. The pen, I learned, was not always used for such innocent purposes. In Texas it is legal to bait resident game, and in the hill country that is the way most hunting is done. The hunting locations are also kept supplied with feed during hard winters to ensure a good crop of fawns—too good, according to Texas wildlife specialists, who note that every year the overpopulated range produces runtier deer and fewer bucks with smaller racks. Ramsey, of course did not manage his ranch primarily as a hunting preserve, as did many of his new neighbors. But he did lease the property to a group of east Texas businessmen each year, hence the feeding pens and the thickets of shinnery oak. The businessmen were permitted a maximum bag of 25 bucks, although some seasons they shot considerably fewer. In return they paid Ramsey a dollar an acre, or $5,000 a year. Since he made an equal sum from leasing the property to an oil company, Ramsey was $10,000 ahead before he sold the first sheep, goat, or cow.

In most parts of the country, the deer a man sees in his pasture today will be on his neighbor's land tomorrow. He understands that livestock is livestock, and wildlife is wildlife. In Texas, however, wildlife *is* livestock; the animals are half-domesticated, raised as a money crop. Unattractive and unsporting as this lease-and-bait syndrome might seem to many people, the practice does assure the presence of large numbers of game animals on the land, even if they behave like red deer in an English park. And without the income they provide, many a thicket of shinnery oak like the one on Ramsey's ranch would soon be cleared away, along with all the nongame wildlife it protects.

This situation may help to explain the vindictive attitude so many southwesterners, Texans in particular, have toward predators. After all,

Incident at Eagle Ranch

if a man considers wildlife as livestock, how can he help but hate those species—including eagles—that insist on behaving as though they are not?

The sun was close to setting when I took my leave of Ramsey after thanking him for the information, much of it inadvertent, that he had given me. Neither of us expected to see the other again.

Night had fallen by the time I arrived at the ranch of the second of the three defendants, Lanny Leinweber. The winding, graded road from the gate to the house seemed to go on for miles, and I looked for road kills as I drove along. It seemed a good way of checking the hypothesis, held by all the local ranchers, that eagles have no natural prey to eat in Real County. I spotted one freshly killed jack rabbit and three live cottontails along a twelve-mile stretch of the road. When I approached the ranch compound, the headlights swept several outbuildings, and I wondered if one of them was the hunting lodge where Heintzelman and Allen had spent the night during that first eagle hunting expedition in December 1975. At the main house I thought at first no one was at home; the only light came from what appeared to be a new wing at the rear. After a couple of minutes, however, Leinweber answered my knock, wearing only his underclothes and an air of perfect self-assurance. This was New Year's Eve, and he and his wife were dressing for a neighbor's party. He asked me into the handsomely furnished parlor, then excused himself long enough to put on his pants.

He was back in a moment, offering me a beer and getting one for himself. At 41, Leinweber was the youngest sheep and goat rancher in these parts, but he had the solidity and composure of a somewhat older man. More than anything else, his voice drew attention. It was the perfect contrast to Pape's nasal tenor—a basso profundo that emerged as from a cavern. This weighty voice carried far in Real County and beyond. Leinweber was one of the county's four commissioners, who, along with Judge Sansom, governed its purse strings and political life. He also was president of the Independent Cattle Raisers Association of Texas, a director of the Texas Sheep and Goat Raisers Association, and a director of the Frio Canyon Chamber of Commerce. He owned or leased four ranches totaling 8,400 acres.

After some preliminary remarks about the trial and its outcome, the conversation turned to the four ranches. Two of them were to the south, near U.S. Highway 90 in what is known as the coyote "buffer zone," that Maginot Line through which coyotes had recently begun to infiltrate the hill country. Chiefly because of the coyotes, but also because of eagles, Leinweber said he now raised only cattle on those properties. The two ranches up here in The Brakes supported some cattle too, but they were chiefly given over to 500 ewes and 1,000 angora goats. Leinweber's estimated loss to predators was a modest one compared with that of other ranchers—a mere 10 percent—and he attributed only half of that to eagles. Furthermore he conceded that sheep and goats did not always have a 100 percent crop, that 3 percent might die of natural causes. "It's hard to tell how many you're shy," he explained, "until the kids and lambs have grown a little and are ready to be docked."

As for eagles: "My home ranch is practically back-to-back with Mr. Auld's. Generally, the eagles stay over there or at the Prade, in the rougher country. But this year my ewes was the first to start lambing, and those eagles went to work on me, by God. Two of the times I got there in time to positively identify the lambs as killed by eagles. I think you can verify that, when they got claw holes in the back. But as soon as Mr. Auld and others started lambing over there, the eagles practically left me." He paused, sipped his beer. "Let me explain something: Mr. Auld's place is so large he can't see after the predators as easy as I can because my place is smaller. Don't misunderstand me—I'd be glad to trade him—but on my 5,000 acres I'm always out in the pastures, driving around. An eagle doesn't like people or pickups. And I hand-feed daily in winter. It helps the problem to be out there in the pasture. But I'm the right age for that. My father ahead of me, and other elderly ranchers, they can't do that."

I then raised a question similar to the one I had asked Auld. If taxpayers' dollars are subsidizing the sheep industry, doesn't the American public have a right to expect some toleration for eagle predation in exchange? Leinweber replied: "I think that's unfair. If they closed the door to imports you might have a point. But as long as they let all that imported meat come in, it's not a fair trade-off." At this point Mrs. Leinweber entered the room and immediately picked up the conversation's drift. "The steel and train industries get subsidies," she interjected scornfully, "but they aren't asked to take a loss for the good of the American bird!"

Mrs. Leinweber, a trim, attractive woman, was modishly dressed for the evening's party. But her expression betrayed considerable tension. My presence could not help but remind her of the trial and its verdict, and she was not as skilled as her husband at preparing a face to meet the faces that she meets. He was very good at that indeed. At the trial, he was the only one of the defendants with the presence of mind to address the jury, not the lawyers, when he was on the stand. After the verdict was handed down, he was criticized by some for his remote indifference to his daughter's tears. And earlier in our own conversation, he, unlike Pape, gazed calmly in my face when he said he was innocent of the charges.

Mrs. Leinweber attempted to remain calm, but couldn't. "Of course," she said, "the trial isn't going to affect us as a family unit. But I do get a little bitter at the federal government for spending at least a quarter of a million dollars to prosecute three law-abiding men for this *little thing*! After all, we *are* the taxpayers, aren't we? We *did* pay for that trial, didn't we? Let the federal government pay our three families on welfare. Let the Audubon people up north go hungry. People have got to realize that we farmers and ranchers are the backbone of the country. Ranching isn't like in the movies like *Giant,* you know. It's a darn hard life."

She paused, leaning forward. "I have two little girls, and they've been growing up in this wonderful community. At one time you could let your children go all around and play with who they pleased. And now we have all this—this *dope*! The feds and the police won't do anything about that. They can send eight federal agents to find out about golden eagles, but they won't send one, not one, to find out about the dope!"

The dope, it seemed, was being brought in by the New People in Real County, the purchasers of the ranchettes into which many of the large ranches have been divided. Mrs. Leinweber seemed prepared to fight the invasion: "Old-time people like us, who have been settled here for 150 years, we aren't selling. But a lot of people are."

"Of course you can't say predators did it all," said Leinweber, "but predators have put most of them out of business."

Leinweber got up to finish dressing. In parting, he decided to be philosophical about the trial: "I feel like I've done nothing real bad. That trial is going to turn out more good than otherwise because it's going to make people wake up to the fact that we do have a problem."

There was time for just one more question. A lot of talk had been going around that John Elliott, Real County's sheriff, was responsible for starting the eagle investigation. Was there any truth to the rumor?

Real County

"We don't know that," said Mrs. Leinweber, doing her best to keep her voice even, "but we suspect it, yes."

In the counties of the rural west, an elected official's attitude towards the predator control issue may have more bearing on his political health than anything he says about abortion or SALT. But in the case of Sheriff John Elliott, that issue—or more exactly, the eagle case— became entangled in a political free-for-all that had little to do with the eagles themselves.

Elliott had no grudge against eagles; he was not especially for or against them, but he granted that they had become a serious complication in his already complicated political life. And his supposed involvement in the investigation had not helped their public image in Real County.

"I never knew anything about the eagle case," said the sheriff, "until a few days before Lanny Leinweber was arrested. Jim Stinebaugh, the federal agent, came to my home to let me know what was going on, you know, as a courtesy. My only role was to show him where Lanny lived."

In accordance with standard federal procedure, Stinebaugh had handcuffed Leinweber in preparation for the drive to San Antonio. The fact that Elliott was present when this act occurred made him inescapably a party to it. The handcuffs may have had more to do with Elliott's subsequent problems than anything else. "The ranchers have to have somebody to blame," he sighed, expectorating tobacco juice into his dashboard spittoon.

We were driving along a ranch road in a valley of the Frio River, amidst a landscape which by the rugged standards of the Brakes seemed almost level, almost verdant. In the distance, a large dark bird was circling. Elliott guessed that it was a buzzard, but he was wrong; it was an eagle.

The sheriff was a large man in the way that former professional football players tend to be large, the massiveness settling like an avalanche at the belt. In a previous incarnation which no longer seemed very real to him, he had been a defensive tackle with the New York Jets, sharing in the team's memorable victory at the 1969 Superbowl. He still wore the enormous diamond and gold ring commemorating that high point in his former career. His winnings from that season also helped to pay for the home he built on a seven acre ranchette in Real County.

Incident at Eagle Ranch

Although from east Texas, and therefore an outsider, his reputation as a football player and his easy-going style had won him the offices of county sheriff and tax assessor in the last county election against considerable opposition. After the eagle trial he continued to have strong support among the New People and the Mexican Americans, who described him as "walking tall;" but among the ranching set, according to his own description, he was "as popular as the bastard at the family reunion." Many ranchers believed he precipitated the investigation of the eagle killings as a way of settling a score with Lanny Leinweber and, through him, with all the county commissioners. The feud stemmed, on the one hand, from the sheriff's efforts to have the county's record books audited for the first time in 45 years and, on the other, from the commissioners' refusal to increase Elliott's salary (from $650 to $950 a month) or to award him the $1,000 bonus paid out recently to every other elected official in the county including the commissioners themselves. Elliott maintained that the salary and bonus dispute arose after he had begun to investigate the county's records, not the other way around. There have been a number of other instances of what the sheriff regarded as harassment: the commissioners limited his phone allowance, refused to subsidize a law-enforcement course he wanted to take, and erased the salary of a deputy sheriff they did not like after Elliott refused to fire him.

Personal vendettas aside, there did seem to be adequate reason for the attorney general's office in San Antonio to take a look at the county's records. There were alleged inequities both in property tax assessments and the distribution of county funds, which usually worked to the advantage of the established ranching families. Bidding on county projects was also suspect; and there were accusations, thus far undisputed, that two county commissioners appointed their wives as election judges in violation of state law, and that on one occasion, a polling booth was set up in a commissioner's home. (In an interview for the *Real County News,* Leinweber, after observing that the federal charge against him was a "political blackmail type of thing," went on to describe complaints about the aforementioned inequities as "picky." He explained that it was hard to run "a small stop-and-shop store [like Real County] the same way you would run . . . Harris County at Houston.")

Elliott was particularly angry that $720 in county funds were used to help pay South Texas Helicopter Service for the aerial predator hunts in the county. As far as he was concerned, the killings were more a political issue than an environmental one, an example of the old ranching families' belief "that they can do just as they please in Real County."

The sheriff refused to make predictions about his political future. From his phlegmatic bearing it was hard to tell whether he was stoical or just tired of the whole thing. But whenever he spoke of the county commissioners, the edge of his voice sharpened. Indeed, if it were all to do again, Elliott would probably not miss the sight of Commissioner Leinweber in handcuffs for all the votes in Real County.

The county courthouse at Leakey, built in the 1930s as a public work project, is a comically squat and homely building. Within its rancid green interior sat Judge W. B. Sansom, who had been its most important occupant since it opened for business. His office was aggressively drab; no one could accuse him of spending county funds on anything as frivolous as interior decoration. The chief embellishment was a series of group pictures of Texas politicians. The photo of Governor Briscoe— for whom the judge served as county campaign manager—smiled down from a prominent place.

According to the testimony of Jerry Heintzelman, the helicopter pilot, Judge Sansom, accompanied by Lanny Leinweber, met with Andrew Allen and himself at a Leakey cafe on December 10, 1975, to discuss where the helicopter would fly that day. The judge, however, had made himself scarce before the shooting started. At the time of the trial, it will be remembered, he also proved elusive when his health took a sudden turn for the worse; but his deposition was obtained and he testified *in absentia* as a character witness for Leinweber and the other defendants. His statements, read aloud during the court proceedings, were flatly contradicted at various points by witnesses for the prosecution. By the end of that performance even spectators sympathetic to the defense were gloomily admitting that the only character on which the judge's testimony had shed much light was his own.

But that had been three weeks ago, and in another county. If recollections of the episode troubled the judge now, he gave no sign. He chewed his cigar, shrewd eyes watching my pen at work, and said a great deal about as little as possible. When I asked about his reactions to changes in the county, he replied, "Forty-one years ago when I first sat down at this desk, I found a bankrupt county. Now we have 160 miles of paved road, we've paid off our debts, and we have 300,000 dollars cash in the bank. We don't own nobody nothing." Asked about his reaction to the New People, he pointed out that although there were a lot more property owners now, most of them lived (and voted) elsewhere. (The county's resident population has actually dropped in the last 30 years, from 2,600 to about 2,000.)

About the trial he said, "These boys were unjustly convicted. I personally have known them [Leinweber and Pape] all my life and I consider them as good citizens as we got." As for the eagles, "They have been a menace as long as I can remember, but not as serious as a predator as they are now." This observation had a certain incidental interest because in his sworn depostion the judge had declared that eagles were not a problem in Real County.

When asked about the altercation between Elliott and himself, Sansom replied, "Money! The sheriff's the type of man who's used to making lots of money, and the county can't pay the funds. . . . Most of his interviews about all that have been with people who haven't lived here very long. Even the sheriff hasn't lived here five years. . . ."

One final question: I had heard that the judge once made the statement that no one would ever be prosecuted for hunting eagles in his county. What about that?

Judge Sansom looked me up and down; the stray thought zipped through my mind that while in Real County I should drive well below the speed limit. "Why," he said, "I'm not a lawyer, but I well know that no federal cases can be prosecuted in county court."

As I was about to leave he remembered something: "They've got proof now, you know. They staked out a lamb, and my understanding is that it was dead by an eagle in less than an hour."

Who staked it out?

"Don't know," said the judge.

As chance would have it, Judge Sansom's parting shot had been anticipated the previous day by Sheriff Elliott's unsalaried deputy, an excitable man named Raymond Hortness who hated the Real County establishment with single-minded fury. According to his account, the county commissioners had deprived him of his wages—the commissioners control the county's purse strings—because he had the temerity to arrest the son of Leakey's mayor for misconduct at a public gathering. While pacing about in the shambles of his kitchen—it was the morning after New Year's Eve—Hortness recited a more profane and vivid litany of the judge's and the commissioners' misdeeds than the one Elliott had given me. A number of allegations were included that he could not substantiate, although at one point he did produce a photograph of a man, purportedly "on the federal manpower program," mowing the lawn in front of Judge Sansom's home "at 10 o'clock in the morning when he's supposed to be taking care of the courthouse square."

There would be no reason to introduce the deputy here at all if he too had not had an afterthought as I was perilously crossing his yard on the way back to my car. Evidently he had remembered why I had come to Real County. "Oh yeah," he called after me, while chucking a rock at a dog that was trying to bite my leg, "about those eagles. I understand from the talk on the street that somebody has been staking out lambs in pastures by theirselves, trying to get pictures of eagles picking them up."

Judge Sansom had said he did not know who the somebody was; but I was beginning to think that I did.

From the very beginning of the trial, it was the Eagle Ranch that most captured my imagination. Heintzelman's testimony of the pursuit and killing of the eagle there, and the corroborating testimony of the Zimmermans, father and son, had been particularly vivid. For a moment, as Mrs. Zimmerman chauffeured me in her pickup along the road her husband and son had taken that important afternoon, I had an eerie sense that I had come this way before. The day was not unlike that other day two years earlier, cold and overcast. The road dipped twice into the same clear stream. A whitetail doe, collared and belled, turned to stare at us, and a herd of axis deer flushed from among the rocks.

Ahead, above the leafless trees, rose the crest of Eagle Bluff. "They could see the copter from here," Alyn Zimmerman explained, pointing through the windshield. We hit the second watercourse without braking, and sheets of spray scudded out on either side of us. "Al started blinking his lights to warn them, you know; but it didn't do no good."

A moment later we were parked under the steep red face of the cliff. In the silence I could imagine the roar of the helicopter, the three shots, the long glide of the mortally wounded eagle toward the stony slope. I remarked that there were no eagles in sight now. "We usually have about six of them hanging around here this time of year," said Mrs. Zimmerman, "but I haven't seen but three this winter. Of course, I been busy; I don't know if there's any here right now."

Incident at Eagle Ranch

The Eagle Ranch was closed to business when I visited it; Zimmerman's employer was making plans to sell it. The plush-looking guest lodges were dark, and in the row of employees' cabins, the only lights came from the house where Cecil's teenage wife waited to cook his supper, and the neighboring one where his parents lived. Zimmerman and his son, who had been away on errands, converged on the latter house at the same time we did, and we assembled in the kitchen. "You can see I don't like housework," said Mrs. Zimmerman as she surveyed her untidy kitchen without apology. "I'd rather be outdoors."

They were a remarkable crew, these Zimmermans. With the exception of their nominal head they were nature's anarchists. Unlike other families I visited in the county, voices here tended to cancel each other out; contradictions flourished; hospitality consisted of the reasonable expectation that if you wanted something badly enough you would open your mouth and ask for it.

Alfred Zimmerman was a stocky man with horn-rimmed glasses, the inevitable cowboy hat worn indoors and out, and a very square face with a wide mouth. He laughed often but nervously; when he was really amused he slapped his knee. His son had the sort of face that Botticelli would have been glad to paint. That—plus the vulnerable name of Cecil —may have accounted for the boy's extravagant and defensive cockiness. As for Alyn Zimmerman, the mother, she was not your typical Real County housewife. She said what she pleased, was indifferent to distinctions in age and sex, and deferred to no one, including her husband. Her face was as inscrutable as a poker player's.

Once, briefly, her expression softened. She was telling me how she and her husband had wrestled down an entire truckload of panicky, sharp-horned black buck at a midwestern zoo while their keepers looked on in dismay. "That herd didn't do themselves or us any damage. Al and I were a real team back then. Not," she added, "that we aren't still a team now."

The Zimmermans seemed at ease with their role as managers of a shooting preserve. They pointed out that the ranch was more often used for conferences than for hunting; but even so, there was a difference between game ranches and game compounds. Mrs. Zimmerman admitted that there were many places like the shooting galleries exposed in the TV special, "The Guns of Autumn," but claimed this place wasn't like that: "A guy can go two or three days without shooting anything." When I remarked that the deer just outside the house were so tame I could have killed them with a stick, the family assured me that these nearby herds were protected. All the same, they admitted, it wasn't like hunting in Colorado or Wyoming or Idaho.

It was during this conversation that the Zimmermans tried to express their reasons, already recounted, for feeling protective of eagles. Mr. Zimmerman found it equally difficult to discuss his reaction to the state of psychological siege in which he and his family had lived for two years. He claimed he was not particularly disturbed by his role in the eagle case, even though it made him and his family social pariahs in the view of many of their neighbors. His main concern, he told me, was how the affair would affect the ranch's business. His wife listened to this, then remarked that "he's had ulcers since all this started," a revelation that caused the embarrassed Zimmerman to thrash about in his chair.

In fact, Zimmerman could hardly have been blamed if he had backed out of his role as government witness. There is little doubt that the situation held the potential for foul play. Many Americans think of violence in terms of highway accidents or random muggings. It requires a certain amount of imagination to bring to life the stress the Zimmermans had endured. One must conceive what it would be like to live in a totally isolated house in the shadowy cedar brakes and then receive secret well-meant warnings that one's life was genuinely in danger. The visible evidence of an anonymous hatred was on hand every time the Zimmermans left their door: The ranch's sign at the turn-off was repeatedly torn down, and the ranch road, although a public thoroughfare, was left ungraded for eighteen months. For a long time, Zimmerman carried a gun with him wherever he went. At times it must have seemed unreal that this should be happening just because he saw an eagle butchered and dared to complain about it.

Even before the eagle incident, however, the irreverent Zimmermans were not especially popular among the county's established families. "We were new here," Mrs. Zimmerman told me, "and if you haven't lived here for a hundred years, you're not good enough for them. The only ones that would be friendly to my daughter at school were the Latin kids; the ranchers' children never were."

Perhaps understandably, Mrs. Zimmerman had had it with sheep and goat ranchers. "I've always heard a lamb is born with a desire to die," she said. "But do you know what else I've always heard? That the only thing stupider than sheep is someone who raises them."

Incident at Eagle Ranch

"Hot damn," replied Zimmerman, laughing nervously, "don't say that now!" Then, to me, "Don't say I said that! We got to live here!"

Mrs. Zimmerman glanced first at her husband, then at me, pressing her lips together. For once this outspoken woman had nothing to say.

When I was about to leave, however, she remarked that she would like to have a copy of whatever I ended up writing. Evidently it was no more apparent to her than it was to me that her strength and will were giving out, that within a few weeks she would try unsuccessfully to take her own life. And that not long afterward, when she and Mr. Zimmerman were officially separated, she would come to his room one night and kill him with a single shotgun blast.

The night had turned viciously cold. Sleet was falling. My car was encased in a thin sheet of ice. Driving along the twisting ranch roads under such conditions was a scary business, not much helped by the fact that I was exhausted. I wondered how many lambs would freeze to death by morning. The image of a dead lamb took shape in my mind —not in Auld's pastures but on the floor of Bob Ramsey's freezer shed. Suddenly I knew what I would do: Since the winding county road back to Leakey was out of the question anyway, I would take the roundabout route via U.S. Highway 83, which passed by the Ramsey ranch.

I must have seemed an apparition, appearing in the Ramsey's doorway unannounced on a night like that. For a few seconds all three of us were at a loss for words. Mrs. Ramsey looked genuinely startled. I explained I was passing by and had thought I might drop in to ask a few more questions. After a few minutes of small talk, the conversation came around, as it had to, to eagles. Ramsey was riffling through a drawer in his hidden file cabinet, looking for clippings about eagle damage. I remarked that I had been wondering where the little lamb in the freezer, the one with just a few talon marks on it, had come from? Ramsey mumbled, almost inaudibly, that it was found on the Auld ranch. Then he brought over some newspaper clippings about predators that he wanted me to look at, and the subject was quickly dropped.

Later Ramsey would say he had had to bite his tongue to keep from telling the truth. However that may be, the truth was this: in the wake of the trial, angered ranchers decided to stake out lambs, separated from their mothers, in a deliberate effort to get eagles to respond to such bait. Apparently on its own initiative, the *San Angelo Standard-Times* in-

Real County

cluded itself in the action. San Angelo is in the heart of the sheep and goat country—it is the hometown of Bill Sims of the Texas Sheep and Goat Raisers Association—and to a considerable extent, its economic life depends on that industry. Somewhat earlier, alarmed community leaders had learned that the Armour Company intended to close its lamb-processing plant there—one more sign that the industry was declining. Eagle predation, of course, had not the slightest bearing on that decline; there were better reasons. But given the high feelings unleashed by the trial in San Antonio, the eagle had become both an emotional target and a newsmaker. So the *Standard-Times* contacted Ramsey and arranged a stakeout. Dan Auld and Buddy Pape would provide the setting, the newspaper would provide the photographer, and Ramsey would provide the lamb.

This lamb was more interesting than most, simply because it was a pet. Ramsey had found it orphaned and had given it to his two grandchildren during their holiday visit. The small children fell in love with it, bottle-fed it, and named it Charlene. They were somewhat puzzled when, one day, their grandfather proposed to take Charlene over to the Auld ranch. They were even invited to help build a blind. The children understood this had something to do with eagles, but not what the consequences would be. While the blind was going up, Ramsey's grandson asked where Charlene would be placed. Ramsey pointed to a spot below the blind, and the child suddenly understood. He dropped the stick he had been about to add to the blind and headed back to the pickup without another word. His sister followed him. When Ramsey finished the blind and approached the truck he found the children wiping their eyes; they had been weeping bitterly.

Tears, alas, would not save Charlene. The next morning she was tied with a 15-foot-long rope, and the newspaper's photographer was installed in the blind. For 45 minutes the lamb was left exposed, bleating, struggling at the tether. Then, as the photographer luridly related, "a pulsating wind . . . signaled the arrival of a killer . . . and its flesh-searing talons did their gruesome damage."

The *San Angelo Standard-Times* eventually published a supplement, cosponsored by numerous ranching and livestock businesses, which featured the "historical" photographs and a series of commentaries by interested parties. The presentation was as reasonable as a newspaper in that place, with that sort of readership, could be expected

to provide. But Dede Armentrout, National Audubon's southwestern
representative, who was invited to comment for the environmental
organizations, later observed that although she was glad her views were
"given a page of coverage, with a minimum of editorial embellishment,"
she did feel "that 15 pages, 12 of which represent [the anti-eagle] side,
two of which represent the other, and one neutral page, do not constitute a fair presentation of an issue."

The photos do prove what even the golden eagle's stoutest defenders admit: that on occasion—especially when the occasion is a
tempting stakeout—eagles do kill lambs. But the supplement did not
suggest that this particular kill occurred within a very small tract, a
single ranch, where there were probably more eagles, certainly more
golden eagles, per square mile than almost anywhere else in the contiguous United States. The *San Angelo Standard-Times* might as well have
tethered a lamb on an urban expressway at five o'clock in the afternoon
to prove that sheep are sometimes hit by cars.

About the intent of the supplement there could be no doubt. Its
purpose was to urge repeal of the federal law that protects the golden
eagle. Congressmen and high government officials were soon swamped
with copies. So, not surprisingly, was the U.S. District Court judge who
would soon pass sentence on the convicted eagle killers.

On February 6, 1978, those sentences were handed down by Judge
John Wood, Jr. Andrew Allen was fined $2,000, given a 60-day sus-
pended jail sentence, and placed on a year's probation. Lanny
Leinweber was fined $1,000, and Buddy Pape, $3,000. Since the three
men could have received a total of 20 years in jail sentences and a total of
$55,000 in fines, many conservationists viewed the sentences as a mere
wrist slap, the more so since none of the men would have to pay the fines
out of his own pocket.

The comments of Judge Wood at the sentencing did little to
mitigate this reaction. In explaining the lightness of the sentences, he admitted he was influenced and "in fact convinced by the very able investigation and reporting of the west Texas area news media that the law in
its present form is probably one that needs congressional attention."
Although he was sharply critical of the defendants for breaking the law
of the land, he left little doubt that he considered the law a bad one. He
also expressed surprise that the defendants' attorneys did not pursue the
defense-of-property argument. If they had, he said, he was prepared to

Real County

instruct the jury that it was "required and compelled" to return a verdict of "not guilty" if it found "the self-defense or self-preservation condition to exist."

Since the judge also called this "the most controversial case I have ever encountered either as a trial lawyer or as a federal judge," environmentalists were disheartened to learn that he researched it by relying on information from just one biased segment of the popular press, notably the supplement in the *San Angelo Standard-Times*. But for all that, conservationists had no reason to be too discouraged. A jury of ordinary citizens had convicted these men, and the fines were at least not as small as they might have been just a couple of years earlier. Moreover, as later events would prove, the Judge himself would have second thoughts about the case.

During my stay in Real County I tried to talk to some of the New People, those who were not personally caught up in the eagle case the way the Zimmermans and Sheriff Elliott were. It was surprisingly difficult to get any of them to express an opinion. They all knew about the trial but were close-mouthed about it. The proprietress of a grocery store in Leakey said that she heard that the defendants were "all nice people, but if they broke the law they should pay for it, shouldn't they?" Then she became flustered, adding by way of disclaimer, "Of course, my husband and I have only been here for seven years so we wouldn't know."

That was about as frank as the comments got—until the advent of Willard Phillips. My editor had passed on a letter written by Phillips some weeks earlier, in which he alluded to a "cover-up" of the eagle killings in Real County, as well as the abuse of county funds. This was my last day in the county. I was feeling a bit burnt-out; and I suspected that at this point I had heard more about local cover-ups and abuses than Mr. Phillips had. Nevertheless, he was one of the New People and apparently more willing to talk than most. Not wanting to leave stones unturned, I paid him a visit.

It was a radiant late afternoon. The valley of the Frio River just outside Leakey was awash with golden light. At a distance, two golden eagles were coasting in the shining air. If they were out hunting it could not have been for sheep since there were none around.

Willard Phillips turned out to be not just one of the New People, but New Person himself. He and his family lived in a pleasantly refurbished barn, around which a large subdivision had lately sprung up. Phillips was formerly employed as an engineer in Houston. Although not temperamentally a radical, he had been blown upon by the sixties' winds of change. He described himself as an "escapee." Four years ago, when he was turning forty, he "dropped out of the ratrace" and had become "a self-employed metalsmith"—actually a sculptor of metal artifacts such as skeletal wire ships. "When I first came up here," he said, speaking of the ranching establishment, "I met a lot of resistance. I told them, 'You may be able to run me off individually but if you try to stop the general ingress, it'll run over you.' Right now we're living on land that was once a ranch as big as Auld's. Now it's a subdivision with room for a hundred families." The roads, however, "are not graded as they ought to be. Even within favored precincts, some people's roads get more attention than others."

Like Elliott, whom he admired, Phillips felt that "the whole foundation of the eagle issue is the arrogance of the county officials. Until the federal investigation there was nothing here to make them stay within the structure of the law. They knew it was against federal law to kill eagles. The way I see the eagle thing, some wealthy rancher said 'I got an eagle problem,' and some county commissioner thought it would be fun to rent a helicopter to kill a lot of eagles. It illustrates their general attitude. They're going to decide what's best."

Phillips was a mild-mannered person but he became somewhat wound-up as he went on: "If the ranchers' intention was to eradicate the eagles, I'm sure I could think of a better way of doing it, using poison or something, which doesn't cost as much as a helicopter. I'm not crying for the eagles. I'm not an extreme environmentalist. But when I see tax funds used to break a federal law, then I have a responsibility to scream about it. . . . Of course, I hate to see anything killed. But I realize that any time an animal or a human stands in the way of civilization, it's going to get ground into the dust. The big rancher is just as dead as the eagle. I have a fatalistic view about the environment. In the long run, saving the eagle is hopeless. Wherever the eagle nests people will probably be sitting in the next thirty years. . . ."

There was quite a bit more of this. By the time I retreated from the Phillips' household much of the Frio valley was in shadow. The golden eagles had departed, and in my present mood their remembered flight had a valedictory eloquence. It struck me that in the cross-fire of com-

Real County

mentary I had been listening to for several weeks, hardly anyone except Stinebaugh, Matlock, and the Zimmermans had expressed much concern for the eagles themselves.

4. New Mexico

SOUTHEASTERN NEW MEXICO is an immense, treeless, generally undulant plateau. The part of it that lies west of the Pecos River has the topography of an unmade bed, covered, on the map, by a crazy quilt of federal, state, and private holdings. There is some farming wherever the ground flattens out enough to balance an irrigation ditch, but most of this land is sheep country, and looks it. Many of the miles-wide pastures have been grazed down to the point where "even the rocks are shiny." Mesquite is omnipresent, and there is some juniper and assorted cacti. In places the ground looks like the dry bed of a stony creek.

One gray afternoon in mid-March, 1979, I explored a bit of this prodigiously empty-looking land west of Roswell in the company of Sam Crowe, a young, scholarly-looking biologist with U.S. Animal Damage Control, and his brand new assistant, an even younger looking redhead named Carl Mitchell. Not long before the San Antonio trial had made the eagle a celebrated cause, or curse, the Southwestern Regional Division of Animal Damage Control had hired Crowe as its "eagle man" in response to rancher discontent (mostly in Texas) with the Eagle Protection Act. As far as the ADC was concerned, Crowe's most compelling qualification for the job was his adolescent experience as a falconer. He had started live-trapping Texas eagles not long after Real County ranchers began taking the law into their own hands.

His home base was San Angelo, Texas. There are no eagles in that immediate area, but sheep ranchers are abundant. No doubt the ADC hoped that Crowe's presence would be construed as evidence of the agency's concern about the eagle problem. Not that the young man was merely on display. He had been travelling around a lot; he was in New Mexico at the moment to investigate a rancher's unusual complaint that eagles were attacking his calves. There was some hitch about getting to the ranch in question, so he and Mitchell, with me in tow, decided to make the most of the delay by checking out a power line near the Two Rivers Reservoir. It was a preferred roosting place for itinerant eagles during the winter months; for some of them it was a last resting place as well, since the birds quite often electrocuted themselves when they made use of it. Alighting or taking off, their outspread wings were apt to touch two of its three wires simultaneously, completing a lethal circuit. Such high-voltage deaths have been a major cause of eagle mortality throughout the West. When the problem was first publicized in the sixties, the power companies, responding to public concern, made the necessary adjustments in some of the more notoriously lethal lines. Since then it had been widely assumed that the problem was no longer a very serious one. Yet even as Crowe, Mitchell, and I were walking this line, Pat Benson, a graduate student at Brigham Young University, was patrolling other power lines in the west and discovering hundreds of dead eagles underneath them. It now seems likely that thousands of the birds are still being electrocuted every year.

It took some time just to find the power line. Crowe had only visited it twice before, and after we had left the highway, one rock strewn ridge looked like another. However, after several miles of ranch road and as many more cross-country—during which I marveled that Crowe's pickup did not shake itself to pieces—the power line at last revealed itself. Several of the poles were capped by perches that resembled homemade gibbets. Crowe explained that they were meant to be inviting from an eagle's point of view, attracting the birds away from the ordinary poles where they might be electrocuted. It struck me as a sensible idea. Unfortunately the eagles did not always catch on. In the months following my visit, Mitchell would find two of them dead under this line.

Incident at Eagle Ranch

For the next hour and a half, we followed the line afoot, cross-country, under sullen skies, pausing at each pole to look for eagle sign. There was a great deal of it: splats of dried "whitewash" on surrounding rocks, and an average of three or four castings (the balls of fur and bone regurgitated by birds of prey during their digestive process) per pole. Judging from the distribution of these tokens, there was little indication that the eagles preferred poles with perches to those without. Other raptors used the poles too, of course—at one point we came upon the desiccated remains of an unidentifiable hawk, cause of death unknown —but the pellets upchucked by eagles are notably larger than those of other birds of prey.

If there had been anyone out in all that emptiness to observe us, we would have made a curious sight, huddled together over these recovered castings, earnestly crumbling them and examining their fusty contents. Most were of indeterminate age; in this arid country, hair and bone and almost everything else except mortal flesh disintegrates slowly. But there was no doubt about what the eagles had been eating: jack rabbits and more jack rabbits, breakfast, lunch, and dinner. And for good reason: almost every concavity turned up another of these lanky creatures, sometimes hightailing it into the mesquite, sometimes freezing in a half crouch in an effort to look rock-like.

Jack rabbits compete seriously with livestock on the western range. Scientists calculate that thirty of them can eat as much in a year as a full grown sheep. Anyone who has seen a jack rabbit will not find this hard to believe. They are a big-looking animal, the size of a young lamb, or three or four cottontails put together. Ironically, they have established a sort of one-sided relationship with sheep; jack rabbits (at least black tailed jack rabbits, which are the kind around here), cannot live where groundcover—grass and forbs as distinguished from scrub—is more than a few inches high; so they thrive on the eaten-up pastures occupied by sheep, aggravating the damage done to the range.

I suggested to Crowe and Mitchell that if this power line traversed a series of sheep pastures, as seemed likely, judging from the copious piles of shiny black scat that were everywhere about, and if it could be established that the lambing season concided with the presence of these eagles, then the power line and its supply of castings could afford a wonderful opportunity to study the diet of the birds in the area when both lambs and jack rabbits were available as prey. The study would be

New Mexico

all the more valuable because eagle diet had been studied only at nesting sites, whereas most predation was said to occur in winter and early spring when the birds were on migration. Crowe, however, did not seem to think much of the idea and mumbled something about the need for "a control group." Phrases like that usually daunt me, but I was prepared to argue that in this case I didn't see the need for one. However, the discussion was interrupted by Crowe's exclamatory "Look!" Mitchell and I snapped to attention in time to see an eagle launching itself from a perch-free pole about fifty yards ahead of us. In an admirable manuever, it stooped to put a ridge between itself and us. When we next saw it, it was almost a quarter of a mile away. I was reminded of Buddy Pape's complaint that, from the ground, "those things are hard to shoot."

Even after we returned to the pickup, the power line was much on my mind. In Texas, eagles tend to crowd up at vertical places like rock outcroppings, steep hills, and the walls of canyons, generally avoiding the open rolling country of the Edwards Plateau or the south Texas plains. Whereas here we were some 40 miles east of the Rocky Mountain interface, and the local ups and downs took the form of unprecipitous, if bumpy, slopes. I wondered aloud if that power line, by providing artificially upright lookout posts, might not attract eagles to these parts. But Crowe said no; eagles liked to use the line if they were in its immediate vicinity, but they would be in this region in any case. As if to prove his point, I unexpectedly spotted an eagle sitting on a nearby ridge. Crowe brought the truck to a rattling halt, but the silhouetted bird refused to budge. If I had been a rancher with a gun, I could have picked this one off from the window of the cab with no trouble at all. Only when the three of us piled out of the truck did it reluctantly take off. Its perch turned out to be a sizeable riddled mound which looked like it harbored mutant ants but was actually home to a colony of kangaroo rats. "There's your 'vertical' in this country," said Crowe with a smile. He was more interested in the fact that we had seen any eagles at all this late in March. Usually, he said, most of them would have headed north by now.

The likelihood was that we saw immature birds. Eagles take their time, about five years, reaching breeding age. Once they do, however, they are on their nests by March, which means that north-bound adults usually leave the wintering grounds by the end of February. Adolescent birds are in no such hurry. Depending on food supply and weather, and maybe the mood they are in, they may linger for several more weeks, or even into the summer months; what happens to them after that is some-

Incident at Eagle Ranch

thing of an ornithological puzzle. The problem is compounded by the fact that no one has as yet sorted out the migrations of golden eagles of the American West from those of their itinerant Canadian relatives. Some biologists believe that the mature American birds do not wander far from their nesting territories even in winter, and that the eagles migrating into New Mexico and Texas each year are a mix of Canadian adults and immatures, plus young eagles from Wyoming and Montana. But so far this is just guesswork.

Crowe, Mitchell, and I were staying at the same Roswell motel, so we had a leisurely after-dinner talk that evening, undistracted by eagles or their castings. Both young men were pleased, even grateful, that U.S. Animal Damage Control had hired them. Openings for wild-life biologists are hard to come by these days, partly because of the number of applicants, partly because of federal cutbacks. Those who are lucky enough to find jobs usually are not fussy about which agency takes them on. Understandably, Crowe and Mitchell were eager to establish reputations in their eagle specialty in order to ensure their professional futures. Mitchell, who would be stationed in the Roswell area, hoped to "get a publication" out of the assignment, and Crowe fretted about the inhibiting ambiguity of his role: "I don't make the policy," he explained. "Right now ADC is debating whether I should be in eagle research, or doing what I can to stop eagle predation by live-trapping, harassment, whatever."

Crowe had several vague ideas concerning eagle research: he had asked for, and was getting, three assistants to monitor and investigate rancher complaints of eagle predation in all the southwestern states. And he wanted more equipment, from high-powered binoculars to land rovers. But perhaps because of the schizophrenia built into his job—scientist or eagle trapper?—as well as his youth and inexperience, his intentions did not add up to a master plan. Almost all of his time was spent checking out rancher claims, trapping eagles, and transplanting them to federal refuges where they might or might not survive and settle down.

Crowe's availability had been well publicized in ranching circles but he had not been exactly beseiged by complaints. He ascribed this slow start to the ranchers' mistrust of the federal government. "They think we're out to make a case against them, or else they believe the problem can't be solved without killing the birds." Of the requests for help that did come in, not many amounted to much. He cited only four cases during the last two years in which there had been evidence of significant predation. One of these was the Auld ranch where five confirmed kills were discovered the previous year during the height of the lambing season. Another was a ranch near Auld's where eagles—bald eagles, interestingly enough—seemed to have killed some lambs while feeding on the carrion of others. However, the lambing operation was so badly managed, abandoned lambs so common, and "natural" mortality so high, that it was difficult to tell what was going on. One thing that was certain: eagle predation was not the major problem. On a third ranch, south of Fort Stockton, Crowe found "some indication" that kids were being preyed upon, but since the goats were breeding at all seasons of the year there was no way to assess the damage. Crowe urged the rancher to restrict kidding to special pastures and a spring season. The fourth case was the most serious. This was a ranch near Marfa, Texas, where Crowe spent some time last year. He confirmed five kills in two weeks during an intensive survey. All were fresh, all exhibited talon punctures with under-skin hemorrhaging (indicating the lambs were alive when the wounds were made), and, in two instances, eagles were flushed from the still bleeding carcasses. Crowe live-trapped several eagles and planned to return this year; but the ranch foreman had left a message for him just a few days earlier telling him not to bother. The place was called the Love Ranch, and I made a note to visit.

Crowe and Mitchell were temperamentally quite different, the former reserved and older-acting than his years, the latter wide-eyed and eager to try out his new job. However, they shared with each other, and apparently most of their generation of western wildlife specialists, a dread of seeming too personally enthusiastic, that is, "unscientific," about the subjects of their studies. They liked eagles, but they subscribed without question to the dogma on which most wildlife management curricula seem to be based, namely that wildlife is simply a resource existing at man's sufferance, and for his use. If these young men had inherited anything of the passionate caring of, say, Aldo Leopold, they kept it to themselves. Also, in the particular case of Crowe and Mitchell, reserve and objectivity may have unconsciously masked understandable personal concerns: aside from a mandate to live-trap eagles (how many? and on what grounds?) they had received little guidance about what they were supposed to be doing; furthermore, if eagle predation proved to be an insignificant problem, how would they keep busy? How would they justify their jobs?

Incident at Eagle Ranch

Interviewing ranchers can be a time consuming business. They often live eight or ten miles from the nearest paved road, and twice that far from each other; and when you show up at their doors they are, more often than not, out doing chores in an unspecified pasture or running errands in the town you just left. One way to beat this problem is to show up at a wool warehouse on a weekday morning. Ranchers, like other professionals, enjoy the company of their own kind, and the manager's office of a wool warehouse is a good place to sit around, drink coffee, and talk shop.

The Roswell Wool and Mohair Warehouse is no exception. On the morning of my visit, a choice selection of the area's sheepmen was on hand. Chief among them were the owner and his wife, Mr. and Mrs. James Goodrum, who ran two large ranches as well as the warehouse, and sold Indian jewelry to tourists on the side. If they were Mystery Guests, I would have guessed the last occupation before the other two; they were a neat, indoor-looking couple, not in the rancher mold. Among those present, Bill Ball came closest to the standard: a beat-up cowboy hat at one end and cowboy boots at the other, with a rugged, sunburned face, muscular shoulders, somewhat protuberant gut, and narrow hips in between. Joining him was Bronson Corn, an older, tidier representative of the type, with graying hair and sun glasses. He was a prominent member of a sizeable sheep-raising clan in the area. Charles Waller, temporarily retired from sheep raising, was the senior member of the group, relaxed, trim, looking fit.

Not counting Mr. Waller who owned land but not sheep, this small gathering controlled 250 square miles of the surrounding countryside through leases and outright ownership, enough to make a medieval nobleman's mouth sag with envy. About 10,000 ewes and 4000 "mother cows" grazed this land, which figured out to roughly one adult head of livestock for every eleven acres.

Despite the baronial statistics, all present confirmed that they were land-poor. Or at any rate sheep-poor. Or at least they had been until the price of wool began going up a few years ago. Mr. Waller had in fact quit the sheep business in 1970 because he was going broke and had stayed out ever since, although he toyed now with the idea of getting back in. Mr. Corn quit raising sheep in 1966, but soon changed his mind and began building up his flocks again. Both Waller and Corn conceded that the market price affected their decisions, but they also put much of the blame on predators. Corn insisted that because of coyotes he was bringing only 50 percent of his lambs to market in the sixties. In Waller's case it was the preventive costs of predator control that wrecked his operation: "I had 6000 sheep up at Clines Corners, surrounded by nothing but cattlemen who wouldn't help me with my coyotes. I wasn't losing sheep to coyotes, because I kept two full-time trappers on the place; and if a coyote did get in, I'd invite all my doctor and lawyer friends from town and we'd have a drive. But trappers were getting harder and harder to find, and the cost was breaking me—fifteen to twenty thousand dollars a year."

However, Waller never had any trouble with eagles. "The weather up there is worse than it is here so we lambed late, after they were gone." In contrast, although the climate at Roswell was more clement, the rancher attitude towards eagles was not. Bill Ball figured he lost twelve lambs to eagles in the last year, though he did not explain how he arrived at that figure. He did volunteer that his ewes sometimes got on their backs to scratch and, "like a turtle," were unable to get back on their feet again, whereupon eagles "will peck their eyes out." Mr. Corn said, "I know they eat on me and my neighbors but we don't have facts and figures. We don't start lambing for three or four more weeks (late April) and by that time they're gone. Every week you put off lambing costs you in the growing season, but you do save from eagles and the weather."

Mrs. Goodrum declared that "we get eagles as predators but nobody will substantiate it. I'm sure the man who works for us has seen them." Her husband, who had a pleasant habit of speaking in tandem with his wife, observed, "Some turkey from Game and Fish goes out for a day and doesn't see any, so they aren't there." He explained that "when it was lawful to control eagles, we controlled them. But the year after they began to be protected we lost 10 to 15 percent of our lamb crop. All we could see was that the lambs were being decreased by something besides weather and coyotes. We've gone into the eagles' nests and broke them up. You'd be surprised how many lamb carcasses you'll find in an older nest. . . ."

I reflected that this news would indeed surprise the biologists who have examined scores of eagle eyries in various Western states and repeatedly come to the opposite conclusion. I was not certain how the eagles could have increased their numbers and appetites so dramatically on Mr. Goodrum's ranch just a year after receiving federal protection. But it seemed an inappropriate moment to raise such questions. Mr. Goodrum was saying ". . . Anyway, after that one year of loss we moved our lambing dates back. We may be dumb, but we're not stupid."

Actually, the weather, more than the eagles, has given New Mexico ranchers reason to wait until May to begin the lambing season. And the eagle census transects that have been flown for the last several years in the state by the U.S. Fish and Wildlife Service do not indicate that the wintering birds gang-up here as they do in some parts of the Texas hill country.[1] There is no reason why they should, since, as already noted, once the southeastern plateau breaks free of the Rockies' massif, there are no attractive "verticals" here like the escarpments and broken hills that characterize Real County and the Trans Pecos—only the nests of Kangaroo rats and an occasional power line; so that depredation, when it occurs, has got to be distributed thinly. The fact is that these Roswell ranchers, given their reflex aversion to all creatures red in tooth and claw, do not seem quite as annoyed with eagles as their compeers in Texas are. Or at least they would not be if the ramifications of the eagle trial had not been felt even at this distance from Real County.

As Mr. Goodrum tells it, the federal investigator, Jim Stinebaugh, not content with riling all the sheep ranchers in Texas, has also aggravated those in New Mexico, especially Mr. Goodrum. It so happened that Clay Hunt, the multi-millionaire rancher who began as a silent partner in South Texas Helicopter Service and ended up as its president, ran sheep in New Mexico as well as Texas. In 1977 he offered the Roswell ranchers reduced rates to do some aerial hunting on their lands while his pilot and aircraft were in the area doing control work on his own property. "Just because this company killed eagles in Texas," fumed Mr. Goodrum, "this Steenbow—whatever his name is—decides they must have killed them here too." As a result of Stinebaugh's investigation, Goodrum's ranch foreman was one of the men brought before a grand jury to be questioned about shooting eagles from a helicopter. "There was harassment you wouldn't believe! One rancher had a heart condition already and he was so upset we were afraid he'd have a heart attack. It cost us money too. We were innocent, but you've got to defend yourself. We had to hire a lawyer for all of us. I've heard that that Steenbow fellow even claimed he found eagle feathers in one guy's driveway, which he probably planted there himself!" Mr. Goodrum looked around as though the walls might have ears. "We have reliable evidence that there have been two federal people out there with binoculars tracking eagles, and they have a tame bald eagle with a transmitter. . . ."

Mr. Goodrum's claims notwithstanding, it must be said that Stinebaugh had a bit more to go on than guilt by association: a pilot who worked for South Texas Helicopter Service, but who was not involved in the Texas case, had belatedly confessed that while he was flying New Mexico sheepmen on coyote hunts, several eagles had been incidentally shot. And Stinebaugh had found some eagle feathers—in a suspect's back yard, not his driveway. But without further corroborating evidence, the investigative grand jury hearing had drawn a blank. (Stinebaugh, no doubt thinking of the long hiatus in the Real County investigation, shrugs and says, "The case is still open.")

Asked whether he knew for certain that the suspected men were innocent, Goodrum and his righteous anger parted company. "Well," he hedged, "there's been shots fired at eagles to *scare* them. But let me put it this way. *I've* never shot one."

M r. Goodrum may never have killed an eagle, but he and the other men present have killed their share of coyotes. When they speak of the Great Coyote War, the listener is reminded of guerrilla warfare, or Indian attacks at dawn: the enemy encircles the defender's camp, outer defenses are infiltrated, strategies of containment and attrition are employed, holding actions are often successful, but the battle is never won. The War rages fitfully throughout the western rangelands, but the fighting is predictably at its most fierce wherever there are sheep. Only about one third of the western counties rate as sheep country, but even in most of that area, the animals are thinly distributed, not more than ten per square mile. The great sheep strongholds—forty or more animals per square mile—occupy only forty counties, or three percent of the total territory of seventeen western states.[2] The largest such area is on the Edwards Plateau in Texas, where one fourth of the West's nine million sheep reside. Some of the other great concentrations are in north central California, eastern Wyoming, southern Idaho, north central Utah, and southeastern New Mexico. But as of the late seventies, sheep and sheep country have been diminished by as much as two-thirds since their halcyon days in the forties.

Incident at Eagle Ranch

Except in ranching circles, this decline has largely gone unnoted. When mules or long horned cattle start getting scarce, there are usually individuals or groups on hand to protest, or at least sound sad. But it is difficult to get exercised about a reduced supply of sheep. The Bible's lovely prose and Mary's little lamb notwithstanding, most knowledgeable people agree that to know sheep is to loathe them. Of all the four-footed creatures man has invented they are the most blandly stupid and incompetent. With only a few exceptions, even the sheep raisers do not seem to like them very much, and frequently echo Mrs. Zimmerman's view that the animals are born looking for a place to die.

By way of compensation, no group of producers is more convinced than sheepmen of the utility of their product: a sheep is "the most practical animal in the world," because it produces both food and fiber, and makes a living where most other livestock would starve. Some sheepmen will also correctly point out that "Sheep don't destroy rangeland; ranchers do," meaning that when sheep are properly managed they are no more destructive to their habitat than any other herbivore. But even the most ardent champions of sheep husbandry, men like Mr. Goodrum, or Mr. Sims of the Texas Sheep and Goat Raisers Association, will admit that sheep can pick the landscape clean if allowed to do so; and they have been allowed more often than not. Economists and historians, as well as environmentalists, have opined that since the days of Solomon, and from central Asia to Nevada, sheep and their associate goats have wreaked more havoc on the surface of the planet than any other creation of Nature or man's—including the axe—since the last Ice Age. From the Old West there are many eyewitness accounts of travellers locating herds of sheep 30 or 40 miles away by means of the dust clouds enveloping defoliated mountain slopes. And early explorers have left numerous descriptions of vast grassy plains where the passer-by now sees only scrub and stone. Species of native western grasses, formerly abundant, have become as threatened as many forms of native wildlife. Throughout all of the sheep country, mesquite, greasewood, creosote bush, and juniper, once the flora of rocky hillsides, are now ubiquitous in the flats and on the rolling plateaus. Some specialists theorize that the control of prairie grass fires by the fire-break effect of roads allowed for this triffid-like invasion, while others argue that overgrazing was all that was necessary to eliminate the natural fire cycles. Still others caution that some of those early descriptions of lush grasslands are suspect, and that the

New Mexico

mesquite-juniper association was perhaps more widespread than is generally supposed. However that may be, even the most conservative authorities on rangeland ecology agree that the impact of too many sheep on the arid western range has been traumatic and, in some cases, terminal.[3] There are millions of acres in the West on which sheep still graze that look like the other side of the moon.

Modern day ranchers like Mr. Sims grant that their predecessors over-grazed the land, because "they didn't know any better," but they argue that those bad old days are gone and good husbandry is now the rule. Skeptics, however, observe that during the forties and early fifties, long after the sheep raisers "knew better," the skyrocketing demand for food-and-fiber induced a no-holds barred increase in western herds and a correlative deterioration of the already depleted range. The same skeptics point out that a depression in the sheep industry, induced by drought and competition from polyester fabrics, explains any recent improvement in range conditions better than the good intentions of the ranching fraternity. But there is even disagreement about how much improvement, if any, has occurred. The consensus seems to be that, given the sharp decline in sheep populations, the recovery of the grasslands has been minimal. There are acreages in South Texas where sheep have not grazed in seventy years that still will not grow a blade of grass.

In the ongoing saga of dust and sheep, the antics of the little prairie wolf, sneaky varmint, God's dog, Brother Coyote have been a persistent leitmotif. The coyote is still home on the range long after the buffalo has ceased to roam and the deer and the antelope have become a managed resource. Like the jack rabbit—indeed, perhaps because of the jack rabbit which is a staple in its diet—it is not inconvenienced by over-grazing and its attendant ecological ills. The adaptability of the animal is proverbial; both folklore and scientific observation attest to its wariness, its incredibly eclectic eating habits, its high reproductive rate, and its elaborate social structure which helps to ensure the survival of its young. It has extended its range, and it sometimes seems able to live anywhere. Even suburbs. The Los Angeles coyotes are famous; and I have myself watched a large dog coyote, looking neurotically harassed and citified, crossing a residential street on the outskirts of Denver.

Mr. Goodrum said, "When the last man dies, a coyote will be howling over his grave." He is probably right. Yet for all that, its gift for survival is overrated. There are vast regions of the West where resident coyotes have been exterminated or are very rare; the 24 million acres of the Edwards Plateau is the most notable example, but there are others, including much of the country around Roswell. These areas are sheep country. Sheep beg to be eaten, and coyotes, once they get the hang of it, are more than willing to oblige. Thus the Great Coyote War, which, in many of the provinces where it is waged, should be perceived as a territorial struggle: On one side, sheepmen and their powerful ally, the U.S. Animal Damage Control, hold great swaths of public and private lands from which they are either trying to expel coyotes or trying to keep them from getting back in. The effort to hold the line is called "preventive control." On the other side is the coyote tribe, supported earnestly but distantly by various conservation groups and, closer in, by the tolerance or neutrality of at least some cattlemen.

From strongholds the coyote still occupies it tries to recover the lands it has lost by means of the annual dispersion of its young. Outlying ranches and "buffer zones" along the perimeter of the sheep country, as well as federally owned rangelands, become the scenes of innumerable skirmishes. As in all guerrilla wars, casualty lists are not reliable, but there is no doubt that tens of thousands of sheep and hundreds of thousands of coyotes die each year. Just who is winning the Great Coyote War remains uncertain. Because the depression in the sheep industry has undermined the integrity of landholding and because some of the weapons once used are now banned, many sheepmen claim that they are in desperate straits. Spokesmen for the coyote argue that much so-called control bears no relation to real sheep losses, and amounts to a sort of canidaic genocide.

Where does truth lie?

Mrs. Goodrum: We never used to have coyotes west of town.

Mr. Goodrum: There are definitely more of them today than ever. In the fifties and sixties we had coyotes under control, but after the government took away 1080 and other poisons, there were large ranchers losing two-thirds of their crop.

Bill Ball: I'm in the center [of sheep country]. I got only two lambs killed on my place, but I hunted fifteen or twenty coyotes.

Bronson Corn: My predators come in from the east. I'm the first rancher on the outside boundary. In the last three or four months we've killed over 240 predators, mostly coyotes but a few other items, three or four bobcats. They [helicopter gunners] killed 147 coyotes in one run of a week's time over Christmas. My crew and I killed about forty. . . . My

New Mexico

losses? I haven't had any losses on my ranch since January, 1979, but I lost fifty or sixty lambs out of 300 on my farm. That's a loss of sixty dollars a head. The coyotes were killing one out of every five that was on the ground. A lot of them don't eat what they kill. . . . Now in 1978, that's a different story. On my ranch last year I lost approximately 300 head of sheep, mostly lambs. . . . Natural mortality? No, I don't have none of that to speak of.

Mr. Goodrum: Have I lost many sheep? Things are getting worse. Four years ago we had our first coyote kill. No, there hasn't been an actual increase in kills, because I'd rather fight them on my neighbors' land than on my own. I belong to two or three predator associations. We probably put in 1000 dollars a year, not counting wear and tear on equipment. I was on a coyote hunt a while ago, I drive a supercab Ford, a 10,000 dollar automobile; and if anyone had said I'd drive it at 60 miles an hour through that rocky country I'd have said they were out of their mind. But I got so excited hunting that coyote after it had killed 22 lambs. . . . Funny part is, we didn't shoot it. Someone ran over it!

Mrs. Goodrum: In one of my ladies' magazines I came across this Sierra Club ad with a coyote in a trap. Well, I felt it would make a great impact and it wasn't fair! They didn't show a mutilated lamb. They didn't show the wool that doesn't reach the market. . . .

Mr. Goodrum: A rancher does get emotional when he sees a sheep, still alive, with its guts hanging out. The big problem with environmentalists is communications. If they came out and we showed them our problems. . . .

Mr. Waller: The worst trouble with ranchers is that they're too individualistic. They're not ever going to get together.

Mr. Goodrum: It's true we're our own worst enemy. We drive a new pickup and car, and leave the impression we have a lot of money. Our ranch is not a money making proposition; it returns less than three percent now. We no sooner recover from one drought than we're in another.

Mrs. Goodrum: Has anyone mentioned how hard it is to get help?

Mr. Goodrum: The trouble is that a lot of young people don't want to put the time in. . . . The only thing that's saving ranchers today is the increase in land values, which increases his borrowing power. That, and the fur industry. The price of furs is keeping the coyote in control; there are all sorts of people out there trapping them now. When the price drops, all hell will break loose. . . . Have many ranchers sold out? Yeah, a lot of them have. Big money, big corporations, buy up the land, raise the price of it. . . .

Mr. Waller: This town is loaded with retirees. The biggest trouble is that they've disrupted our city government. Christ, we hardly ever had anybody going to city council meetings, and now all these retirees are changing our charter!

Mrs. Goodrum: They come out here because they didn't like where they were living, and then they find fault.

Mr. Goodrum: As long as they have the green stuff, we welcome them with open arms.

When I was about to leave, Mr. Goodrum escorted me over to a yellowing *Denver Post* cartoon tacked to his office door. It pictured a grinning hunter, shotgun in hand, emerging from an aircraft that has just landed. The hunter is addressing a bemused cowboy-looking bystander: "I finally solved the eagle problem," says the caption. "I shot all the sheep." I grinned. Mr. Goodrum grinned. "The only thing I'll say about environmentalists," he observed, "is that I thank God they weren't around when there were dinosaurs."

There are a few official reports to which the predation complaints of Mr. Goodrum and his circle can be compared. One of them is a 1974 U.S. Economic Research Service Survey of lamb and sheep losses in fifteen western states, based on a mail questionnaire sent to 38,000 sheepmen.[4] According to its findings, the average loss of that year's lamb crop to all causes was 23 percent. Just about half of this loss, 11.4 percent, was attributed to predation. Interestingly, New Mexico suffered a much greater total loss of lambs (47.1 percent) in 1974 than any other state, perhaps because of the kind of bad weather that has convinced Goodrum, Corn, and others, more than eagles ever could, to set back their lambing dates. But New Mexico also includes in that loss rate a higher than average loss to predators (17 percent).

The ERS predation loss figure for New Mexico has a special interest, because it can be compared with the figures in a similar, equally detailed survey conducted in southeastern New Mexico for 1972 and 1973, under the auspices of New Mexico State University's Agriculture Experiment Station.[5] During those two years, when weather conditions were evidently more favorable than in 1974, the wool growers reported losing only an average 7.3 percent of their marked lambs to all causes each year. Predators, however, were held responsible for almost all of this lamb mortality (5.5 percent). (In a breakdown of estimated deaths caused by different predator species, the eagle is accused of killing only 1 percent of the lambs; the coyote gets the lion's share of the blame.)

In other words, in the NMSU survey New Mexico sheepmen were claiming less than one third the predator losses they reported one year later in the federally sponsored ERS survey. At a first—even a second—glance, it would appear that the New Mexico ranchers are talking out of different corners of their mouths to the "feds" and their own people. Certainly the difference of a single year cannot explain that sudden orgy of predation reported to the ERS in 1974.

However, there is a complication. The state Experiment Station Survey concentrates on losses after the lambs have been rounded up and marked—that is, after the lambing season is about over. This is because the round up provides the ranchers with their first accurate count of the new crop. (Most sheepmen avoid visiting the lambing pastures more than they have to. Ewes will often desert newborn lambs if a man afoot or in a pickup inadvertently sets them running.) Therefore, estimated lamb mortality before marking is a haphazard business, based on what-ever cadavers might be found days or weeks later, plus sheer guessing.

Nevertheless, the ERS survey, unlike the Experiment Station one, encourages the sheep raisers to estimate the losses to predators that occurred *before* as well as after marking. In New Mexico, therefore, the 1974 ERS survey's reported loss of lambs to predators (17 percent) pre-sumably includes the estimated pre-marking losses, whereas the Exper-iment Station's predator loss figure (an average 5.5 percent) does not.

A bit of arithmetic is called for here. Assuming that predation loss figures do not fluctuate too radically from one year to the next—and evi-dence indicates they do not[6]—we can also assume that, if both surveys are on the level, the difference between the ERS's 17 percent and the Experiment Station's 5.5 percent, that is, 11.5 percent, must be accounted for by all the lambs devoured by predators before they were marked. But the figures do not add up. In 1972 and 1973, good weather years, the lamb survival rate in New Mexico was extremely high: 93 per-cent and 94 percent respectively. That is, for every 100 ewes in a herd, 93 or 94 lambs survived until marking time. Negatively stated, this means that there was a theoretical 6 percent mortality before marking—theoretical because many ewes have twins and others are barren.

Let us suppose that every ewe in southeastern New Mexico had given birth to one healthy lamb and that not one of these had died of natural causes before marking time—that, in fact, every one of the missing lambs had been slain by predators. If we add this impossible 6 percent predator loss before marking to the 5.5 percent reportedly killed by predators after marking, the total adds up to only 11.5 percent—still a far cry from the total loss of lambs to predators reported by New Mexico ranchers one year later in the ERS survey.

A Department of the Interior Advisory Report, *Predator Damage in the West* (which gets closer attention in a later section of this book), notes that the "comparatively high loss rates" reported by all the western states in the ERS survey "have led to questions about its accuracy."[7] The Advisory Report then proceeds to discuss the case of California, remarkably analogous to that of New Mexico; there too, an extreme discrepancy exists between the predator losses reported in a state comprehensive survey (for the same year, 1974) and those reported in the ERS survey, the latter being much higher. Therefore, the Advisory Report politely suggests that although the ERS survey is the most comprehensive report of predator related losses of sheep in the West, its tallies should be considered with "caution." It would be fairer to say that they must be considered worthless.

Which leaves us with the New Mexico Experiment Station's survey report. The reported average of 5.5 percent of marked lambs reportedly killed by predators in southeastern New Mexico is a serious economic loss, especially when it is understood to represent three-fourths of all the marked lambs lost to all causes (7.3 percent) for 1972 and 1973. Unfortunately, there is not much chance that it is accurate either, despite the fact that the compilers of the survey accept it at face value.

The discrepancy exists in the relation of the number of marked lambs killed by predators (5.5 percent) to those that died from all other causes (average 1.8 percent) during the last two years covered by the survey. Now it is certainly true that a lamb has a better chance of surviving into adulthood by the time it is marked than it had during its first two or three weeks of life. Nevertheless, we are still dealing with one of the most accident prone creatures on the face of the earth, subject, as it is, to myriad ailments and afflictions, from pneumonia and peritonitis, to malnutrition and orphanhood. Since management practises in southeastern New Mexico, as in the hill country of Texas, usually preclude close supervision of range flocks, the remains of lambs, marked or un-marked, are usually recovered, if at all, days or weeks after death has occurred. By that time they usually have been worked-over by carrion birds. Nevertheless, the survey uncritically reports that 70 percent of these casualties are the victims of predators.

The unlikelihood of this supposition is borne out—unintention-ally—by another study concerning southeastern New Mexico, published by the same Agriculture Experiment Station that produced the survey of predator losses.[8] Considering the intense controversy generated by the predator issue, it is surprising that only a handful of in-the-field studies of predation on sheep exist. This New Mexico study is one of them, and better researched than most. It is an "Evaluation of Sheep Losses on a Range Lambing Operation in Southeastern New Mexico" during 1974 and 1975. The site chosen for study, the McKnight Ranch, was about as close as the researchers could get to a perfect set-up for predation loss: a small holding in rough, wild country on the east slope of the Rockies, supplied with more than its share of visiting coyotes, bears, wildcats, and eagles. No predator control was exercised on the ranch itself, and little or none on adjoining areas during the first half of the study period. Under these conditions, predation was extremely high—an average loss of 13.8 percent of the recorded lamb crop, before and after marking, for each of the two years (but not as high, it should be noted, as the average 17 percent predator loss reported for New Mexico in the ERS survey). More to the point, however, is the fact that the study accurately, if indi-rectly, indicates the number of marked lambs (those tallied after June 1st) killed by predators compared to those that died of other causes dur-ing 1974 and 1975. According to this detailed survey, which employed every possible surveillance method, including some use of mortality transmitters, the average ratio of predator kills to other types of death was high—58 percent to 42 percent, or well over half the total deaths of marked lambs—but it was still much less, even under these conditions of maximum predation, than the average mortality among marked lambs (75 percent) that is attributed to predators by a representative sampling of New Mexico sheepmen in the Experiment Station Survey.

There are a number of other interesting conclusions to be extracted from this study. Among them: no lambs were attacked by eagles, even though time and place were conducive; coyotes did about as much kill-ing during the second year, when trapping at the ranch perimeter was greatly intensified, as they had done the previous year when it was

Incident at Eagle Ranch

minimal—which suggested that in vulnerable areas heavy predation loss is inevitable even with control; and accidents, starvation, and disease killed more of the total herd (5 percent of ewes, 12 percent of lambs) than predators did—indicating that rough country, poor range, and bad weather conditions are decisive factors in sheep mortality even when predators are operating at full force.

The report concludes that it has "verified that the problem of predation on domestic sheep, specifically that of coyotes, in southeastern New Mexico is real." It would perhaps be more accurate to say that it is real on a minority of ranch holdings that are as isolated and susceptible to predation as the one studied. But our concern is still with averages: on the average, sheepmen in southeastern New Mexico acknowledge that they suffered much smaller total losses of marked lambs (7.3 percent) than did the ranch in the research project (26 percent); yet they blamed a much higher percentage of those losses on predators (75 percent) than proved to be the case on the study ranch (58 percent), even though the ranch, far from being representative, has got to be a paradigm of predator problems at their most extreme. It seems fair to conclude that the average real loss of marked lambs to predators in southeastern New Mexico has got to be less than half of the loss discovered in the field study, no more than 30–35 percent of total losses. When the 5.5 percent loss figures in the 1972–73 Experiment Station's survey report are adjusted accordingly, only a little more than a 2.2 percent loss of marked lambs is attributable to predators.

Studies in other states support similar findings. For example, in four in-the-field studies conducted on ranches in Texas, Nevada, Idaho, and Wyoming, where predator control was in effect, the average predation loss was 4.5 percent, despite the fact that all of these ranches were considered to have serious predator problems.[9] Equally interesting, on three out of the four ranches for which total mortality figures are available, two to three times as many lambs died from natural causes as from predation.

The results of various state and regional questionnaires are also revealing.[10] All are more modest in their estimates of loss than the federal survey. State surveys in Utah, Idaho, Kansas, California, and Oregon, and a four-state canvass of Texas, Colorado, Wyoming, and Montana indicate an average loss to predators of 3 percent of the lamb crop compared to an average loss due to other causes of 10.3 percent. In other words, the ranchers were acknowledging that they were losing more than three times as many lambs to natural causes as to predators, even though the survey method is likely to produce at least some bias in favor of high claims of predator loss. Given that bias, even in state surveys, it is also reasonable to reduce the reported 3 percent predator loss by at least a few tenths of a percent. (This is particularly justified when one considers than even in the field studies mentioned above, all of them involving ranchers with significant predator problems, the average predation loss was only 4.5 percent.) Figuring in the majority of ranches that have little or no predation problem, the real average of mortality due to predators in the states surveyed is therefore probably closer to 2 than 3 percent. In short, it seems likely that few areas in the West exceed—on the average —a loss rate due to predators of more than 3 percent, and in most areas the loss is probably 2 percent or less.

Admittedly, these conclusions are based on limited evidence—all that is available—but the line of reasoning makes more sense than the ball-park guesses predicated solely on survey figures, or on the general inferences (as in the New Mexico field study) that are drawn from the built-in bias of the few in-the-field studies that are available, most of which deal with ranches that are highly susceptible to predation. Moreover, the two to three percent predation loss tends to be borne out by the New Mexico ranchers I spoke with, once the facts and figures are separated from the rhetoric. In this respect, the symposium at the Roswell Wool and Mohair warehouse is representative: A coyote killed one sheep on Mr. Goodrum's ranch in 1975, apparently the first and last to do so (in effect, zero losses in a herd of 3000 ewes). Mr. Ball said he lost only two sheep on his place in 1979 (out of a herd of 800 ewes). Mr. Waller used to ranch 6000 sheep, and although he understandably feels that the cost of preventive trapping was very high, the fact is that he had no predator loss to speak of ("I wasn't losing any"). Mr. Corn, who is on the territorial border in the Great Coyote War, but not so vulnerably placed, perhaps, as the McKnight ranch in the research study, claims to have lost about 5 percent of his range flocks in 1978–79 (300 head, mostly lambs, out of a herd containing 3,500 adult ewes); but then, he also discounts natural mortality among lambs as a significant problem. In the case of Corn's farm flock the loss was much more severe, about 17 percent (50–60 lambs out of 300) and there is no reason to assume he is exaggerating, at least not much. The farm operation was supervised, and Corn claims that he found almost all the bodies. The fact is that a single coyote with mayhem on its mind, or more likely, a denning pair, can create havoc in a small flock if the owner does not catch them in a hurry.

If we take these men at their word about their losses, and add up their various herds, including Mr. Waller's for the sake of argument (but granting him a fairly generous predator loss of, say, 150 lambs, on the assumption that he would have had to give up one of his trappers to stay in business), then figure in a better-than-average lamb crop of 90 percent, we end up with a hypothetical but plausible loss figure of about 2 percent. In practise, of course, that averaged figure has relevance only to agricultural economists and other general estimators, including, sometimes, environmentalists. What it means on the range is that a sheepman who lives in an area where coyotes are absent or heavily controlled may have no losses at all, whereas one who lives in a locality that is heavy on coyotes and light on control may have losses of 6 percent or more.

Ralph Simpson owns a relatively small (11,000 acre) ranch midway between Roswell and Vaughn. The moment the dirt road leading to his property crosses the guard and begins its mile long way across the pastures to the ranch house, even an uneducated eye notices the difference between this operation and others nearby: the rolling slopes are more green than brown; if there were not sheep in view, the visitor would guess that this was pretty good cattle range, not sheep country at all.

Simpson is remarkable in that he genuinely cares about his sheep. "I just enjoy them," he says. "I believe if you're going to choose livestock as a profession, then you have a responsibility, you know, a moral responsibility, to take care of your animals. I think I could probably make the same profit from cattle, but I'm a sheepman. Some people will tell you sheep are all alike, but that's not true. They have different faces. I think a sheep is smarter than a cow, if you want to know the truth. At least the sheep has the sense to come to water in the early morning when it's cool. The damn cow will wait till high noon; then she comes in, clomp, clomp, in the heat and dust. All the same, the West developed with the glamour of cattle, certainly not sheep. Cattlemen hated sheepmen from the beginning, and I think a lot of ranchers have clung to that old idea that cattlemen have more status. My dad was of that opinion. He kept the sheep so he could indulge himself with his cattle."

When he was young, Ralph Simpson considered other options. He went off to college, studied music, and for a while considered trying to make a living as a pianist. When that did not work out, he took a government job for a few years, long enough to "prove something to myself about holding nine-to-five employment." But although he did well at the bureaucratic routine and was soon promoted, he found himself increasingly "homesick for the ranching lifestyle," and in time he returned to it. He is a well-preserved sixty-four now, with fine eyes set off by crow's feet, neat close cropped gray hair and a three day stubble on his chin, soiled baggy trousers and a clean denim shirt that is neatly tucked-in in front and hangs out behind. His accent ranges from cultivated academic to country-western in a single sentence. He is addicted to Camel cigarettes, football, and western art. The walls of the long living room in the old ranch house are covered with original oils, watercolors, and sketches by Peter Hurd, R. C. Groman, and others; for variety there is a loud Picasso watercolor in one corner. But Simpson's greatest enthusiasm is for sheep. He is modest about it, but he is the only sheepraiser I would meet in my travels who, on an open range operation, consistently achieves that *sine qua non* of the sheepraisers' world, a better-than-100 percent lamb crop. In 1979 he marked 107 lambs for every 100 ewes, and the year before, even with a severe drought in this part of New Mexico, he managed a 104 percent crop.

One reason for his success is that he understocks: "The University of New Mexico's Agricultural College recommends 80 sheep to the section around here, but I only put 65 or 70. Then if you have a drought your forage will carry you longer." On the western range such an approach is unimaginably rare. "My father," Simpson admits, "was one of those who believed in overstocking. There was a time this place looked like a gravel pile."

However, a lot more than range management is involved in Simpson's success. "The few weeks of lambing season will make or break you," he said. Unlike almost all the other sheepmen I encounter who engage in range lambing, and who believe that ewes should not be disturbed lest they desert their young, Simpson is convinced that "you have to live with your sheep" during this critical period. He has arranged his pastures for the most efficient supervision, not more than 200 ewes to a single enclosure, with only one watering place per pasture so that he can observe each flock when it gathers to drink. He is on the lambing grounds at daybreak, and discovers at once if a ewe has not nursed. "Her udder gets big, you know; you spot her right away. Sometimes her lamb is just plain lost; or maybe it's in a badger hole. That ewe will lead you right to the hole, you know; she'll talk to her baby. . . ."

Nevertheless, Simpson admitted that ewes—especially the Rambouillets that he stocks and which produce the finest wool—are deplorable mothers. His efforts to offset this fact are herculean. Behind the ranch house are dozens of small pens which house orphaned lambs or, more often, confine reluctant ewes that will not allow their offspring to nurse. The recalcitrant mothers are tied with a wire that tightens when they try to kick their lambs away. And when a lamb dies, its skin is wrapped around an orphaned lamb in need of a mother, so that the lambless ewe is tricked into thinking it is her own.

These elaborate manipulations require much time and effort but they work; and Simpson, for all his modesty, takes pride in his success. He is uncensorious of the lambing philosophy of his fellow ranchers, but once or twice his dismay at their actual practise gets the better of him. He recalls one evening when he drove over to a neighbor's ranch for dinner: "I found this little orphaned lamb in the road, so thin there was no flesh on him. I picked him up and brought him to the house. Do you know what my neighbor told me? He said, 'take it back where you got it. Its mother will find it.' I was really embarrassed that he wouldn't feed that lamb, but I took it back like he said. In six hours it was sure to be dead."

A sheep is old at five years, so flocks must include a large number of two-year old replacement ewes, inexperienced mothers that are notorious for rejecting their young. "A lot of ranchers just don't feel they'll get many lambs out of their two-year olds," says Simpson, "but I don't feel that way." In a single year he has saved as many as 40 of the replacement ewes' rejected young. Since his herd numbers only 650 adult sheep, those 40 make a large part of the difference between his better-than-100-percent lamb crops and the "around 80 percent" crops that he estimates are typical for the area. He grants that if he had a larger ranch it would be much harder to keep a close eye on the lambing operation, but he would still do it his way, even if he had "to hire high school kids or more wetbacks" to help. In any case, he makes a better living with 650 sheep than do many ranchers with operations twice as large. "We don't make too much profit," he observes, "even the way we operate. There's inflation; and every time you're going to bank a few thousand some damn capital improvement rears its ugly head. But I do make a gain each year. And of course the real estate value continues to rise." This last fact is a potent element, for good and ill, in the economics of modern ranching. Not only does the inflated worth of land tempt many ranchers to sell their property even when they are making a satisfactory living, but it encourages others to over-extend their credit by borrowing on the increased real estate value not only to finance the next year's operations but to purchase more land or install capital improvements that are not always needed. Many of them find themselves hopelessly in debt to the banks. Simpson, like most other successful ranchers I encountered, borrows money only on his livestock. "No loan company has a paper on my land."

Simpson counts himself lucky in that he has no predator problems. His ranch is flanked on three sides by other sheep operations, but on the fourth there is a cattle ranch whose owner is "unsympathetic" to sheepmen. "Any coyote that reaches his fence is home free." Nevertheless, there have been only four or five coyotes on his ranch in the last twenty years. In his youth, he remembers, they were far more numerous, but in those fenceless days the flocks were tended by herders and dogs, and predators were kept more or less at bay. Now, he says, although coyotes are not as abundant as they once were, the fencing of pastures and the shortage of labor make sheepmen more vulnerable to attack. Some of his neighbors to the north and east have real problems and he occasionally participates in coyote drives on their lands. As for himself, "If I were living in real coyote country, I don't know whether I could make it or not."

My own feeling is that he would still do all right. He would know the minute a coyote took a lamb. As it is, he or one of his "wetbacks" regularly patrols the boundary fence of the neighboring cattle ranch, on the look-out for the first coyote track. Usually when ranchers experience heavy losses to coyotes it is either because they discover belatedly that killings are taking place, or, once the discovery is made, they do not know how to initiate their own controls and wait for the government trappers to bail them out. Judging from Simpson's performance in other respects, it seems likely that he would deal as effectively with an invading coyote as with a ewe that will not nurse its young.

As for eagles, Simpson's views flatly contradict those of his colleagues at the Roswell Wool and Mohair Warehouse. "I've seen eagles, a lot of eagles," he says, "and I've never seen one kill a lamb. I would know if they did. And yet folks around here just go into a tail spin about eagles. I don't understand it." He believes that, to the extent that the Eagle Act is enforced, it serves as a deterrent to any large scale eagle killing. "A rancher north of here set traps on a pole and caught an eagle a few years back, but the wardens flying over saw it and caught him. He was real worried because the fine could be thousands of dollars. They took him to Roswell for the hearing, and the judge fined him the minimum, a few hundred dollars. He came back tickled to death he got off as light as he did. . . ."

Simpson may have no problems with coyotes and eagles, but there is one species of wildlife that sometimes costs him dozens of lambs a year, and which he fights not with a gun or traps but with a hoe. This is the prairie rattler. "They're worse than a coyote to me. A little lamb will go right up to one, curious, you know, and it'll bite him right in the face. I once found five lambs bit in one morning. This year I've already lost five." Remarkably, however, the indefatigable Simpson manages to save about half of the snake-bitten lambs he finds. He brings in the paralyzed animals, as well as their mothers, and keeps the ewes lactating by compelling them to nurse other orphaned lambs while their own offspring recover, if they can, in a cool pen with a ready supply of water. If a lamb dies, its skin becomes a temporary jacket for an orphaned substitute which the ewe adopts as its own.

Simpson was the only sheepman I met who volunteered rattle-snakes as a hazard to the lambing pastures. Yet during field studies of predator loss, researchers have discovered that rattlers are a significant cause of lamb mortality on some ranches. It occurred to me that a ranch-er probably would not notice that sheep were dying of snake bite unless he spent as much time with them as Simpson does.

The drowsy light of a Sunday afternoon filled up the living room of the ranch house. Simpson had been up since the crack of dawn making the rounds of his pastures, arriving back at the house just a few minutes before I showed up at 11 A.M., but if he felt his sixty-four years it did not show. He puffed his cigarette, drank instant coffee, looked relaxed. I remembered Lanny Leinweber's remark about those elderly ranchers who are too old to "be out there in the pastures" all the time. And I thought of some of the ranchers I had talked with, lazing away their mornings over coffee in the cafes of Leakey, Vaughn, and Roswell. As with any other occupation, some ranchers work hard and others do not. The difference, I was beginning to learn, is that ranching is not really an occupation at all, like that 9-to-5 job Simpson tried for a while; it is a way of life. It requires hard work and sound management, of course. But it also requires the kind of intense personal involvement that shades

New Mexico

out the difference between what a person works at and what he is. Simpson's "moral responsibility" is not just something he owes his livestock; it has to do with his idea of himself. He is the rare good shepherd, the one who finds the lost lamb and brings it to the fold.

When I was about to take my leave, I looked around at as much of the ranch as could be seen, wondering what would eventually become of it. Simpson has no issue; his nephews are not enthusiastic about "the ranching lifestyle" and Simpson evidently is not very enthusiastic about them. "I don't plan to sell," he said stoutly. Then he added, "But if I ever have to, I won't be helpless. I have other prospects, you know, other interests I can turn to."

Incident at Eagle Ranch

5. The Trans Pecos

IN THE LAST CENTURY the wilder reaches of the Trans Pecos were much frequented by intractable Apaches, Mexican bandits, notorious renegades, and other human outcasts because they were such a good place to hide. For the same reason, a considerable number of furred and feathered outlaws still hold out in them, to the aggravation of ranchers in the area. No where else in the West has there been such a hue and cry about the misconduct of assorted varmints, especially eagles. During the fifties, aerial hunts for eagles were conducted out here on an imposing scale, and if the records of the hunting clubs are accurate, more than a thousand birds were slain each year. The publicity that attached to these killings eventually led to the protection of the golden eagle in 1962 under the provisions of the Bald Eagle Act. Since then, while prospects for the eagle have perhaps improved, they have worsened for the sheep industry in the area—there are now only a half dozen big sheep ranches operating west of Alpine—and many sheepmen see a causal relationship between the eagles' ascent on fortune's wheel and their own come-down.

It was early spring in west Texas. The valley I was passing through on the way from Van Horn to Marfa is part of the Chihuahuan Desert, but this early in the Spring the air is cool, and there are great yellow splashes of bladderpod beside the road. Ten miles to the north are the Davis Mountains, and to the south, a little further off, is the Sierra Vieja range. As western mountains go, these are not all that high—the Davis Mountains are in fact described as the southernmost foothills of the Rockies, barely reaching 5000 feet in elevation. But they make up in ungentleness for what they lack in size. They are dun colored or mauve, depending on the distribution of sunlight and shadow, and their contours vary greatly: long, folded slopes dotted with juniper, conical hills like the breasts of young girls, buttes, spurs, and prolonged divides surmounted by snaggled rimrock, arranged one behind the other like flats in a stage set. Now and again the ridge erupts into an imposing tor from which earth and shale have peeled away, exposing the limestone underpinning as a series of vertical ribs.

The sense of space takes some getting used to. Out here twenty miles, fifty miles, mean almost nothing. Roads, mountains, valleys, sky go on and on, and around the corner or just down the road or over the hill always seems a long way off. But it is not only the sense of space that gives this landscape its special language; a lot of other western places, including southeastern New Mexico, have their share of that. I was reminded here of the title of a novel I read when I was young, Paul Bowles' *The Sheltering Sky.* The Trans Pecos is one of those places where the sky is all the shelter there is. Everything else lies exposed; but the very nakedness of the terrain creates an unanswering privacy, like those daguerreotype faces of elderly Indian chiefs that reveal everything except expression. Further east, landscapes tend to be relatively intimate; the middle ground holds the eye. To the west, majesty takes over; everything is so grand and looked-at that one enjoys feeling insignificant or exalted. Whereas the Trans Pecos demands an ascetic rather than an esthetic response, or none at all. Here the stony heart of things— more daunting than any jungly, libidinous heart of darkness—lies right on the surface, uncaring, expressionless, where anyone can see it. It is no wonder that the desert fathers came to places similar to this to get rid of themselves. I am surprised that more west Texans are not mystics.

Most southwestern towns are one-half filling station-motel-and-McDonald's, and one-half suburban Anywhere. But Marfa is not like that, at least not once you get two steps away from Highway 90. There is a grand gothic pile of a courthouse, a selection of old-timey store fronts, and quiet streets lined with modest, country-looking stucco homes.

Incident at Eagle Ranch

There is also the stately Paisano Hotel. Ex-hotel. It was being converted into condominiums for retirees; but at least it had not been torn down. And its restaurant was still a going concern. When I showed up it was two minutes after nine; the restaurant was about to shut down for the night. After a succession of chrome and fluorescent eateries, the dining room looked like an appealing change, a dignified pale yellow space with neatly lined-up tables covered by shining white tablecloths. The solitary occupant, an elderly, petite waitress with bright red hair, read my disappointed expression, and after telling me I was too late, trotted off to the kitchen and asked the cook to open up again.

After a day of the stony heart of things I was feeling as gregarious as the most extroverted Texan, and as soon as my benefactress had served up a hearty plate of roast beef, mashed potatoes, and green beans, I invited her to join me at the table with a cup of coffee. She proved a companionable, talkative person; before long I discovered that she was a native New Yorker, and that she had showed up in Marfa during World War II for no better reason than that some friends had asked her to come along with them. There was a military base here at the time, and "a lot was going on." She had been self-stranded here ever since.

She liked Marfa and its people, but saw them with a New Yorker's appraising eye. The town hadn't grown much, she said, because the ranchers liked it the way it was and had seen to it that it stayed that way. "Which makes it nice and peaceful; but it's kind of hard if you're not a rancher and need a job." The ranchers "are the friendliest people in the world," and she is popular with them: "I'm welcome in all their homes." She recalled a recent occasion when she was catering a wedding reception for a rancher's daughter and had more orders for drinks than she could handle. Without being asked, the sheriff and one of the ranchers had helped her out, staying with her at the bar until the rush was over. "In New York, they would've let you drop dead," she added. "Here, if you need anything, they'll help you—*if* they like you. If they don't, you might as well move on."

Yet Marfa's social structure was not as static as these preliminary observations might suggest. In fact, as my waitress-companion pointed out, there was considerable flux and flow. Young people left for larger towns and cities, and "New People," retirees, moved in and bought up homes. Even more significant, another kind of New People, the Mexican-Americans, were "taking-over" numerically and politically.

The Trans Pecos

The school system, which used to be segregated at the primary school level, was now wholly integrated and "there's a lot of use of drugs." There was also considerable intermarriage. "The ranchers don't like it, but they don't say anything."

The dying adobe hamlet of Valentine, Texas, is "not far" from Marfa, and Clay Miller owns a 33,000 acre ranch "near" Valentine. Not far means 35 miles; near means about 10 miles from the closest paved road. My Corolla, already much put-upon by expeditions to other ranches, was showing signs of serious nervous disorder by the time the ranch headquarters, announced by locust trees and windmill, came into view. It was a pleasant, homely place, and pleasant, homely things were going on: Mrs. Miller was just leaving, on her way to deliver a Siamese kitten to a neighbor's home; and Clay Miller and one of his grown sons were gently urging a cow and calf into a corral.

Miller was in his early fifties, overweight, with bushy gray eyebrows and heavily lidded eyes. He was short of wind and had a slow moving voice that came from somewhere in his stomach. Instead of the usual cowboy garb he wore a gray hooded sweat shirt and loose-fitting trousers, comfort taking precedence over custom. Miller tends to go his own way in more than just his choice of apparel. This was never more evident than in 1962, when hearings were being held in Washington to determine whether or not the golden eagle should receive federal protection. Miller, like a number of other ranchers, including Dan Auld and his own cousin, Fritz Kahl, was on hand to testify, but with a notable difference. To the delight of conservationists and the chagrin of his peers, he endorsed protective legislation. He told the Congressional committee that although some ranchers undoubtedly lost lambs to eagles, the birds were not generally a serious problem. On the other hand, they were a vulnerable and much decimated species. He did not go so far as to advocate their complete protection; but he was against the kind of wholesale aerial gunning that was going on in west Texas at the time. As with Alfred Zimmerman, personal experience had goaded him to action. He had watched eagles being shot over his own property once too often; and it was this spectacle, more than a concern for abstract ecological concepts, that had brought him to Washington to testify.

Not that he was indifferent to the larger issues. Compared to most ranchers, he was unusually well informed about them. He studied zoology at the University of Texas; his wife was an enthusiastic bird watcher;

Incident at Eagle Ranch

but mostly it was a matter of temperament. Almost all the ranchers I met
enjoyed having non-predatory wildlife on their property; and notwithstanding the radical effect their operations often had on wildlife habitat,
they were right in claiming that the water and salt they provided for
livestock benefitted wild species, too. So did the protection that many of
them afforded for game species, even if it was frequently in the interests
of their own hunting pleasure or that of their paying guests. And unlike
so many westerners from the towns and cities, they were selective about
what they shot. But most ranchers take wildlife for granted because they
live so close to it, and their expertise is often confined to where and when
it can be hunted. Miller's interest is more active and more general. He
does not let folklore or a built-in bias against predators get in the way of
hard facts; he is a careful, unhurried observer; and when he is not sure of
something he says he is not sure.

He is pretty sure about eagles. For many years he has kept track, in
a casual way, of those that frequent the vicinity. He believes that nesting
pairs of golden eagles in West Texas are almost gone, and that the
numbers of winter migrants have gradually decreased in the last decade.
Not long after the ban on killing eagles went into effect, he was host to a
distinguished authority on birds of prey, Dr. Walter Spofford, who had
come to West Texas, sponsored by the Audubon Society, to study eagle
predation.[1] (Spofford would eventually report that there were not very
many eagles in the area, and that those that were present were doing the
sheepmen, of whom there were still a good many, more good than harm
because they were feeding chiefly on jack rabbits.) Miller recalled that
Spofford did find at least two ranches where eagles tended to congregate
and where he suspected they might cause trouble. "But one of the places,
in the Davis Mountains, still has sheep on it," he said. "The other, in the
Chinati Mountains, I don't know about. Spofford said he never got
enough cooperation from the rancher to find out if he had a problem
or not."

According to Miller, most of the sheep raisers—former sheep
raisers—in his area grew up as cattlemen. In the forties when wool prices
boomed, they packed their pastures with fence-to-fence sheep. During
the mid-fifties, however, the entire West was stricken by year after year
of drought, and west Texas was especially hard hit. "People around here
were caught in a bind. There were bad weather conditions, a declining
market, and the prospect of permanent damage to the range. To top it
off, there were expanding labor opportunities for young people at the

The Trans Pecos

time, which left ranchers at a disadvantage. So," he added laconically, "a lot of folks decided they were in the wrong business."

His post mortem on sheep operations in the Trans Pecos is supported by the report of a U.S. Fish and Wildlife supervisor, Kenard P. Baer, written on May 2, 1963: "A reliable rancher and good cooperator at Marfa [not Miller] told us that the very best sheep range in the area . . . could not support over 100 head of sheep per section [640 acres]. In spite of this, some range was being stocked at 200+ per section. He said that it was an impossible situation resulting in destruction of range that would *never* come back [Baer's italics]. We saw some of this and agreed with him."

Clay Miller sticks exclusively to cattle, but unlike most of his contemporaries, he did grow up on a sheep ranch. In spite of the great expansion in the sheep industry that still lay ahead, he is convinced that the worst abuse of the range occurred in the early thirties, "just before my earliest memories." He remembers great dust storms, and a time when his earliest chore as a small boy was to cut up sotol, a spiny plant with a nutritious, cabbage-like core, for the stock to eat. In those days, mountain lions killed more sheep on his father's ranch than any other predator. "Coyotes usually wouldn't kill more than one a night or one every other night. But lions go into a killing frenzy sometimes. It wasn't always a slaughter; under range conditions, the sheep aren't always together. Sometimes a lion would find an old ewe and her lamb, kill her, and go about his business. But I personally once found 63 dead sheep scattered around on one hillside, and it wasn't too uncommon to find a dozen or more. . . . But then you might go a month, sometimes two or three months, without trouble."

There are still lions on the rimrock, but there are not enough of them, or else not enough sheep, to cause problems in the immediate area. Miller suspects lions have increased in numbers since a low point in the fifties, partly because a decline in hunting pressure accompanied the decline in the sheep industry, and partly because the deer population grew rapidly in the early sixties. In any case, he bears no grudge against the ones that visit him now. They sometimes pass along the ridge above his house; they do not bother his cattle and he does not bother them.

Miller's attitude towards coyotes, however, is close to the orthodox rancher line. (At least nowadays that is the case. According to one source, he was as tolerant of coyotes once upon a time as he still is of eagles. But if that was ever true, it is not now.) He told me that during the heyday of the sheepmen, coyotes were effectively controlled with traps and poisons. "In the late fifties there was only one federal trapper who worked this part of the Valley. Even then there weren't as many sheep ranches as there had been, and he would pretty much confine himself to those that were left. He'd maybe trap 20 coyotes a year, average, in an area of 500 square miles. The breeding population was so low because the sheepmen kept it that way themselves." Since then, he said, the population has increased to one or two animals per square mile. "There isn't the manpower now to keep them in check. A trapper I know told me he used to get along fine when they gave him 150 dollars a month and a pickup, but these days his family can't live on that. Now he's working in a filling station."

There are conflicting reports about the relative abundance of coyotes. The experts, basing their estimates on probable densities per square mile, come up with a guess—they admit it is only that—that in the western states there are about one and a half million animals in a winter population, more or less evenly divided between adults and juveniles.[2] During the last six or seven years, the U.S. Animal Damage Control has maintained scent post surveys throughout the West that suggest trends in overall coyote abundance. According to this rather sketchy index the species' numbers have bottomed out after declining by about fifteen or twenty percent since a relative high point in 1974.[3] By no coincidence, the drop corresponded with the boom in "fun furs," in which coyote pelts figure prominently. Miller, like Goodrum, confirmed that "everybody with a little spare time is out there setting traps."

Nevertheless, not only Clay Miller but every rancher I talked with in Texas and New Mexico insisted that coyote populations were positively blooming. There is no reason to assume that all of these people were mistaken. Clay Miller, for one, is probably correct about the increase of coyotes in his own neighborhood. I would be inclined to believe this careful and observant man in any case, but his claim had been substantiated by an incident earlier that same day. At a cattle ranch further up the road, I had been visiting with the owner's son, a thickset, snub nosed young fellow with the wonderfully western name of Beau White; and our conversation had turned from eagles (no real problem) to coyotes (also no problem as far as the cattle were concerned, although a lot of antelope fawns were being killed). White unsurprisingly assured me that coyotes were thick as fleas hereabouts; then, on impulse, he suggested that we try to call one up to prove the point. He warned me that he did not have much time to spare, and in any case the wind was blowing too strongly to make success likely; but it was worth a try. For the next half hour we waited beside an arroyo, not more than a hundred yards from the ranch house, while the ghastly taped screams of a jack rabbit—I have often wondered how the recorded animals are made to go on like that—were caught by the wind and snatched away. I watched a harris hawk hunting a real jack rabbit on the nearby mesquite flat, but nothing else happened. It was, I would later learn, a pretty amateur effort. No matter. The fact that Beau White thought there was at least a chance a coyote might show up in that half hour, that close to the house, in a wrong-blowing wind, had its own significance.

Later on, I checked the Animal Damage Control coyote indices for 1977 and 1978 and discovered that two scent post lines were being run in the Valentine-Marfa area. The number of coyote visitations of these lines suggested that, although the animals are on the increase in the area, they have a long way to go before they approach anything like the population in south and east Texas where visitations are two to five times as frequent. (On the sheep-crowded Edwards Plateau, significantly, the lines indicate an almost total absence of coyotes.) But what was most striking about the data was its variability. For example, in 1977, the irresistably smelly scent posts on line #3, apparently not far from Valentine, were visited 70 times by an unknown number of coyotes, while those on line #4, south of Marfa, were savored during only 27 visits. In 1978, however, exactly zero visitations were counted at #3, while those at #4 almost doubled to 57. A likely inference, in the case of line #3, is that the Animal Damage Control people, having lately received a fat increase in their aerial gunning allocation, had put it to use. But the more general implication is that in local situations, coyote numbers may wax and wane from one year, and one square mile, to the next, depending on food supply and the degree of predator control.

Clay Miller would prefer to see them wane. "I'd be perfectly happy to reduce coyotes by 50 percent," he said, "I'm not interested in eliminating them or even reducing them to sheep country levels . . ." He paused, gave me a dry grin, ". . . but I hope you've gathered that my feelings about control of eagles and coyotes are entirely different. There is no possibility of endangering coyotes as a species, whereas eagles. . ." and here he

sounded as though he still remembered his Washington statement word
for word, ". . . are highly visible, have low productivity, and it's highly
possible to endanger them.

"It's been documented"—a favorite phrase of Miller's—"that some
coyotes will live in a sheep pasture for years and not kill sheep. But you
have to say that sheep raising and coyotes are essentially incompatible.
It's essential to control coyotes at a very low population level. And when
there's a shift out of sheep—primarily due to economic factors—there's a
blockbuster effect: As one rancher goes out of business, it increases problems for his neighbors." He added that he would never get into the sheep
business now, assuming he were the only one in the neighborhood to try
it, because he was convinced that losses to coyotes would be too severe.

But the reason Miller is down on coyotes is because, like Beau
White, he believes the animals are taking more than their share of antelope fawns. Although most of the sheep are gone, the ranch pastures—
immense by eastern standards but still delimiting—have retained their
mesh wire fencing, which restricts the movements of pronghorns as well
as livestock. Beau White, for example, knew he had exactly 22 doe antelope on the small ranch he operated for his father. He had seen coyotes
distracting one of them, and later discovered the remains of her fawn.
Last year the herd raised only two fawns, and he was convinced that
coyotes got most of the rest. Clay Miller, and several other ranchers I
would talk to later, had similar stories, though the claimed losses were
not usually so high. A lot of money rides on the issue. In these parts,
a guest-hunter will pay three to five hundred dollars for the privilege
of picking-off a decent pronghorn trophy. There is no sport involved;
the hunter is taxied out to the herd in a jeep or pickup, which is often
equipped with a shooting platform; when he sights the animal he wants
or is willing to pay for, he knocks it down with the help of a telescopic
sight. My little red headed waitress had deplored this local practise: "The
antelope aren't like deer you know; the poor things hate to jump fences,
so they don't have a chance." Even so, Valentine and Marfa are the only
places in Texas where considerable numbers of them can be seen. You
could see still more, say the ranchers and the state wildlife people, if it
were not for the coyotes.

A couple of studies indicate they may well be right. But there has
got to be a little more to the equation than so-many-coyotes-more equals
so-many-antelope-less. After all, in Wyoming there are a lot of coyotes

The Trans Pecos

and swarms of human hunters; yet in places the pronghorns are coming out of the rocks. Although the Trans Pecos did once have a native stock of antelope, some biologists suspect they were never very plentiful (the present population has been re-introduced) because of food supply, the composition of soils, above all, the frequency of droughts. Nobody knows. But it is at least possible that the prevalence of mesh wire sheep fences on the West Texas pastures is now a critical factor as well. The antelope tend to exist hereabouts as isolated bands rather than contiguous, interacting, exchangeable units of a large regional herd. In these circumstances, it seems likely that the effect of coyote predation upon the limited prey base is more traumatic than it would be under more natural conditions, especially in instances where a small nucleus herd, like Beau White's, is just getting started. This is an amateur's guess, of course. But the really odd thing is that there is apparently no one in the world of antelope expertise who can tell me whether it is right or wrong. In fact, although the mesh wire fence is known to cause the deaths of antelope during hard winters in the northern tier of western states, its effect on the overall ecology of the species, including its influence on predation, has not been studied. Meantime, the coyote, no doubt a factor in the shaky condition of some southwestern antelope herds, carries the brunt of blame.

Clay Miller is a slow speaking, slow moving man, but in his interesting company time hurries; noonday had come and gone. While he hunted in the refrigerator for cheese and coldcuts, I was free to look around. From where I sat in the kitchen, much of the tiny living room was in view. Its most riveting feature was the skin of an enormous rattlesnake, mounted, like the one in Bob Ramsey's house, on a red velvet mat. But there the resemblance between the two establishments ended. Most of the ranch homes I visited ranged from the opulent to the modestly comfortable. The Miller household was almost humble. This was surprising, since the ranch appeared to be a flourishing operation, with fat cattle and what passed in this arid country for a luxuriant display of grasses and forbs in the flatland pastures. When Miller settled down in his chair again, he explained that in fact this dwelling was originally used by hired hands. The main ranch building, "a pretty nice house," burned a few years earlier and, what with sons to send through college and a recent drought to contend with, there had not been enough money

Incident at Eagle Ranch

to rebuild. But he was unquerulous about his lot. "It is eminently feasible," he said with wry ponderosity, "to make more dollars in a lot of other fields. But we're getting along. It's cyclical. We'll do all right if we don't get another drought. But there's mighty few ranchers who get rich ranching. However, there are a lot of rich folks who like to get into the ranching business. Which is not the same thing." This brought up a theme that had recurred often in my travels: the effect of sociological change on the ranchers' world, of outsiders moving in and ranchers' children moving out. Miller quickly made clear that his problem was not how to keep his sons down on the ranch after they'd seen Dallas: "All of my four boys love the ranching life," he sighed. "But in this country, 33,000 acres is not much land to divide four ways. . . ."

The Love Ranch, southwest of Marfa, faces an even more typical dilemma. The previous owner, W. F. Love, died in a plane crash some years back, and although his widow has remarried, most people still refer to the ranch by its former name. This is only fair, since from all accounts the senior Love was the last of his line to take a personal interest in the property. His two children live a long way off. One comes to visit maybe once every other year, the other almost never.

This seems a great pity, for the Love Ranch is an awesomely lovely place. It is a sort of private national park, fifty square miles of high wild country, much of it as austere and remote as anything in Big Bend, which lies about 80 miles to the southeast. The bumpity ranch road climbs, imperceptibly at first, across the introductory foothills of the Cuesto del Burro Mountains. The ranch buildings are clumped against the first serious slope of the mountains themselves; but because there is no view beyond, the impact of this topographical change is postponed for several minutes while the road cuts to the right, by-passing a metal silo and several staring horses, then climbs for a mile to a high divide. At the top, the field of vision opens on a prospect that is magnificent but also startling: the country ahead seems to have been petrified in an epileptic siezure. It is unable to decide whether it is falling up or climbing down, whether it is canyonland or mountain. It is rimrock, seen close up: spires, round towers, ampitheatres, small valleys and ravines, granite chairs and tables, cliffs, spurs, and acres of gravelly outwash. Yet the fractious details of this geological three ring circus unite, when seen at a distance, into a manifestation of pure hostility. Even mountain lions and eagles might wonder if they are welcome here. In its wild, unkind way, this place is as lovely as any on earth, but it is also the sort of country where you could break a leg sitting down.

At the ranch headquarters, Mrs. "Buster" Holland, the wife of the manager, told me about the disaffection of the senior Love's heirs: "There's a lot of that," she said. "Right in this area I know of only two or three ranchers' children who are on the ranches and helping out. A lot of them go to college and don't come back. Or the families move into town with the kids and let Mexicans run the ranches." She confirmed the red-headed waitress's view that the Mexicans also run Marfa. "Any time a political job comes up—that has a salary attached to it, you under-stand—they pull together." But she granted that most of Marfa's Mexican Americans are good people. "Not too intelligent, you understand; but they can't help that."

We had been waiting for Mrs. Holland's husband to show up for lunch, and a few minutes after this, he did, a middle aged man with a weathered looking face, accompanied by a younger neighbor who had been helping him with the morning's chores.

To anyone interested in the eating habits of the golden eagle, the Love Ranch is a place of some importance. The same landscape that inspires intimations of existential nothingness in human visitors is a refuge to migrant eagles, and for as long as anyone can remember they have settled here during winter months. It is at the center of an area where eagle predation on lambs has been considered very serious indeed. Spofford came here; and so did another researcher, Leo G. Heugly, who conducted further studies for the Audubon Society in the late sixties.[4] In 1978, the previous year, Sam Crowe, Animal Damage Control's "eagle man," visited the ranch in response to Mr. Holland's complaints and live-trapped three eagles after discovering evidence of several kills. He had expected to be summoned again this year, but Mr. Holland had left word at the last minute that he was not to bother. Crowe had wondered about that, and so had I.

Mr. Holland's explanation was simple enough: "We haven't had any eagle problems this spring," he said, although the lambing season had begun. For some reason, few eagles showed up, "but," he added, "we sure have had problems in the past."

Incident at Eagle Ranch

Although it may have no connection with the message Holland had
left for Crowe, the manager did feel miffed with the young biologist
earlier this year: "We heard he was quoted as saying we have more eagles
than anybody, but that we still have a 90 percent lamb crop!" Holland
has since decided to give Crowe the benefit of the doubt: "I think Sam
was innocent on this; I think he was misquoted." But he still bridled at
the idea of a 90 percent lamb crop these days. Although he assured me
that back in the sixties, "when coyotes were under control," the lamb
crop at marking time could range from the low 80s to almost 100 percent. When asked about more current survival rates, Holland checked
his record book and produced figures for eight of the last ten years, explaining that he couldn't find those for 1971 and 1974. Here they are:

1969–82%; 1970–81%; 1972–92%; 1973–63%; 1975–89%;
1976–38%; 1977–81%; 1978–73%.

Field studies of general lamb mortality in unsupervised range operations, with and without benefit of predators, are few in number. There
are enough of them, however, to indicate that even without predation,
losses of 10 to 20 percent of the lamb crop are the rule. Ranchers like
New Mexico's Ralph Simpson who regularly achieve a better-than-100
percent lamb crop are so few that their numbers have almost no statistical significance. According to data collected by Heugly, an 80 percent
survival rate at marking is average for most range operations.[5] As far as
west Texas is concerned, the most useful information available is data
provided by the U.S. Department of Agriculture's office at Austin. According to its calculations, the Texas lamb crop at the time of marketing
averages between 80 and 85 percent or less. (This average is based on
the number of adult sheep on hand at the beginning of the lambing
season.) It should also be kept in mind that since most of the lambs produced in Texas come from the relatively predator-free Edwards Plateau,
predators can have little bearing on the total survival rate.

Given the hostile terrain of much of the Love Ranch and its vulnerability to predators as it becomes more isolated from other sheep operations, as well as the missing averages for two years, the figures cited by
Holland would not seem all that out of line, not even with his recollections of the more productive sixties, if it were not for the lows in 1973
and especially 1976. When asked about the poor lamb crops for those
years, Holland was a bit sketchy, mentioning drought and the exceptional prevalence of locoweed as "having something to do with it."

The Trans Pecos

As for eagles, Holland became a bit vexed just thinking of them. "We've had three different people in here to see whether eagles were killing lambs, and I told them all that if they really wanted to find out, they should get in the sheep business with their own money and they'd learn pretty fast whether there was a problem or not." In contrast to Clay Miller, he believed their numbers had increased, at least until the current season. "Used to be, when I started here, we'd just get on the phone and call an eagle hunter, and he'd get rid of them." Now, he said, the eagles were year round residents.

Holland had no idea what percentage of his lambs were killed by eagles, but it is likely that he belongs to that apparently select group of sheepmen who have a genuine problem. Heugly, almost unique among eagle researchers in that he set up observation posts in sheep pastures, watched eagles attacking two lambs and one kid not far from the Love Ranch; and he eventually concluded that eagle predation on selected pastures in the area accounted for one or two percent of the total lamb crop. (A kidding operation which he observed suffered much higher casualties.) Crowe found five eagle-killed lambs on the Love Ranch during a two-week search. However, he would acknowledge during a subsequent conversation that two of the lambs had been abandoned. This fact might be coincidental, were it not that Heugly, in his more extensive surveys in the area, determined that out of seven lambs killed by golden eagles, five were rejected by their mothers or orphaned. Abandoned lambs were also a prominent feature on two other ranches that Crowe explored in response to complaints about eagle predation, and although he did not quite say as much, it seems clear that some, if not all, of the lambs killed in those cases were motherless. It is hardly surprising that this should be the case. One of the few predictable laws of predator behavior is the marked inclination of the predator to select, when available, prey that is already in trouble; and nothing is more blatantly in trouble than a bleating, solitary lamb (a fact borne out, in the aftermath of the eagle trial, by the swift attack on Ramsey's tethered "bait"). Since abandoned lambs are a not uncommon feature of even well-run operations, and are present in large numbers on badly managed pastures, they no doubt receive a disproportionate share of attention from any eagles in the neighborhood unless, of course, there is someone around like Ralph Simpson to collect them.

However, Buster Holland was not likely to give much credence to the abandoned lamb theory; and I was not about to press it. Instead I

added up the three unabandoned lambs which Crowe found during two
weeks of searching, and the three times as many that he might have
missed in that rough country, multiplied the total by four or five weeks
of the lambing season, and came up with a pretty arbitrary loss to eagles
of about 30 lambs. If that loss is substracted from the (maximum) 3000
lambs born alive on the Love Ranch it comes within the minimum
range—one percent—of Heugly's estimate. One percent does not seem
like much, but the cash value of 30 lambs, about $1,800, sounds more
impressive.

Even so, this was only about one-third of the amount that the Love
Ranch paid out to control coyotes, which Holland admitted were much
the greater problem. Without that investment, he said, "there's no way
we could make it." The cost included the services of a trapper who worked
a vast territory around the ranch as well as the ranch itself, plus periodic
aerial hunts sponsored in part by the U.S. Animal Damage Control.
These preventive measures accounted for about 100 coyotes a year.

Bobcats were not a problem nor were the occasional lions. In the
past ten years, Holland could recall only two occasions when an itinerant lion might have killed a few sheep. Like all ranchers, he insisted that
he did not want to see any animal become extinct; but he believed that
the only reasonable solution to the predator problem was "to lift all government restrictions."

Holland's temporary helper was a native of east Texas. While Mrs.
Holland prepared lunch, and her husband and I talked, he sat quietly in
a corner, only occasionally joining in the conversation. At one point, he
remarked that he was among those who feel that eagles are hard to shoot
from the ground; he had "wasted a box of shells trying to hit them." At
another, he echoed a belief widely held by west Texas ranchers that
wintering golden eagles derive from Mexico and are therefore an alien
species:"What I don't see," he said,"is why there's all this fuss over killing
Mexican eagles!"

The Marfa airport north of town looked silent and empty in the
late afternoon sun. A lone buck antelope browsed just across the road,
and behind it the conical foothills of the Davis Mountains stood out like
red kilns in the almost horizontal light. Fritz Kahl was running a little
late; but presently his small plane hummed into view, alighted, and taxied
to a standstill. He jumped out, attended to a little business, and invited
me to settle down in the hangar office where he managed the airport as

The Trans Pecos

well as his own flying service. He remained standing, a heavy featured man with a considerable gut superimposed on a powerful frame. He looked like he might coach the local high school football team in his spare time.

Years ago he was part-owner of a large combination sheep-and-cattle ranch in the nearby hills. The ranch was still there but Kahl was no longer raising sheep. "Everybody knows that predators were part of the problem," he said, talking to the window. "I'm not saying where they fit in—first, second, or third place—in the total causes why sheep are practically gone from this country; but they were a major factor." He stared moodily at the setting sun, which stared back, turning his face orange. He looked out over the grassy flats that extend beyond the runway. "Five years ago you could come out here at 6 A.M. and not hear a coyote barking. Now we've got two coyote dens right by the airport."

Fritz Kahl is Clay Miller's cousin. The two men like and respect each other, which perhaps attaches a special force to the fact that they spoke on opposing sides at the Washington eagle hearings. Kahl was still resentful about the Congressional decision to protect eagles. Since I had often heard environmentalists lamenting, not without reason, their own inexpertise concerning the political process, and the excessive influence of the special interests that oppose them, it was instructive to hear Kahl's point of view: "We found out that it doesn't matter what side you're on as long as you got the numbers. It was like sending the Boy Scouts out to fight a war. We had no idea how deeply the Audubon Society was involved in our government. . . ."

We were briefly interrupted at this point by the arrival of a Border Patrolman whose plane had just landed. Since coming to the Trans Pecos, I had noticed several of the Patrol's airplanes waltzing dangerously with the hilltops. At first I ignorantly supposed they were ADC aircraft hunting predators; actually, they were hunting men. From the patrolman's comments, it seemed that the "wetbacks" were even less susceptible to control than coyotes. He caught his share of them, he said, but the whole operation, underfunded and neutered by diplomatic considerations, was "a bad joke." At best it barely kept the lid on. His sardonic, shrug-of-the-shoulders mood became part of the room's atmosphere after the man himself had left.

Kahl returned to our subject: "The environmentalists and ranchers have reached an impasse. They've worn each other out." But his tone belied this. He could still get bitter when he talked about eagles. "No," he

Incident at Eagle Ranch

said, "they're not increasing around here now. And we don't have many nesting pairs either. The reason is that they've gone where the feeding is easier. They've decreased in the last ten years, but it's due entirely to the lack of kids and lambs. Lockhart [Michael Lockhart, a biologist and eagle specialist with U.S. Fish and Wildlife Experimental Service] tells me that they're moving to New Mexico."

If this were so, New Mexico's own eagles had to be moving elsewhere, since the number of wintering birds in the state had remained fairly stable during the 1970's according to Fish and Wildlife transect surveys. (This was, incidentally, an improvement on the overall survey findings which indicated a distinct downward trend of both nesting and wintering golden eagle populations in the Western states.) Since Lockhart had taken an active part in the surveys, it was not likely he would have made the remark Kahl ascribed to him except as a joke. In any case, Kahl's memory was apt to play tricks on him. For example, he told me that during the Washington hearings in 1962 he testified that he lost 15 percent of his lamb crop to eagles. Yet there is still a memorandum in existence, dated February 12, 1963, written by a U.S. Fish and Wildlife biologist, William D. Fitzwater—a man by no means unsympathetic to the ranchers' interests—and addressed to the Regional Director of Fish and Wildlife (then called the Bureau of Sports Fisheries and Wildlife) which quotes Kahl as saying that he "lost 120 lambs to eagles from a herd of 2000 ewes in 1962." This would be a loss of 6 percent, not 15. But in the same interview, Kahl also told Fitzwater that there was only a 1 percent natural mortality rate of lambs in the area, an estimate that seems phenomenally low, especially when one considers there was a recurrence of severe drought in West Texas during the early sixties which, according to a U.S. Department of Agriculture spokesman at Austin, seriously affected lamb production from 1961 to 1963.

Still later, in 1964, in a transcribed telephone conversation with the USFW supervisor of management and enforcement in the area, Kahl said that he had lost "over 100" lambs the previous year to both "eagles and coyotes." Since all ranchers in West Texas agree that coyotes are an even more perfidious nuisance than eagles, it is unlikely that the latter would have accounted for more than half the hundred-plus lambs Kahl claimed he lost, assuming the estimate had any relation to reality at all. In other words, within a span of a couple of years, Kahl was variously claiming that he was losing 300 (15%), 120, and (presumably) not more than 50 of his lambs to eagles.

The Trans Pecos

It is also worth noting that in the same memorandum in which Kahl is quoted as saying he lost "over 100" lambs, he was more precise than he is now about where predators "fit in" when blame is allocated for the decline in the West Texas sheep industry: "75 percent of the reason is because of the increase in prices [of mohair, as compared to wool], 25 percent because of the loss of lambs to eagles and coyotes."

Clearly, Kahl has no idea how many lambs he lost to eagles when he was in the sheep business. Driven by frustration and anger, he resorts to the same sort of quasi-syllogistic logic, understandable but unacceptable, that so many ranchers construe as evidence: eagles are known to eat lambs; I am producing fewer lambs than I should; therefore, eagles have eaten the missing lambs. The flaws in this deduction do not necessarily exonerate the eagle—but they do suggest that Kahl's estimates of the extent of eagle predation were sheer guesswork.

Dr. Walter Spofford granted that Kahl's operation may have been one of the few he visited in 1963 which were having trouble, although he also flatly stated that "the claims ranchers make that eagles are primarily responsible for their problems are ridiculous." Spofford was in the Trans Pecos under the auspices of the Audubon Society, researching eagle predation in response to the hue and cry raised by Auld, Kahl, and other West Texas ranchers after the golden eagle had received protection the previous year. Kahl said he flew the scientist over his ranch: "I showed him eleven eagles on my place in less than an hour. Eleven eagles! Eleven eagles will eat eleven lambs a day. Do you know what Spofford said to me? He said 'You do have a problem. What you should do is take your sheep to Kentucky. They don't have eagles there.'"

Kahl swore by this story. Some weeks later I would check it out with Spofford himself. The biologist acknowledged that he might have said "some such thing." At first he explained that he had meant it only as a joke, but on second thought he provided a somewhat revised interpretation of that long-ago remark. "Oh, it was a joke, all right," he said, "but it was a half serious joke. After all, there are only a handful of places in this country where eagles are concentrated enough to prey significantly on sheep; whereas there are thousands of places with no eagles where you can raise sheep. In a way I suppose I did feel that if Kahl was convinced eagles were that much of a problem, he ought to move his operation to some place where there weren't any." For his part, Kahl might respond that he has gone Spofford one better by quitting the business entirely.

Incident at Eagle Ranch

During the forty mile drive to Fort Davis, I composed a letter in my head. It is one that I never wrote, but if I had, I would have addressed it to Buddy Pape's wife, Reba. It was about mountain lions. During my interview with her husband, soon after his conviction for killing eagles, I had made an offhand remark that revealed my partiality for these beautiful and exclusive animals. Mrs. Pape kept her peace at the time, but several weeks later she sent me a clipping from a Texas newspaper which reported that lions were causing trouble in the state's Black Gap Management Area near Big Bend National Park. The article cited the following instances: the cats were wrecking the Texas Parks and Wildlife Department's efforts to maintain a captive herd of desert bighorn sheep, and they were preventing a severely depleted herd of mule deer from making a comeback. Mrs. Pape's intent, as the accompanying letter made clear, was to prove to me just how pestilential mountain lions could be. But the newspaper story inadvertently sabotaged her case with more information: no doubt the state biologists had good reasons for establishing the nucleus bighorn herd at Black Gap, but they had chosen the one spot in Texas where a fenced-in herd would be most susceptible to predation by lions. (There was, of course, the additional point that if the bighorns had not been nearly hunted out in the first place. . .) As for the mule deer, the state people had deliberately and drastically reduced the animals on the management area so they could find out how long it would take the herd to recover from excessive hunting pressure—again without noting that resident lions, their numbers evidently increasing, might have some effect on the remnant herd. (In the hill country of Real County, where the Papes live, all game biologists agree that the deer populations could stand some thinning by lions or anything else on hand.) I was just asking Mrs. Pape who should really take the rap, men or lions, for the Black Gap fiasco, when a small sign announcing Fort Davis came into view.

It was because of mountain lions that I had come here. I wanted to learn as much as I could about their present status in the Southwest, as well as the problems they might be causing, and consequently having. In west Texas the authority on such matters was a lion hunter named Roy McBride, who I would not have a chance to meet until some months later. Meantime I had heard of the Espy family, which owned and leased an enormous spread, 100 square miles more or less, adjoining and with-

The Trans Pecos

in the Davis range. The Espys are mentioned in U.S. Fish and Wildlife correspondence from the sixties as being among those opposed to the ban on the aerial killing of eagles. More recently, trouble with lions has inspired the family to build up its own pack of lion dogs.

Jim Espy, Sr., was not available; and Jim Espy, Jr. had come into town from the ranch just long enough to get a night's rest before heading out again. He explained that he was too tired to invite me over, but he would talk for a while on the phone. The voice was young, tenor, and sounded convincingly weary. Yes indeed, he told me, lions were increasing in the Davis Mountains. The Espys run 11,000 angora goats—worth more than a gold mine since the recent leap in mohair prices—and "up until this year," according to the wan voice, "I imagine lions were costing us 200 goats a year. In one pasture we had 1000 goats and we came up 275 short."

During the forties and fifties, all the ranching families in the mountain country had lion dogs, with the result that lions were few and far between. But with the lions and the ranchers subsequently going out of business for different reasons, the dogs went out of business too—until about two years ago when young Espy "worked up" his own pack. Since then, "we've got where we keep the lions off the goats. We've caught lions right off the kill. I don't hunt them for sport, you know. I do it for self-protection."

Espy believes the lions must also answer for the decline in the numbers of deer and other game. "You ask any rancher if they're having trouble with their deer populations. The deer are down 25 percent. There's hardly any deer high up in the mountains anymore. Lions would rather eat them than anything." Espy is certainly correct about the mule deer being "down." Unlike the abundant whitetails of south and east Texas, their numbers have declined significantly from an all-time high in the mid-sixties. No official explanations for this phenomenon are as yet forthcoming. But one thing is clear: the reduction has impartially occurred both in and out of lion country.

As for his goats, Espy was convinced that disease, drought, and accident had nothing to do with his losses. "We've got country you can't imagine how rough it is, but we don't keep it overstocked!" Here again, Espy's assessment may not have been altogether accurate. His family had something of a reputation in the area for being "hard on their range," and given the harsh terrain, young Espy's own statistics (11,000 goats/64,000 acres) seemed to bear this out.

Incident at Eagle Ranch

One final question: now that he had been hunting lions for two years, were their numbers still increasing? He hesitated, then said, a little doubtfully, "I imagine they're holding their own."

Espy had said that during the last two years he killed 37 mountain lions. By any measure, that seemed a lot of lions; and because hunters, like most mortals, are known to exaggerate on occasion, I was a little skeptical, even though Espy sounded too worn out to be boastful, or anything else except eager to get off the phone. Later that night I learned that he could not have exaggerated very much. In my travels I had found that a visit with a local taxidermist—in this case Ray Duncan, an insomniac young emigre from New Orleans—was often a handy way to pick up gossip about hunting and hunters in an area. Duncan told me that he had prepared more than twenty lion skins for Espy. Interestingly, although the goat raiser had mentioned having some trouble with female lions raising young, all but one of the hides Duncan had handled belonged to males. I am incorrigibly given to amateur speculation about stray items like this. Why so many males? Did it mean that a large percentage of Espy's lions were the outriders of more permanent populations, perhaps in the Guadalupe National Park area, or the more inaccessible reaches of the Davis Range? Researchers have lately suggested that successfully established male lions maintain large exclusive districts in which several females also reside; this leaves a surplus of males to strike out on their own. Were these bachelor animals trying to set up their own territories in areas occupied by the Espy goats? If so, they had not had much luck. Lions are not coyotes. According to Espy, it had taken only two years and a single pack of dogs to quell the invasion on a 100 square mile front, in country that is "I can't tell you how rough."

I regretted being unable to talk with Jim Espy face to face, but I was certainly not sorry that I had come to Fort Davis. It was a snug, quiet little place. The few dozen homes and public buildings had been built so close to the surrounding cliffs and hills that the latter looked as if they had shouldered their way right into town. The Courthouse was less imposing than the one in Marfa, but handsome nonetheless; and the redstone hotel was a wonder of solidly built, old fashioned comfort. After decades during which its population declined, there were signs that the town was being rediscovered by the outside world: tasteful and not so tasteful gift shops, and a comfy-looking restaurant with steep prices and undistinguished food. The managers of the hotel were a middle-aged couple from the Texas midlands who, like Willard Phillips in Leakey and Ray Duncan down the road, had wanted to get away from where they were. They felt modestly adventurous and excited about changing professions and localities in the middle of their lives. They had bought a few acres and built a house in an enormous ranchette development near Fort Davis, the brain-child of an east Texas speculator. It was located on one of the highest mountains in the Davis chain, a former ranch, remarkable for its rare stands of yellow pine and aspen which in west Texas grow only on a few high peaks. They disliked hunting and were pleased that the ranchette development was a wildlife refuge and that deer and raccoons were often on view. There was even a mountain lion still in residence. Its tracks had been found several times near the neighbors' garbage cans, and it had been seen at least once. "I don't really think it would hurt anyone," said the manager's wife, a little doubtfully, "but our neighbors are elderly and it makes them nervous. They think it might be an old lion that can't hunt for itself anymore. Anyway, one of the local people, a nice young man named James Espy, has told them that anytime they want, he'll bring his dogs and get rid of it."

On the approach to Sanderson, my love affair with west Texas began to reach its eastern limits. Dry pale ochre bluffs, the southwestern demarcation of the Edwards Plateau, crowd the highway; the intermittent flats are picked-clean of grass and invaded by scrub. Even the approach of Spring does nothing to soften this wasted, bitter looking country. Sanderson itself is no beauty spot. The bare slope it occupies is not very conducive to shade. Many residents try hard for a garden, but in the noon day sun the overall impression is a blaze of yellow dust and stone.

As in all small Texas towns, the inhabitants are courteous and helpful. It was a Saturday, and the wool and mohair warehouse was not open, but I was soon directed to the office of Dudley Harrison, the local Ford dealer and a prominent rancher. Just inside the display windows, two of his rancher friends were drinking coffee and passing the time of day, and Harrison invited me to talk with them while he finished up some paper work in his private office.

One of the ranchers was Sid Harkins, a man in late middle age, well known and much respected in these parts. He smoked cigars, wore a baseball cap, and ran 5000 sheep and 2000 goats on 56 sections north of

Incident at Eagle Ranch

town. The other was Lee Dudley, an old-timer pushing seventy, with a cowboy hat tipped far back on his head. His sheep and goat operation was also north of town on the Edwards Plateau.

Either age and experience, or the drowsy peace of a weekend afternoon, made these men more mellow, less absolutist, than many of the ranchers I had spoken with in New Mexico and other parts of Texas. Some of their observations were variations on themes already heard, while others were new:

"What sense is there in having one branch of government paying us subsidies, and another that won't let us protect ourselves from predators?". . ."Ranchers used to hang coyotes and eagles on their fences. It was a little-boy brag, but it offended people. Even now, everytime they kill a mountain lion it gets in the local papers. We should do our own killing and mind our own business". . ."The Animal Damage Control isn't doing a damn thing. They're spending millions of dollars to see if coyotes kill sheep! Our local club has fired the ADC trapper and hired one of our own. Those government boys spent half their time making out reports". . ."About fifteen years ago the land rush came. Those new people weren't interested in sheep. Any livestock would do. They were just buying for investment". . ."And the younger people in the ranching families wanted an easier life". . ."In 1933, when I went to work on a ranch, one of my jobs was to set baited traps on high spots near the road to catch eagles. It was a common practice". . ."Six weeks ago, my wife and son and I watched an eagle hit a young fawn, still with its mother. That thing would go in at brush level, and when it got to the fawn it would just drop down. It didn't dive bomb like you'd think". . . "We used to have so many jack rabbits you could shoot 50 or 60 in an afternoon. But then they had a die-off. We've never had that many since" . . ."Oh yeah, the range has improved. When they first fenced it they overloaded it, but since the big drought in the 50's people take better care of it. I run about one third the sheep I used to". . ."To my notion, the range has grown up a lot more in mesquite. There were flats that didn't hardly have any mesquite at all, where now it's all over". . ."They say the prairie dogs kept the mesquite killed back; but then they were poisoned out. I got in on the tail end of that". . ."My wife says there used to be just acres of prairie dogs. . . ."

Occasionally the two men seemed to contradict themselves or each other. Harkins said at one point that "since the government has taken our tools away, predators have become our number one problem," and described how in one of his smaller pastures, where he had marked 241 lambs, only 92 were left by September. "We knew we had one coyote in there, maybe more, but he had killed that many before we got him." Yet later in our conversation he remarked that he had only seen one coyote on his ranch; "We don't have that many." When reminded that he had said they were the "number one problem," he grinned good naturedly, "Well, I told you we had that one coyote and he did all that damage." Harkins also believed "that we have more eagles now than we ever had." But Dudley, who used to lose 6 percent more lambs in the rougher sections of his ranch than in the flatter pastures, and blamed the difference on eagles, now observed that "I don't see that many; I couldn't say what's happening to them." As an afterthought, he suggested that it might be because he was lambing later, after the eagles were gone—not because he wanted to avoid a confrontation with them, but because he has been "looking for a hard winter."

Harkins is no man's fool. He was aware that he and his friend might have overstated the case a little. "We can't help what drought and low prices do to us," he said; "but predators we can do something about." He paused. "It's not that we have that many problems down here anymore, but—maybe I shouldn't say this—we do feel we have to support the ranchers further east." He meant Real County ranchers, of course, whose recent problems with eagles had more to do with the San Antonio trial than with the loss of lambs.

Dudley Harrison had time to see me now. His ranch, unlike those of his friends and most other Sanderson sheepmen, lay to the south, 65,000 acres stretching from highway 90 to the Rio Grande, a distance of some twenty miles. Harrison himself said it was "sorry-looking country," and when I visited it later at his invitation I was forced to agree. The whole area around Dryden would be an instructive place for anyone to visit who wants to see what sheep can do to land. No English heath could look more blasted than this plateau, with its infinitude of buff colored rock and black brush on which a dragon might have breathed. The dominant vegetation is greasewood. As an indicator of range quality, this scrub is a sort of vegetable cockroach. It lives where nothing else will, greedily sucks up all available moisture, and is inedible to wildlife and livestock; even sheep can't live on it.

Incident at Eagle Ranch

In fairness, I saw Harrison's ranch at its end-of-winter worst. In another week or two the scrub would have quickened, coloring the monotony green. Also, this land of Mordor supported a greater variety of vegetation and more animal life than a first glance might imply; not just Harrison's 6,500 sheep and goats, some of which were usually in view, but lots of jack rabbits. On Highway 90 their flattened remains had been on display every hundred yards or so. On the ranch road, the living animals were as much in evidence. I wondered what it must have been like before the great die-off that Mr. Harkins had mentioned, when maximum overgrazing and maximum predator control had, like spontaneous combustion, produced an explosion of rabbits. The current supply was still more than enough to attract raptors; I spotted two red tails checking things out from utility poles along the road.

Closer to the hills there would no doubt be deer and javelina. And eagles and lions. The view of these hills, a dozen miles away, was the great mercy in this forbidding landscape, a blue and lavendar range of them accompanying the Rio Grande as it emerges from the Big Bend country and begins swerving south towards Laredo and the Gulf. This entire stretch of the Rio Grande had been recently designated a national scenic river, much to the outrage of Mr. Harrison, who feels that federal easements along the banks will create an increase in wetback coyotes and mountain lions. And throwaway beer cans.

I longed to reach those hills and that river, but the sun was setting fast; and the Corolla, springs gone, tires going, could do no better than a five-minute mile on all this splintered rock. Reminding myself that I was not on a camping trip, I turned the car around and headed back to the highway.

Highway 90 is the Maginot Line, the Great Wall of China, that divides coyote-and-cattle country from the sheep-and-mostly-coyoteless steppes of the Edwards Plateau. It is along this line that Heintzelman and Andrew Allen and many other combatants in the Great Coyote War have ceaselessly patrolled. Obviously, Mr. Harrison was on the wrong side of the tracks. During our meeting, I had asked him how much stock he lost to predation. "I can't give you an honest answer. We've had eagles, bobcats, and coyotes, and lions coming in from Mexico all my life. But now I'm also faced with invasion from the east, because the big investors have replaced sheep with cattle; and from the west, because of Big Bend Park." Eagles? "They're a definite problem.

The Trans Pecos

I saw three of them down by the river not long ago eating on a mohair kid." Lions? "We catch about five a year." Coyotes? "They're definitely the worst."

Yet in spite of his exceptional vulnerability to predators, he did not seem to regard them as more than one more cross to bear. Harrison was a young looking 50, with frizzy red hair, gold rimmed spectacles, and the harried, preoccupied air of a man with so many problems on his mind that all of them have begun to blur together. It was the malaise of ambitious and successful people, not life's losers; and Harrison admitted that he had so many irons in the fire that he could not keep track of them all. He could be ambivalent, too. At one point he complained bitterly that inflating land values—thanks to those big investors in search of tax breaks—had wrecked the sheep industry because ranchers could no longer afford to lease land, much less buy it. Yet later he remarked that "appreciating land values over the years have made the ranch industry profitable." When confronted with this inconsistency he laughed impatiently. "The irony is that the very increase in value that makes ranching profitable makes it more profitable to sell out, get the interest on the money, and do something else." He took off his glasses and rubbed his eyes. "You get tired of being harassed—by government, by the shortage of labor, by the lack of product profitability, by the lack of predator control. Ten years ago there were 124 operating sheep-ranching units in Terrell county. You know how many are left? Exactly 64. Some ranches are larger—I've gobbled up a few smaller ones myself—but a lot are just not operating. Take the ranch I'm on. In 1940, there were six families on those 65,000 acres, all operating units. Some died out and their children didn't want to fight that kind of life. The hardiest and toughest survive; the others don't. My daddy put this operation together. I can assure you I could make more money on the ranch by selling it and investing the money than by operating it." He leaned forward, pushing papers toward the edge of his desk. "But I don't want to sell! That's why I'm in this office today; I can't make a living in the manner I'm accustomed to down there. Sure, if I wanted to live on that ranch and eat beans and trap coyotes and come to town once a week, I could make it fine! . . . My children? They'd like to hold on to it, but I don't think they're capable. They live in town; they have other interests. I'm going to stay, but my children, I don't know what they'll do." He looked at some point beyond my shoulder. "It's sad," he said, but he sounded angry.

Incident at Eagle Ranch

6. Salt of the Earth

IN THIS WESTERN JOURNEY, it is not yet time to draw any conclusions about the status of predators, their present and future, or about the policies and agencies that are meant to control them. But it is possible to offer some generalizations about the ranching community, its attitudes on the subject, and the real extent of predator damage.

It should be obvious by now from the testimony that the war against predators is being fought by sheep (and goat) raisers, not ranchers generally. The entire livestock industry and its lobbyists support sheepmen in this battle, but it is also true that on the range the traditional animosity between cattlemen and sheepmen still lingers and many of the former prefer coyotes to sheep. The attitude of individual cattlemen towards predators varies markedly from a generalized hatred of all wild carnivores, to vague tolerance, to an active appreciation of their usefulness in rodent control. According to their own report, 75 percent of western cattlemen experience no loss to predators, and only 1.5 per cent claim a loss of more than 5 per cent. There are areas where a local population of coyotes acquires a taste for veal; and there are many more where cattlemen's associations pay hard cash to control coyotes. But the fact remains that sheepmen are the militants, the front line fighters, in the Great Coyote War.

Within the ranks of the sheep raisers themselves, however, there are considerable gradations in attitude. To a man, they are fiercely intolerant of predators, but the basis of their animosity varies. For some,

128   like Dan Auld, Bronson Corn, and Buster Holland, the killing of sheep and goats by predators is a vivid, indisputable fact. Although such ranchers sometimes, indeed, often, exaggerate their losses, the losses do occur and they can be serious. Other sheep raisers, like James Goodrum and Charles Waller, have only occasionally lost a lamb to predators, but the threat of loss and the cost of preventive control are a continuing vexation. Finally there are the majority of sheepmen, people like Bill Sims, Ralph Simpson, Sid Harkins, and Lee Dudley, who support predator control more as a matter of committment and safety insurance than because they are experiencing serious losses themselves.

Yet whatever the difference in their individual situations, all of the ranchers I conversed with were as one in their passionate conviction that "varmints" are a scourge and an invading horde, and that they, the sheepmen, are losing the battle against them. This conviction has impelled one after another of these decent, normally honest men to imply that most of their problems are due to coyotes and other predators—when in fact bad weather, insufficient forage, assorted parasites and diseases, toxic weeds, stillbirths, abandonment, poor management, and the predilection of sheep to become the victims of any potential accident that presents itself are almost always more general and consistent causes of livestock mortality.

This pervasive attitude cannot be adequately accounted for, at least in most cases, simply by the statistics of economic loss. A better explanation can be found in the recent economic history of the industry, and, even more, in the changes that have affected sheep ranching as a way of life. In bits and pieces, these changes have surfaced in this book as recurring themes in the testimony of the ranchers themselves; but perhaps a somewhat more coherent summary is in order here.

In the 1940's, the Second World War created an escalating demand for fiber and meat products. The sheep industry boomed. Throughout the Western rangelands, populations of sheep increased by staggering percentages; and in many areas, like the Trans Pecos, they were established in former cattle country almost overnight. Many cattlemen particularly welcomed the change because cattle had so overgrazed the range that much of it was now unfit for anything but sheep. Post-war prosperity sustained this expansion well into the fifties. Also during this period, the federal government's predation and rodent control program, begun in the thirties, was conducted in a no-holds-barred fashion, eliminating coyotes, bobcats, and eagles (as well as non-target species)

Incident at Eagle Ranch

in enormous numbers. However, the reduction of predator populations throughout most of the West had no perceivable effect on the fortunes of the sheep industry. Indeed, during the fifties, when conservationists' had as yet made no headway in their objections to federal control programs, the sheep industry was already beginning its long decline. The great drought of that decade, which affected all of the western rangelands to varying degrees and which was particularly hurtful in the Southwest, caught thousands of producers at the worst possible moment. The over-stocking of both publicly and privately owned grazing lands had already severely depleted the range. Millions of sheep perished or were sold at ruinously low prices. (This same syndrome, incidentally, had annihi-lated the sheep industry in south Texas a half-century earlier; and neither the industry nor the range in that area has ever recovered.) Economic factors compounded the debacle. The development of poly-ester and other synthetic fabrics reduced the demand for natural fibers in the market place.[1] (A similar displacement was occurring in the case of mohair, which had previously been used by automobile manufacturers in the upholstering of car seats.) Ironically, the government's substantial efforts to subsidize American sheep growers, while at the same time not imposing prohibitive tariffs on the importation of Australian wool, had the effect of increasing the consumer price of both the domestic and foreign product, thereby hastening the acceptance of cheaper synthetics. As a final straw, the ranchers found their labor supply dwindling (sheep husbandry requires a much larger seasonal work force than cattle raising) as a result of the expanding job opportunities in the rural West during the fifties and sixties.

By the mid-fifties, thousands of operators were "getting out of sheep," and that exodus has continued until the late seventies. Recently, a renewed demand for natural fiber, plus an even more generous price support system, has stimulated a revival in the industry. During the interim, however, only the strong have survived, as Dudley Harrison says; or at any rate, only the stubborn. Those who did hold out have been usually able to make a quite good living, in spite of depressed prices, simply because there were fewer of them. Nevertheless, con-cerning the matter of the industry's overall decline, statistics have their own eloquence: In 1950 there were perhaps 200,000 producers and 36,900,000 stock sheep in 17 western states.[2] By 1960 the number had dropped to 115,000 and 21,497,000 respectively. By 1972, the totals had been nearly halved again, to 59,700 and 12,601,000. And

Salt of the Earth

130   in 1978 the figures were 46,600 and 8,745,000. By this time, however, the decline had bottomed-out. Now the numbers of sheep raisers and sheep are on the rise again,³ and there is at least a possibility that the entire cycle, including the further devastation of the western range, will repeat itself.

In the meantime, the lifestyle of the ranching community has been greatly altered, and there is little likelihood that these changes will be reversed. For one thing, the ranchers themselves grow older; two thirds of them are over 40, a fifth of them are in their sixties or seventies. Their sons and daughters "go away to college" or "have other interests," or else they face ruinous inheritance taxes and/or the subdividing between heirs of their parents' holdings. Even the older ranchers, in this glimmering age of still rising expectations and television commercials, have no wish to "eat beans, trap coyotes, and come to town once a week," nor, as Larry Leinweber says, can they "be out there in the pastures" as often as they once were. So they sell out, or move to Marfa or Roswell and let "Mexicans" run the ranches.

Incursion has an impact at least as great as excursion. The ranch country is being invaded by more than coyotes. Throughout the West, the phenomenon of investment buying of ranch lands has reached epidemic proportions. Both domestic and foreign buyers, corporate and individual, are heavily involved. The motivation in many cases is tax write-offs on long term investment; meanwhile, cattle or game ranching pays the property taxes. Often, however, these ventures are meant to produce immediate gains in the form of real estate development, which subdivides vast holdings into 6-to-60 acre ranchettes; or farming, using dry land cultivation or irrigation, which is depleting underground water tables at an awesome rate. But in terms of social consequences, even absentee landlordship has had less impact than the encroachment of the New People upon the ranchers' domain. For generations, the ranching families have lived not unlike a feudal ruling class, owning vast tracts of land, overseeing sizeable work forces, presiding absolutely over all political and economic decisions at the county level, making their influence felt in the Western state capitols, and even Washington, to an extent greatly disproportionate to their actual numbers. The Dukes of Duval—and Real—have had a long run for their money, and they have not vanished yet. But everywhere the New People—Mexican Americans, retirees, ranchette owners—are moving in and "taking over." They change city charters, assume control of local politics, alter

Incident at Eagle Ranch

the tax structures, have large numbers of children, provide havens for coyotes, and import new customs and attitudes, even including, as Mrs. Leinweber says, the use of "dope." About these New People, more anon, in a different context. For the moment, it suffices to observe that because of them the older order is changing, for good and ill; the old-line ranching families understandably have a hard time changing with it.

The ranchers are a true social class, not a new fangled "ordered social segment." As a class they are everything that the little red-headed waitress in Marfa—one of the first of the current wave of New People—claims them to be: "The friendliest people in the world. If you need anything, they'll help you—if they like you." They are also, as many other New People aver, used to having their own way. They differ from the planter class of the Old South, to which their own class is in some ways analogous, in retaining a considerable economic and social vitality; nor are they tainted by association with peculiar institutions and Faulknerian notions of decadence. They are still the "backbone of the country," independent, hard-working, stable family people (though not quite as much so as they once were). But their attitudes are also eroded by ambivalence. They detest government handouts even while they accept their share of them; they believe in personal honesty and law-abidingness, but not when a law like the Eagle Act contravenes their interests; they do not want to sell their land, but cannot resist the investors' tempting offers; they resent the value systems and lifestyles of the various sorts of New People who now outnumber them, but they depend on the cheap labor or the "green stuff" these newcomers provide; they usually enjoy the presence of huntable wildlife on their lands, but regard it as private property to be exploited like livestock when it behaves, and eliminated when it does not; and finally, they genuinely love the often harsh, spacious land they have inherited, and subscribe in theory to the Old West virtues it inspires, but in practise they have abused it dreadfully; many of them will go on abusing it now that the demand for wool and mohair encourages them to do so.

These factors—the pressures of a changing social order, and the vicissitudes induced by weather, mismanagement, and the market place—have created the sort of class paranoia that afflicts any minority group that has not yet acquired power or, as in this case, is losing the power it once possessed. In the insular world of the sheepmen there is a subtle failure of nerve, and a corresponding need to find someone or something to blame. But the weather is God's affair; the government,

Salt of the Earth

though blameable, is remote; the market is beyond anyone's control; the New People are an irresistible force; and the destruction of the rangeland, being the ranchers' own sin, is something for which they must forgive themselves.

When all these exceptions have been made, there is nothing much left on which the ranching community can vent its frustrations except that bloody-minded thief and perfect scapegoat, the predator. Here, at least, is a culprit one can "do something about." It is on the scene, it cannot make excuses for itself, it attacks in perceptible, gory ways, it does real damage in numerous instances, and—as in the case of the fly which the harassed housewife swats instead of the bill collector—it can be rendered satisfyingly dead. Until ranchers became worried about their public image, it could even be displayed on the fence as a "little boy brag." In short, the eagle, the coyote, the bobcat, and, where available, the mountain lion, must be made to pay not only for their own real and imagined mischief, but for all the more intractable difficulties created by God, government, the New People, the marketplace, and the rancher himself.

The need to use the predator as a sort of conductor for a variety of rancher discontents inevitably obscures the question of just how serious the predator problem really is. But some facts should be self-evident by now. Conservationists have long suspected that sheep raisers as a group grossly overstate their losses to predators, but they have had as much trouble proving their case as the ranchers have had proving the opposite. Most of the evidence confirms that the suspicions of the conservationists are correct. In a confidential memorandum, dated May 2, 1963, the U.S. Fish and Wildlife team that had been investigating rancher reports of eagle depredation in Texas and New Mexico advised the regional director in Albuquerque that "it was agreed by us that, almost without exception, claims of very heavy loss to eagles were greatly exaggerated." That finding was never published, but the evaluation still stands not just in the case of eagles but for most other general claims of predation loss as well. The emphasis here is on that word "general," for there can be no doubt that some individual ranchers suffer predation losses that hardly need to be exaggerated.

In my own journey to the West, I was determined to give the sheepmen the benefit of every doubt precisely because I distrusted my own environmental bias. When I visited the Auld ranch and saw far more eagles than the opinions of the experts had led me to expect, I was that

Incident at Eagle Ranch

much more willing to take the ranchers' views seriously. But the evidence of exaggeration and misstatement during the course of the scores of interviews that followed soon became so clear that I could not have ignored it, at least in the privacy of my own thoughts, even if I had been a charter member of the Woolgrowers Association. Again and again it was evident that the ranchers were playing a guessing game in which they themselves were hopelessly prejudiced. Again and again, their guesses were at odds with objective data when the latter were available; and their own facts and figures were sometimes at variance with the generalizations they were making.

Of the many ranchers I interviewed, those who have appeared in the preceding pages were singled out, with a couple of exceptions, because they seemed to have the most evident problems with predators and/or because they were candid and articulate in their views. They are certainly representative, yet they include very few of the considerable number of individuals who told me, for example, that they were losing more than 40 or 50 per cent of their flocks to predators, or who claimed that they could regularly market a more-than-100 per cent lamb crop if it were not for predation. (I have also weighted the included-testimony away from the amazing commentaries on the natural history of predators: the rancher's story of the baby that was carried off by an eagle way back when; the several accounts of eagles lugging 15 pound lambs aloft with the greatest of ease; the claims that eagles will kill a fresh lamb for breakfast and another for dinner, and that neither they nor coyotes will eat carrion if they can help it; the contrary and highly imaginative ways in which the various predators are said to make their kills; etcetera.)

Some few ranchers made statements that were deliberately meant to mislead, but with most the intent was less calculated, a matter of being carried away by strong feeling. To listen to Sid Harkins or James Goodrum, a person would at first suppose that their ranches were being overrun by swarms of ravening coyotes. Only after considerable questioning and clarification does the fact emerge that they may have had no more than a single coyote in their pastures in the last five years. Other ranchers, like Fritz Kahl, Charles Waller, and Bronson Corn, who have quit raising sheep at one time or another, have convinced themselves that predators or the cost of predator control was largely responsible for putting them out of the sheep business, when the overwhelming reason was the depressed market—as is evidenced by the

Salt of the Earth

fact that some of them have "gotten back in" or are thinking about it, now that the prices are going up. But most often, the sheepmen's hyperbolic guesses at predation loss are based on an assumption of guilt by association and/or extrapolation. The rancher, on one of the minimum occasions when he ventures into the lambing pastures, sees one or more eagles in the sky overhead, and discovers the partly eaten remains of a lamb. Possibly he may even spook an eagle from the carcass. The lamb may have died an hour or a day or several days earlier of any one of several natural causes and the eagle may have been making a carrion meal. (Spofford relates how he once found an eagle on one of Espy's lambs shortly after dawn. The animal was recently dead and appearances suggested that the eagle had killed it. But examinations showed that rigor mortis was already well advanced and the lamb had obviously died during the night, when the eagle was perforce inactive.) Or the lamb may have been killed by an eagle because it was orphaned, since there is evidence to suggest that eagles (and, to some degrees, coyotes) are disposed to attack prey that behaves in an agitated, abnormal way.[4] Or the victim may have been a perfectly healthy, ordinary lamb that was killed because it was the handiest prey around, and because eagles do take healthy normal lambs. The point is that with all these possible alternatives, the rancher will almost certainly choose the last explanation as the only one worth considering. Moreover he will assume that eagles are devouring lambs right and left and that they have accounted for all or most of those lambs that are missing before and after marking. The same assumptions are made when a coyote is seen in a sheep pasture. Certainly coyote predation is a frequent occurrence in areas where both sheep and coyotes abound. The problem of accuracy arises when the factual or circumstantial evidence of two or three—or even a dozen—coyote kills is used to explain the overall mortality rate in that year's lamb crop, regardless of any other factors that may account for it.

Some ranchers frankly admit that all they can do is guess since the lambing grounds are often very large tracts in rough country, which the rancher has no opportunity to search thoroughly, unless, like Ralph Simpson, he believes in "living with his sheep." In fact, very few bodies of recently dead animals are found on range operations. The problems of terrain, incomplete body counts, and ranching "philosophy" are compounded by the typical rancher's inexpertise at accurately assign-

ing a cause of death, as well as by his natural prejudice against predators. But the most critical factor is his reluctance to credit "natural" mortality as a reason for his losses if there is any way he can avoid doing so.
Trying to find a rancher who will concede that starvation, disease, and
mischance figure importantly in his losses—as long as there are
predators around to blame—is as difficult as finding a mother who will
admit that her baby is not particularly cute or bright. All the evidence,
from in-the-field body counts to the U.S. Department of Agriculture's
statistics of lamb/ewe ratios at marking and marketing, indicate that,
even in an average year, from 12 to 25 percent of a lamb crop will die
before it leaves the ranch, whether the ranch is located in predator country or not. Yet I have met only one or two ranchers in coyote-and-eagle
country who would concede a natural loss of more than 2 or 3 percent.

Exaggeration of predation loss also prevails in general discussions
of the past, present, and future of the sheep raising industry. Ranchers,
and some bureaucrats, will frequently cite coyotes in the same breath
as the depressed price of wool as the reason for the industry's decline,
and some will insist that predation is the more immediate cause. In fact,
the prevalence of "varmints" has almost nothing to do with the decrease
in the number of sheep and sheepmen. Hard data proves inarguably
that this falling-off occurred as impartially in areas like the Edwards
Plateau which were totally free of predators as in those where they were
present in substantial numbers. Furthermore, the most precipitate decline occurred during the fifties and sixties, which, according to the ranchers themselves, were the golden age of predator control, with ADC
operations almost totally unrestricted, and populations of coyotes and
eagles at an all-time low. What is true of the entire industry is also true
of individual large operations. While there is no doubt that, as Clay
Miller points out, the breaking-up of large blocks of once contiguous
sheep country has had the effect of isolating some sheep operations
like the Love Ranch, thereby compounding predator problems, it is
certain that no large operation has gone under primarily because of
predation losses. The fact that many of these isolated ranches are still
money–making enterprises, especially now that the market for wool
is reviving, and that some former sheepmen are getting back into the
business in spite of the supposed increase of coyotes and eagles, is con-
clusive evidence, if any more were needed, that management and market
prices are the decisive factors.[5]

Salt of the Earth

Yet when these observations have been made, fairness requires a further clarification of the rancher view. I have already suggested that the average loss of lambs to predators in the Western states is probably not much more than 2 percent of the total crop and is certainly less than 3 percent. But this loss rate would certainly be much higher—perhaps almost as high as many ranchers claim it is now—if it were not for some control operations presently in effect. Moreover, my travels have also served as a useful reminder that averages, even adjusted ones, contain only limited quantities of truth. To borrow Reba Pape's analogy of a theft, it is small comfort to a person who has just been robbed to know that, according to the averages, the likelihood of the robbery happening to him or her was fairly slim. Nor is the victim consoled by well-meant criticism: that he, or she should not live in a high-crime area, or leave the property unguarded, or yield to a natural temptation to exaggerate the harm done. For the victim, the obvious solution is to catch the thief before he strikes again.

Rationally considered, this predator-thief analogy does not stand up very well; in academic circles it would be called a pathetic fallacy. Unlike thieves, coyotes and mountain lions and eagles are not able to function even within the limited range of choices available to humans. Their activities more correctly belong under the heading of "acts of God," along with drought and sudden storms—the only difference being that they are one act of God that, as Dan Auld observed, the rancher can "latch on to."

The predator is not a thief, but then, neither is the rancher a statistic in a graph of averaged losses. In some cases, coyotes, particularly denning pairs, can kill an amazing number of sheep in a relatively short period, and a significant minority of sheepmen do suffer serious losses. For ranchers like Bronson Corn, Buster Holland, Buddy Pape, and the owner of that isolated McKnight ranch in New Mexico, it is not consoling or very relevant to know that the average predator loss of lambs in the West is not much more than 2 percent, or for that matter, 5.5 or 17 per cent. It is their own loss that matters, at a going rate of 60 or 70 dollars a lamb. They will not feel chastened to know that in accusing a coyote of theft they are guilty of a pathetic fallacy. Nor will their tempers cool when they are told they have been using the predator as a whipping boy for an assortment of unrelated frustrations. The fact is they have a telling argument on their side, their right of self-defense—a right which, in the West especially, is still very much revered.

Incident at Eagle Ranch

Ironically, the ranchers themselves are largely responsible for be-clouding this basic issue. In claiming that predators are driving them out of business, and that environmentalists are embarked on a sort of class warfare that is meant to undermine their right to exist, the sheep raisers themselves sometimes forget the fundamental question of wheth-er or not they have the right to protect their property from predator loss, as long as the possibility of such loss, great or small, exists.

The eagle case, which in so many ways is a paradigm of the larger predator controversy, is representative in this respect also. At the San Antonio trial the defendants' counsel had the opportunity to fight the legal battle on the defense-of-property issue. The judge would later observe that this was the strategy that should have been followed; and it was certainly the one the prosecution planned to rebut. Instead the defense built its entire case on the unimpeachable moral character of the accused men. In other words, the jury was not being asked to find them innocent or guilty of the specific charges, but to vindicate their claim that they are the salt-of-the-earth-and-backbone-of-the-nation sort of citizens they perceive themselves as being, with the attendent inference that if people like themselves kill eagles, then killing eagles is an all right thing to do. The presentation of the defendants in this light indirectly bears out the bitter contention of Jim Stinebaugh, Sheriff Elliott, and the New People that the ranchers believe they "can do just as they please in Real Country," and elsewhere in the West, simply because they are who they are.

The jury, in effect, said that they could not do as they please. But this still leaves unanswered the question of where the legitimate right of self-defense, in this case the defense of property, leaves off, and the unacceptable manipulation of an important group of wildlife species, the predators, begins. Although only a minority of ranchers lose sig-nificant numbers of sheep to predators, all ranchers resent restrictions on their right to protect themselves from real or imagined loss, much as members of the NRA abhor limitations on the use of handguns, and Right-to-Lifers object to any restrictions on the right of a fetus to be brought to term. As with these other issues, irrational argument and emotion interfere with a clear understanding of what is really at stake. In this case, the essential issue, much obscured by all the *sturm und drang,* is to define a just accommodation between the ranchers' legiti-mate right to protect their interests and the environmentalists' right to protect predator species from pointless slaughter.

Salt of the Earth

A discussion of how much predator control is actually needed in the West, or, perhaps more exactly, how much control of the predator controllers is needed, will be the subject of a later chapter. This much can be said now: the sheepmen's anti-predator bias is so strong and irrational that it would be folly to permit this special interest group to dictate predator control policies in the future as it has in the past. But solutions to the controversy—at least any that fall short of shooting all coyotes and eagles, or all the sheep—must take into account the right of a shepherd, even a not very good shepherd, to protect his flock. And they must also deal with the unstatistical anger and frustration that impels a sober-sided person like Jim Goodrum to risk his expensive pickup in pursuit of an offending coyote, that inspires a normally easy going fellow like Bob Ramsey to use his grandchildren's pet as eagle-bait, and that convinces a model of social propriety like Buddy Pape that he should break a federal law.

Above all, any solutions must cope with the fact—difficult for many environmentalists to accept—that in the case of coyotes, at least, the "war" described in the previous pages is a real territorial struggle: if most sheepmen do not suffer serious predation losses in that war now, it is mainly because they are "behind the lines," occupying areas from which most or all coyotes have been eliminated. This is the harsh truth of the status-quo. As shall be seen, however, there is reason to hope that the status-quo may yet be changed to the advantage of both the predators and the men who prey upon them.

Part Three

The Controllers

7. Caroline's Fief

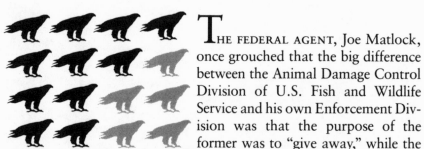

THE FEDERAL AGENT, Joe Matlock, once grouched that the big difference between the Animal Damage Control Division of U.S. Fish and Wildlife Service and his own Enforcement Division was that the purpose of the former was to "give away," while the purpose of the latter was to "take away." It is hard to argue with this view. The ADC is to ranchers what the Corps of Engineers, for example, is to barge companies and soybean growers: a federal service that will do all it can to please an influential constituency in order to ensure its own survival. Unlike the Corps, the ADC deals in millions of dollars ($14 million in 1978), not billions. After all, it does not cost as much to do away with pesky coyotes and other predators as it does to dispose of inconvenient swamps, marshes, and river valleys. On the other hand, predators are to some degree renewable; wetlands are not. It is entirely possible that in another 30 or 40 years, when the Corps has been relegated to some government graveyard for defunct bureaucracies or has at least dwindled to a repair and maintenance operation, the ADC will still be a thriving enterprise. The division has had its ups and downs; its budgets depend to some extent on how badly politicians in Washington, including presidents, need the ranching community's votes. But as long as a growing population requires meat and natural fiber, and as long as there are sheep and coyotes, there will be a market for ADC's services.

My own interest in the agency began in the weeks following the San Antonio eagle trial, when I listened to the investigative agents, Jim Stinebaugh and Joe Matlock, describe their dealings with the convicted

ADC trapper, Andrew Allen, his district supervisor, Jim Beavers, and the chief of ADC operations in Texas, Milton Caroline.

Allen was the G. Gordon Liddy of the eagle Watergate. Unlike the two other defendants in the case, Buddy Pape and Lanny Leinweber, who belonged to the closed world of sheep ranching and county politics, Allen's professional life was linked in its modest way with state and federal bureaucracies and the political forces that often govern their policies. I remembered Matlock's description of the day he and Stinebaugh had played the tape of Heintzelman's deposition while Allen listened, and how the ADC trapper had mysteriously referred to the "big ones" who never got caught.

I had the idea that revelations denied to others might be mine for the asking, but when I phoned Allen from a Uvalde motel in January 1978, he squelched that small fantasy in no uncertain terms. This was between the time of the conviction and sentencing, and Allen was still scheduled to stand trial for perjury at the investigative grand jury two years earlier; so I should not have been surprised that he was in an uncooperative frame of mind. No, he said, he did not want to meet with me or be interviewed on the phone; nor did he wish to tell me what he had been doing since the ADC had fired him. His only comment, when I asked him how he felt about the jury's verdict, was that he guessed he would "turn into a little green frog."

The next day, I stopped by his home in the hope that a bit of person-to-person might break the ice. No one answered my knock. The house was at the very edge of town, with nothing beyond it but a vast plowed dry-farm field, and nothing behind it but a small trailer park, owned by Allen, where perhaps a dozen weathered mobile homes were lined up in two uneven rows. The *tout ensemble* was pretty dismal: the unfinished-looking back of Allen's house, the blank wintry field, and the trailer park in which nothing stirred but a cold wind blowing trash and dust around. I waited for a chilly hour and a half before giving up.

Allen, meanwhile, was off in the wild blue yonder, doing what he did best, which was blowing coyotes "right into the ground." This information was gleaned later that afternoon from the conversational wreckage of a meeting with Al Barnes, the former president of South Texas Helicopter Service, now its vice president. (The reshuffling of titles had occurred when the "silent partner," Clay Hunt, assumed control of the company.) Barnes was in the act of leaving his suburban home when I appeared on his door step. He was a heavyset man, fortyish, wearing a

Caroline's Fief

once white cowboy hat that had turned black around the head band from sweat and mildew. He was scowling even before I identified myself. From all reports he could be a turbulent sort of person when aroused, and he aroused easily as I soon discovered for myself; but reports of his character contained a number of contradictions. His erratic financial arrangements, his not always tranquil domestic situation, his frequently stormy relations with employees and associates were often mentioned, and not just by foes like Heintzelman; yet he was also known for his impulsive generosity, his willingness to take chances, and his chauvinistic belief in the values of the Old West. In private moments he painted landscapes and action scenes, always with a Western theme.

He did not wish to be interviewed but he did want to tell me a thing or two. About Heintzelman: "If they're going to put anyone in jail it should be that little son-of-a-bitch. He was gun crazy, always wanting to kill something . . . Sure I owe him money but he'll never get it now." About Stinebaugh: "He used to be a state warden in south Texas. He was after a friend of mine for shooting deer from helicopters—that's why he has such a hard-on for helicopter companies. It got where my friend had a shotgun levelled at the bastard's head. He should have shot him when he had the chance." About wildlife biologists: "Those damn scientists! There's one of them in Houston says we got only one eagle in 300 square miles. Hell, I'd have shown him 300 in 100 square miles!" About federal government: "I'm telling you, I spent 10 years in the Army. I think it's a sad place we live in when a man can't protect his livelihood. Seems like people's rights got a god-damned question mark in front and behind them . . ."

Only when he spoke of Andrew Allen did this barrage of angry opinion soften to a tone of almost poignant concern. On a hunch, I had asked Barnes how Allen was doing, working for the company, instead of asking whether he was working for it or not. "He's doing fine now. We keep him busy. But it's a shame, poor fellah. Andy was just a 500 dollar-a-month government trapper trying to feed his family, and look what they done to him!"

My next question was not a happy choice. Somewhat gingerly, I asked Barnes if political influence might in some way account for the fact that, even after a trial in which it had been demonstrated that one of the helicopter service's aircraft and pilots had been involved in the eagle killings, the company still retained its state aerial hunting permit. Barnes looked so furious that I prepared to duck. "Governor Dolph Briscoe ain't done a damn thing but try to run this state," he roared. A moment later he was in his pickup, backing rapidly out of the drive.

I had been told that Barnes had aged greatly in the last year because of the worries that beset him. Certainly he behaved rather like a man at bay. The company in which he had taken great pride had lost its federal predator control contracts, and the government agents had seized the helicopter Heintzelman had used in the eagle hunts, as well as the trailer and pickup that went with it. Nor were his troubles over. Within a month, the state, with an open show of reluctance, would finally feel compelled to withdraw the company's aerial hunting permit, and soon after that, on March 27th, Barnes would plead guilty of one count, and the helicopter service guilty of two counts, of aiding and abetting the killing of eagles. The occasion was the perjury trial of Andrew Allen. Barnes would show up with Allen when the trial was about to begin, and through a plea-bargaining arrangement, the charges against Allen would be dropped as soon as Barnes pleaded guilty. It is not known whether Barnes acted on his own initiative, or Allen's. In any case, he was later fined $5,000 and the company $10,000. Judge John Wood, who presided, had evidently rethought his views about eagle killing since the earlier trial.

The home of Jim Beavers, Allen's former district supervisor, was a small bungalow on a dead end street in Uvalde. I arrived there early in the morning; I remembered how elusive this man had been when Stinebaugh and Matlock wanted to see him, so I wanted to be sure he would be at home. He was. He looked a little doubtful when I introduced myself, but after a second's hesitation he asked me into the tiny living room. Mrs. Beavers, still in her housecoat, brought me a cup of coffee.

They were an elderly, appealing looking pair, a softer, south Texas alternative to Pennsylvania Gothic. Mrs. Beavers was grey haired but trim and lively. During the subsequent conversation, she maintained an apparently habitual solicitude for her husband's welfare which she expressed by patting his shoulder from time to time, and sometimes answering questions for him, always beginning her replies with "we." Beavers was white haired, but wore the dazed, hangdog look of an adolescent who had been blamed for something he did not do. Usually

Caroline's Fief

he stared at the floor when he spoke. As soon as I mentioned the investigation he shook his head and clasped his hands between his knees.

"We weren't involved at all," Mrs. Beavers declared. "I told them federal agents right out that Jim didn't kill an eagle. He was just supervisor at the time. My gosh, he's not going to know what everybody is doing all the time."

Remembering Beavers' near-breakdown, I asked if the agents had been rude or threatening. "Well no, they weren't too bad," Mrs. Beavers said, "but of course we were disturbed just knowing they'd come." To which Mr. Beavers appended: "It's a little unfair that they was two against one. They seemed to think there was something I wasn't telling them."

I suggested that perhaps the agents' skepticism had something to do with Beavers taking the fifth amendment, or, even more, with Allen's blank and near-blank travel vouchers and itinerary forms. How had these deficiencies escaped Mr. Beavers' notice? "I don't know," he answered. "There was one that was entirely blank. Pretty hard for me to believe that the one with the blank day got by me. But if that report was blank when if left here, how come it got through the San Antonio office too?" A good question. The form should have been scrutinized at Milton Caroline's office before being forwarded to Texas A & M and then the Treasurer's Office in Austin. Somehow the blank report and all those other inadequately made-out forms had managed to be processed through all those stops without any questions being asked.

The couple did not hold Andrew Allen accountable for the suspicion that later fell on Jim Beavers. "We don't know whether him and those others are guilty or not," Mrs. Beavers exclaimed, "but everybody knows they're not criminals! They're good people." They still saw the Allens regularly. "Andy tries to be 'up' about all this trouble because of his wife. They're quiet people, you know, and it's harder with people who can't express theirselves. Her hands are all broke out." But both the Beavers looked vague when asked if Allen was currently employed. "He's always known how to be a ranch hand," said Mr. Beavers, tentatively.

For a while we spoke of Beavers' profession. It was not easy to see this gentle, shy looking man as a person whose livelihood involved the trapping and killing of countless wild creatures. But from all accounts, he was a master at this trade. Mrs. Beavers patted her husband's thin shoulder: "Jim is very knowledgeable about wildlife," she said. "There's just lots in his head what he ain't ever told about. It's not just what somebody else said. It's his own knowledge. Of course I'm prejudiced, but it's a fact."

Beavers all but blushed. "Now don't put it too strong," he said. But it was clear that he shared his wife's prejudice. "It takes experience to trap, and you have to like doing it. Very few people have the knowledge of animals and movements and tracks. It's hard to hire a good trapper now. Everything is paperwork and rules. It's your trapper that's the endangered species!"

Like the ranchers in the Southwest, he spoke of coyotes as an invading army. In spite of the efforts of 16 trappers working the eight counties in the Uvalde district, the animals were "crossing the line," that is, Highway 90, and were infiltrating the hill country that buttressed the Edwards Plateau. Eagles, he admitted, were uncommon in the district with the exception of Real County, and he assured me it would have been foolish for a government employee to risk killing one. "I had all the correspondence on a case in Wyoming a few years back. It never came to trial because the man they were after got killed first. But I knew what those people went through up there and I didn't want any part of it. I told Andy if he flew up in that hill country he better not even look at an eagle or they'd hang us all." Which, unless Beavers knew more about Allen's intentions than he was telling me, seemed an oddly gratuitous, or prescient, bit of advice to volunteer.

In fact, it was hard not to take with a grain of salt much of what Beavers said. His resort to the fifth amendment soon after Stinebaugh and Matlock showed up and his subsequent efforts to avoid any contact with them betokened more than natural shyness. And it was difficult to accept the idea that in the modest confines of the community center at Garvin's Store, he had not heard Judge Sansom and others talking about the killing of eagles. It also seemed unlikely that, while gathering signatures for permit forms for the proposed aerial hunts, with Allen at his side, he would have been ignorant of Allen's subsequent participation in the hunts themselves. Finally, his relationship with Allen clearly had been less formal than that of supervisor and trapper. Each man had demonstrated a protective concern for the other's welfare; it seemed implausible, therefore, that Allen would violate that mutual concern by flying all over Real County, gunning down eagles, forging expense accounts, and turning in blank reports, unless he assumed that Beavers

Caroline's Fief

was willing to look the other way. Certainly Beavers had no active role to play in the eagle conspiracy, but in spite of his wife's disclaimer, he would have had to have been even more incompetent than Joe Matlock deemed him not to have some idea what was going on. This would have been all the more the case because, whatever his managerial faults, all the trappers he supervised are known to have trusted and confided in him.

I asked him how he was getting along now. He had been doing fine, he said, until he was suspended. I was surprised to hear this—not that he had been suspended, but that he had a job to be suspended from. I had understood that his boss, Milton Caroline, had retired him in June, 1976, a year and a half ago, not long after the first phase of the investigation had come to an end. Indeed, only a few weeks earlier Caroline had assured me this was so, that Beavers' "nervous condition" and general mismanagement had compelled him to take the district supervisor out of circulation. If he was safely retired, how could he have been suspended?

"Being retired meant living on half salary," Beavers explained, "so Mr. Caroline right away hired me back as a trouble shooter to make up the other half of my pay." Trouble shooters are a special category of ADC trapper. Instead of operating a regular trapline within an assigned territory, they respond to urgent requests for help over a large area. Ordinarily there would have been nothing unusual in this sort of arrangement. However, the job normally requires a lot of travelling and Beavers allowed as how he "stays pretty well put." There was also the fact that this was not an ordinary case. Caroline had often insisted that he would get rid of anyone in his organization at the merest suspicion of wrongdoing, a category which had to include Beavers. But the real reason for my surprise was simply that Caroline had given me the impression when I spoke with him that he had gotten rid of the district supervisor for good by retiring him; he had not mentioned that he transferred the man to a different job.

Beavers' suspension from this new position as trouble-shooter had occurred the previous summer, on August 17, 1977. He produced Caroline's letter which stated that Beavers would remain suspended until cleared of all suspicion "in the eagle matter." Under the signature was Caroline's hand written postscript saying he was sorry he had to take this action and hoped everything would "soon be cleared up."

Beavers was at a loss to understand why the suspension came when it did; but the explanation was simple enough: the helicopter pilot, Heintzelman, had contacted Jim Stinebaugh just a few weeks earlier, and his revelations had blown the lid off the case. The regional office in Albuquerque had reacted by ordering Caroline to suspend Allen and Beavers, both of them still on the ADC payroll at the time.

"Why do they keep him hanging?" Mrs. Beavers asked the room at large. Added Mr. Beavers, "I'm between a rock and a hard place, I can tell you! I'd rather be fired outright so I could pick up the pieces than waiting around like this." But then he added, "I did see Mr. Caroline a couple of weeks ago and he said that now that the trial was over they'd probably release me from suspicion in a few more days."

When I took my leave soon after this, Beavers saw me to the door. Unaware of any irony, he remarked, "I don't want any of the bait. I just want out of the trap."

I had met with Milton Caroline late in December 1977, not long after the jury had delivered its verdict in the eagle trial, and a few weeks before I spoke with Beavers. The setting was Caroline's private office at ADC headquarters in San Antonio. In contrast to the anterior regions where secretaries and clerks worked under the reprinted gaze of appealing looking wild animals, the walls here were covered with certificates and other testimonials awarded to the Director by grateful rancher associations during the course of his very long career. I was accompanied by Dede Armentrout, National Audubon's Southwest representative; Caroline was seconded by his office manager, Tom Fowler, who during the subsequent conversation was frequently sent off into adjoining rooms to collect facts and figures.

"We took a lot from those people," Joe Matlock had grumped when referring to the Texas Division of ADC, and particularly to Milton Caroline. Under the best of circumstances there was little love lost between the control and enforcement divisions; on occasion they referred to each other as "rat-chokers" and "rabbit wardens" respectively. In their accounts of the investigation, both Matlock and Stinebaugh referred repeatedly to Caroline's efforts to derail it and obstruct them. So I was prepared to meet a hard-nosed, contentious looking man, perhaps on the order of Dan Auld or even Al Barnes. Whereas in the flesh Mr. Caroline came across as a solemn, pedagogical sort of person with a rather melancholy expression and a high cerebral forehead from which the hair had long ago departed. Substantial folds of skin were crimped worriedly between his brows and gathered slackly at the down-turned corners of his mouth. His voice was deep, resonant, somewhat pontifical.

Caroline's Fief

Caroline had been born in Connecticut 60 years earlier and had joined the U.S. Fish and Wildlife Service when he was still a young man, starting out in the wildlife refuge division but soon transferring to what was then the Division of Predator and Rodent Control. He had been occupying his present position for many years, and I had been told that he had few other interests.

Federal ADC programs in all of the western states depend in large part on state and local funding, but in Texas the degree of this dependence is exceptional. In almost all other states, the federal government contributes well over 50 percent of the total funds. In Texas it provides only about 25 percent. Not that the U.S. government is discriminating against Texas. On the contrary, the state currently receives more funding than any other, in keeping with its rank as number one sheep producer. The difference is perhaps best explained by the existence in Texas of a unique non-governmental agency, the Texas Animal Damage Control Association, composed of representatives of rancher interests, which maintains powerful ties with the state legislature, and channels more than a million dollars in state funds into Caroline's control programs. Hundreds of thousands of dollars in additional cooperative funds are provided by rancher associations and county commissions. All told, state and local dollars outnumber federal dollars three to one, and the total budget is, on the average, in excess of 2 million dollars a year, more than twice the amount utilized by ADC in Wyoming, the runner-up in sheep production. Caroline was therefore preeminent among ADC's state directors, supervising a work force of more than 150 people, most of them trappers, and administering a budget which, because of its diverse sources, was almost byzantine in its complexity.

For a while Caroline and I chatted about budgetary matters, including President Ford's "gift" to the Western ranching community in the 1976–77 fiscal year of $1.2 million for an accelerated program in predator control. Caroline's office had received about $200,000 of this supplement and had used most of it for aerial hunting. "It wasn't designed to be spent helter-skelter," the director explained. "We wanted to use it in areas that our trappers couldn't ordinarily cover." I remarked that that was not the way South Texas Helicopter Service had used all of its share. (The helicopter service had received $58,000 in ADC funds during 1975–76 in the Uvalde district. Nearly three-quarters of this sum was paid out while the federal investigation of the company was in progress.)

Incident at Eagle Ranch

Now that that conversational cat was out of the bag, the atmosphere became noticeably more taut, Caroline's replies less direct. "We used the money wherever our trappers and trouble-shooters said coyotes were causing trouble," he said.

The conversation soon shifted to Jim Beavers. It was at this point that Caroline mentioned that Beavers was retired, without also noting that he had been immediately reinstated as trouble-shooter or that Caroline had since been required to suspend him on orders from the Albuquerque office. What Caroline did say was that Beavers was "a rather nervous man. He needed to retire."

I asked Caroline why Beavers had been so inaccessible to the agents, supposedly because of illness, when in fact he had claimed only two days of sick leave during the period. The director explained that Beavers had called him after Stinebaugh and Matlock's first visitation, claiming the investigators had instructed him not to tell Caroline the investigation was underway. Caroline, angered by this failure to proceed through proper channels, instructed Beavers not to say anything to the agents until they contacted the San Antonio office. Several days later, after Stinebaugh and Matlock had called Caroline and persuaded him to meet them in Hondo, midway between San Antonio and Uvalde, Beavers had phoned his boss again. "He began to sob," Caroline recalled. "He told me his nerves were shot and he couldn't take anymore. I advised his wife to take him to a doctor. . . . We got a letter from the doctor telling us not to have him involved in this kind of harassment."

When asked whether he really wanted to use the word "harassment," Caroline replied, "Well, there are ways of talking to people! You need to have Stinebaugh talking to you to know what I'm talking about. It got pretty rough!"

Since Caroline had at the time spoken to Stinebaugh only once or twice on the telephone, it was not clear how the director could have come to that conclusion at such an early date. But even if he had, was he not being a bit over-protective of Beavers? Not at all, he answered. "Most of what I went by was what the doctor wrote."

Well then, had Caroline himself tried to interview the distraught Beavers? Caroline stared very hard at me as though the question were rude. "No," he said, somewhat bewilderingly, "I didn't want to interfere."

Caroline had this peculiar gift of suggesting that the logic of a question-and-answer session was contained solely in his replies, that

Caroline's Fief

questions were somehow in poor taste if they did not conform in advance to the answers he had ready. An extract from our taped conversation will perhaps suggest this trait better than any commentary:

When did you tell the agents that you had fired the trapper, Andrew Allen?

Caroline: I suspended him and wrote a letter to that effect.

According to others, the word you used was "fired" at the time. You said that you had fired him.

Caroline: No; suspension. He was under suspension. He hadn't been found guilty.

But didn't you say that you would fire someone if he were under suspicion?

Caroline: But not in this case. We wanted to be able to have him where we could have our hands on him. Between suspension and firing, I might have been using a word a little loosely. In the usual case we just get rid of the person but in this case it was suspension.

Weren't you aware that by using the word "fire" you made the agents think that Allen was more or less out of their jurisdiction?

Caroline: Yeh, well, see, I was doing business with my boss in the [Albuquerque] regional office. That decision was made there to suspend him. Then we reviewed the decision of what was taking place and put him back on the job again.

Who was "we"?

Caroline: The regional supervisor. [George Rost, southwestern regional supervisor of ADC. When contacted later, Rost first said that the decision to reinstate Allen was made after South Texas Helicopter Service was "cleared" by the state of violating its aerial hunting permit. Since Allen had been reinstated two months before the hearing for the helicopter service had occurred, I suggested that Rost recheck his information. He did so, called back, and now explained that the evidence against Allen had seemed circumstantial at the time, apparently according to Caroline's report. The fact that Allen had confessed to forging an expense account was not, he said, in his jurisdiction.] It just didn't appear there was any case there. . . . We had been told that they [the agents] were after Al Barnes, not our own people. I felt that if they were after Al Barnes, then galdarn it, work on Al Barnes, not one of our trappers.

Hadn't it been established at this time that Allen had unquestionably falsified his expense account?

Incident at Eagle Ranch

Caroline: He told us that, yes.

Yet you put him back on the job and George Rost agreed?

Caroline: No, no. I don't think we knew at the time.

But that information came up early in the investigation, didn't it?

Caroline: Yeah, we did, we did know it. But we felt it was better to put him back on the job and let them go ahead with the investigation. Stinebaugh got mad at me because I didn't tell him I'd put Allen back on the job again.

Well, why didn't you tell him?

Caroline: Why should I?

Well, if the idea was to put Allen back on the job so they could go on with the investigation—

Caroline: I didn't see any difference whether he was working for us or not as far as their investigation was concerned.

Hadn't they explained that he would be technically out of their reach if he was fired?

Caroline: The man lives in Uvalde. He wasn't out of reach.

Do you feel it's advisable for the federal government to be employing people when it knows they've been cheating on their expense accounts and when there is considerable indication that they may be guilty of killing eagles?

Caroline: Well, you'll find that back then Allen told them he was on a ranch rather than in a helicopter. Now I did ask him about that. He said yes, and the reason he falsified the records was because the paperwork Mr. Beavers had to handle was getting to be such a task to him that if he [Allen] told him [Beavers] he was flying in a helicopter those reports would just about kill him. I had to believe that, because I'd had conversations with Mr. Beavers for about two years before that about those reports.

Allen's excuse seems pretty—

Caroline: I could believe what Allen was saying. I could not believe him entirely guilty. Except I did give the report to the people at Texas A & M that he had falsified reports. . . .

But since all the evidence indicated that Beavers' bookkeeping was, to put it mildly, not very thorough, how could he be worn down by it?

Caroline: That's a good question. As far as it was required, the way in which they handled it, when they were aerial hunting, they could call into the office to the lady here and tell how many hours they had flown

Caroline's Fief

and tell whether on federal or cooperative funds. They'd tell her how many bobcats were caught, how many coyotes were shot. Those were the records we would keep.

Surely that wasn't too exhausting a procedure for Beavers? But in any case, was everything left to the word of the trappers? Even when the trapper demonstrates that he lies and cheats on his expense account?

Caroline: First of all there was nothing but suspicion. I was afraid that they were going to get them [Allen and Beavers] just because they were trying to get Al Barnes, and these people were just pawns in the game.

Well, isn't it legitimate for them [the investigators] to use them, if Allen was in cahoots? Aren't you operating in a judgmental way yourself?

Caroline: Well, let me tell you what happened. [To Dede Armentrout:] Are you an ornithologist? Well, they [the agents] were really talking to me about how *terrible* that eagle looked. [Caroline was referring to the eagle carcass Stinebaugh recovered from the Davenport brothers, who had shot the already dying bird at the Prade Ranch.] They sounded as though it was a *live* eagle. . . . He [Matlock] said he had never seen a bird have such a terrible infection! All I know is that I majored in poultry husbandry, I've worked with birds all my life . . . and I've never seen bird skin to become infected! If they tell me a story like *that*, well, they might tell me stories about all sorts of things. . . .

Throughout almost all of this colloquy, Caroline maintained a dignified but somewhat injured tone. However, there was one moment when his manner visibly altered. I had asked him if he was absolutely certain that he had made no effort to keep Beavers and Allen out of the investigation.

In a voice dark with anger, Caroline replied, "Stinebaugh was telling me what my job was. He shouldn't have done that."

While Mr. Caroline and I were going round and round, with Dede Armentrout frequently joining in, Caroline's administrative officer, Tom Fowler, was being seen but not heard except when his boss asked him for facts and figures.

Fowler was a quiet, retiring sort of person. He had a rather soft round face which one non-admirer of the ADC in Texas once likened to "a tree full of owls." This was a gross exaggeration, although Fowler did have a wide-eyed, surprised way of staring at people. Almost everyone interested in the ADC's involvement in the eagle affair took it for granted that he was an innocent bystander; and it was certainly true that he knew very little about eagles and other predators and cared less. His metier was bookkeeping and other paper work, as he was the first to admit. But he was something of a puzzle. Much later he would acknowledge that, as far as ADC was concerned, he was Caroline's creation: "Anything I know about ADC I learned from Milton Caroline. I had no other perspective." Yet as Caroline's administrative assistant, it was his responsibility to examine the incoming reports, expense vouchers, trapping permits, and itineraries that were forwarded by the various district supervisors, including Beavers, to his office. More than any other person, he would have known whether at least the letter, if not the spirit, of ADC regulations was being followed in those supervisors' reports or not. It is on this account that he seemed a puzzle.

A few days after the interview with Caroline I called the ADC office to request some further information about Allen's forged voucher, which I had heard a lot about but had not seen. I was told Caroline was not in, so I spoke with Fowler instead. During this conversation, Fowler made a surprising statement: he said that except for the three eagle-hunting days in December 1975, when Allen had falsified his records, all the reports from Beavers' district were complete, with the ranches, hours worked, predators taken, all filled in as policy required. I protested that Stinebaugh and Matlock had repeatedly said the exact opposite was the case. Curiously, Fowler offered, rather irrelevantly, to pull the files on some less controversial control district as a means of proving his point. Before I could object, he put me on hold. A moment later he was back, announcing that Mr. Caroline had coincidentally "just called in" and instructed him that further inquiries from me would have to be cleared through the Albuquerque office. Not for the first time, I felt I was reliving some part of Stinebaugh and Matlock's experience in trying to deal with the ADC in Texas.

After the necessary clearance was obtained, I got back in touch with Fowler. He did a complete about-face. Now that he had checked, he said, he found that the records from Beavers' office were indeed woefully incomplete compared with those from other districts. Which left a question that it was useless to ask: had Fowler, even after all the fuss of the eagle trial, really not known that Beavers' record keeping was a mess; or had he known and hoped I did not? Either way, the incident suggested that Fowler had not been too efficient about checking the

Caroline's Fief

supervisor's reports. And if Fowler did not know what the supervisors were doing, or at least what they said they were doing, who in the San Antonio office did?

More than a year later, I would get a sort of answer to the question I had not asked. By that time, Fowler had been transferred to the Albuquerque regional office of U.S Fish and Wildlife, where he was now working as a program analyst. When I talked with him in his small tucked-away office, he had evidently forgotten the gist of our earlier telephone conversation, during which he had first denied there was general mismanagement in Beavers' district. Either that, or he felt more free to speak now that he was no longer working for Caroline. At any rate, it was clear that he had known all along that the administration in the Uvalde district was a farce: "The main problem in Uvalde was that there was an incompetent supervisor there. Andrew Allen seemed to be a self-appointed assistant to Beavers. My gut feeling is that all Beavers knew was what Allen told him. Beavers didn't do much travelling to see what the men were doing."

When I asked Fowler why he had not done anything about Beavers' incompetence, he replied somewhat vaguely, "Beavers was scared silly of Caroline; I don't know why. I eventually told him if he didn't understand something he should call me, but he never did."

From his subsequent remarks it was evident that Fowler had also been aware, long before the eagle trial, of the way other districts were handling their paperwork: "Lubbock, San Angelo, and Fort Worth probably did a pretty good job of documenting. There was a good man in Fort Worth. San Antonio wasn't much better than Uvalde, but we were right there so we could help him. Marfa could have done better with its paper work. . . ."

(Later I confronted Jodie Webb, the ADC district supervisor at Marfa, with this last assessment and he boldly acknowledged it was true. He is very popular with the ranchers in his area and can perhaps afford such candor. At any rate, he explained that he didn't much like paperwork and there was too much of it. He spends much of his time aloft, serving as aerial gunner on virtually all the aerial flights in his district—a non-supervisory activity that he much prefers to his administrative duties.)

I returned to my earlier question: Since Fowler had known that some of the district supervisors were doing a bad job, at least of handling reports, why had he not done something about it? Fowler hesitated, intently staring. "Well," he replied, "to an extent I'm to blame. I'd try to perceive what the district supervisors' problems were. I'd then pass on comments—not complaints—to Caroline. If I didn't see something positive would occur, I didn't approach him. He had a different priority on these things. He probably didn't perceive paperwork as being as important as I did. I didn't want to seem to be beating a dead horse. If you understand what I mean."

Whether it was what he meant or not, the main thing I understood was that Jim Beavers was not the only one scared silly of Milton Caroline. Of course there was no excuse for running a government office, any office, the way the one in San Antonio had evidently been run; but I could see Fowler's side of it. I remembered the look on Caroline's face when he said, "Stinebaugh was telling me what my job was. He shouldn't have done that."

When I visited with the federal agent, Joe Matlock, at his home in Victoria, Texas, the mere mention of Milton Caroline's name was enough to rout him from his chair and set him pacing back and forth in front of the fire screen like a caged bear. A salty, straightforward man, he made no secret of his suspicions concerning the ADC supervisor: "Why did he cover up for Allen and Beavers? When we had to force him to call the regional office and make him bring Allen and Beavers in for serious questioning, at that moment I knew Caroline had wet feet in all this, some guilty knowledge. It's one thing to stick by your men; another to lie for them! And why did he go on hiring South Texas Helicopter when he knew damn well they were at least guilty of breaking the permit laws? He knew they were, too. He knew what we knew because we told him! And why did he write letters to the Albuquerque office telling them we were pressuring his employees, being overbearing, the lying. . . ."

These were interesting questions, some of them. But Matlock was probably wrong in suspecting that Caroline was privy to the eagle-killing conspiracy. At least there is a more apparent explanation of his conduct. All the evidence indicates that from first to last he did nothing to help the federal investigators and as much as he dared to hinder them. He was angry, of course, that they had questioned his underlings without first asking his permission. But even if they had consulted him before going to Beavers' office, it is doubtful that he would have behaved very

Caroline's Fief

differently. At no point was the guilt or innocence of Allen and Beavers a pressing concern to him. His subsequent actions, and inaction—"firing" Allen, encouraging Beavers to make himself scarce, resisting the agents' efforts to interview the men, refusing to take any action of his own against either them or the helicopter company, above all, exhibiting a profound disinterest in any evidence that came to light—all of this might suggest a cover-up. But not of the eagle conspiracy. The more likely explanation is that Stinebaugh and Matlock made the diplomatic mistake of being openly shocked not just by the chaos they discovered in Beavers' district but by the general way in which Caroline was running the ADC operation in Texas. They admit as much. To Caroline, their dismay must have seemed not only an insult but a revelation. If he wanted to conceal anything, it was most likely the administrative policies and priorities he had fostered for so many years, which, in a sudden moment, he was forced to see through the agents' critical eyes.

Milton Caroline was the Animal Damage Control Division in Texas; had been for twenty years. From all reports, he regarded his bureaucratic bailiwick with the same pride of possession his rancher friends felt for their territorial fiefs. Until Stinebaugh and Matlock showed up, it had never occurred to him that anyone might consider it poorly run. And in a sense, his self-satisfaction with the job he was doing was justified. Although Caroline was a federal employee, Fowler had remarked of him: "He perceived his responsibility as being to Texas, to the ranchers. The federal government was only paying 25 percent of the state's ADC funding. All the rest came from the state, the rancher cooperatives, and the county commissioners. Caroline perceived that his mandate was more from the state legislature, from Texas, than from the United States government."

From Texas' point of view he was, in fact, doing a first rate job. He was personally liked by the people who counted. Even an autocratic old rancher like Dan Auld, not free with praise, had called him a "fine fellah." The complaints by the Sanderson ranchers notwithstanding, most of the ranching community, especially the very wealthy and influential ranchers, including Governor Dolph Briscoe, appreciated his efforts in their behalf. Even the Sanderson ranchers had complained, ironically, that his trappers were doing too much paper work, not too little. True, he was not much liked by the district supervisors I spoke with. According to them, although he knew nothing about the mechanics of

Incident at Eagle Ranch

control work, he was forever requiring them to adjust their operations to suit the whim of some influential rancher or other who had called him up. Nevertheless, if the proof of a successful enterprise was to be measured in terms of its financial assets, the size of its work force, and the satisfaction of its customers, then Caroline's operation had no peer among the ADC's state programs.

Admittedly, office records were badly kept. Yet a recent U.S. Government audit report of ADC programs in the West, which will be discussed in more detail presently,[1] seems to suggest that although book-keeping procedures are deplorable throughout the ADC operation, they are not quite so bad in Texas as in some other states. Also true, control programs were often based on the willingness of rancher associations and county commissions to help fund them rather than on the basis of real need (in spite of both Caroline's and Fowler's insistence that they did turn down some requests for aid). But the same practice was common in various other Western states, if not on such a large scale.

And truest of all, the activities of trappers and aerial gunners were rarely if ever scrutinized, not just in the Uvalde district but, according to Fowler, in the others as well. In fact, from the safety of Albuquerque Fowler would rather strikingly observe: "What was needed was stronger supervision. I wouldn't even call it better inspection, because we both know there's little real inspection in the program."

But these drawbacks would not loom very large in the view of the Texas state legislature, the Texas Animal Damage Control Association, the Texas Parks and Wildlife Department, or the Texas Agricultural Extension Service, all of which powerfully influenced the control program, and all of which were concerned with keeping the ranchers happy. In fact, these shortcomings had the virtue of diminishing federal influence on the program, a fact that would not have unduly distressed state and local interests. (Indeed much of the hostility towards the federal investigation of the eagle killings is best understood as resistance to the U.S. government's assertion of its jurisdictional rights.) On the other hand, except for a handful of individuals like Dede Armentrout and a few chapters of conservation groups in the larger cities, the constituency that supported the interests of coyotes, eagles, and other predators in Texas was very small.

Inevitably, the Texas "environmentalist" constituency asserts itself at the federal level. In the case of predator control operations, its interests are expressed in the U.S. Fish and Wildlife Service's "Statement of Philosophy and Policy for Animal Damage Control." Granted the bureaucratic prose, the intent of this document is plain enough:

> We recognize that attitudes and perspectives are changing rapidly as a result of the complexity of modern-day civilization. Wildlife conservation must be practiced not only for the consumer . . . but also for the ever-increasing proportion of people who simply enjoy seeing and hearing wild animals in their native habitat, or for that matter, simply enjoy the knowledge that these animals exist. . . . [ADC] programs will be conducted where and when necessary, in the most intelligent and responsible manner possible. . . . They should emphasize removal of the offending individual animal wherever and whenever possible. . . . The animal damage control program will be conducted when and where there is a demonstrated need, as determined by the Bureau, after a careful review of all available evidence. It will be developed and supervised by professional personnel who are aware of the ecological, social, and economic aspects of wild animal population manipulation. This program will be selective and humane to the extent possible. . . .

How well the U.S. Fish and Wildlife Service generally fulfills its own committment remains to be seen. For the moment it is enough to point out that this statement of federal philosophy was one to which Caroline had given very little thought during his long reign. He "perceived his responsibility as being to Texas, to the ranchers," not to that "ever-increasing proportion of people who simply enjoy seeing and hearing wild animals," to whom the guilt or innocence, competence or incompetence, of people like Beavers and Allen really mattered.

But then, the sudden appearance of Stinebaugh and Matlock on the scene, their dismay at what was occurring in the Uvalde district office, must have made Caroline aware in some corner of his mind that, as Matlock had said of Beavers, he was "taking the king's shilling" but not doing the king's job. If Beavers and Allen were incompetent or worse, so perhaps was he. Surely this was reason enough for him to resent the federal investigation.

8. Kilgo's District

On THE AFTERNOON of my visit to the ADC district office in Roswell, New Mexico, one of Larry Kilgo's men was missing. The trapper had gone up to an Indian reservation, "some pretty rough country," a day and a half earlier, and his wife had called in to advise Kilgo that he should have been home by now. It was not the sort of crisis-in-the-making that occurs often in ADC operations. Most trappers are old hands who know their territories as well or better than the people who own the land. And they never get caught in their own traps. The most risky control method is aerial gunning; pilots sometimes get so carried away by the excitement of sticking with their fleeing quarry that they fail to notice when a hilltop gets in the way. In the last six or seven years there have been about a dozen accidents involving aircraft on ADC control flights but only two fatalities. The score is somewhat higher among ranchers doing their own aerial control.

Kilgo's missing trapper was an experienced hand; moreover, his wife had reported that another man was with him when he left for the reservation. Kilgo made a couple of calls to check about the weather and reports of accidents, then decided to postpone a search until the next morning. More than likely, the man's truck had just gotten stuck someplace. During the process of making up his mind, the district supervisor remained admirably calm, almost cavalier. It did not occur to him to doubt his ability to handle the situation.

There was a considerable surface difference between Kilgo and some of his counterparts in Texas. He was young, 33, and looked and acted younger than he was in ways that suggested energy and ambition rather than inexperience. He was sharp, had a degree in wildlife management, and by ADC standards ran a tight ship. "We feel like we have a high quality employee working for us. And we ride with them. One of the first things that happens if they aren't doing their job is that the ranchers will call you and complain. And of course we get their weekly reports. *Carefully* filled out reports," he added with a snappy grin. "If we don't have confidence in a trapper, well. . . ." Another grin and a shrug.

Kilgo grew up in west Texas, but unlike so many of his exiled compatriots he was not homesick for his native state. "I like New Mexico," he said. "And I like my job. I've been interested in wildlife all my life. I intended to get into the wildlife world and I didn't care where. I broke into Texas ADC and worked in rodent control for four years. Then I was fortunate enough to break into the predator end of it. It's challenging and rewarding. And it's a good feeling to take an animal that's destroying livestock."

He paused, considering other positive things to say. "We don't really consider it killing. We consider it management. We don't want to extirpate a species. I think a coyote is a beautiful animal, and I like to see him as much as anyone. But when he starts killing somebody's property, we got to get a holt of him."

As in other ADC districts, however, it was not customary here in southeastern New Mexico to wait until a coyote started killing before getting "a holt of him." Preventive medicine was the rule. "All our sixteen trappers work the sheep ranches, and in sheep country we like to pick up the coyotes before they get on the sheep. Bobcats? Well, we take all bobcats on the sheep pastures but there aren't but a few of them."

This last sentence came as something of a surprise, since Kilgo was the sort of fellow who seemed to know his ADC manual by heart; and ADC's stated policy was that bobcats could be taken on a preventive basis only "in those areas with a history of high bobcat predation losses." Yet my conversations with local ranchers, and Kilgo's own estimate of bobcat numbers, suggested that there were no "high bobcat predation losses" in his district. "Well," said Kilgo, "compared to the total fur

Incident at Eagle Ranch

harvest, we take but only a very small percent. In cattle country our policy is to release bobcats when they step in a coyote trap."

Then, I asked, the Roswell ADC did trap coyotes in cattle country as well as on the sheep ranches?

"We work a buffer area in cattle country around the sheep pastures, hoping to stop the drift," Kilgo explained. "We work right along the Pecos River. We don't have the funds to work the eastern part of the district. It's cattle country, but we do have quite a few complaints." Coyotes, said Kilgo, tend to kill cattle only in certain "historical areas." When their populations are high and they travel in groups of three or four they are more apt to gang up on an available calf. "Complaints go to a trapper and he will try to kill a coyote if it's killing cattle."

Then in cattle country only offending animals are taken?

Kilgo frowned thoughtfully. "Well," he admitted, "sometimes a rancher will call in to say 'I'm calving in a month; come on in and help reduce my loss.' So we will do that if we can. But on something like that we work on a request basis only."

The real need for this service is perhaps best indicated by the fact that at least 30 percent of the cattle ranchers in Kilgo's district will not let ADC trappers on their property. Nevertheless, most coyotes are, in fact, "picked-up" in cattle country during fall and winter, when trappers, helicopters, and a fixed wing airplane—this last recently acquired by the Southwestern regional ADC—all work the buffer zones around the sheep pastures. During this last season, some 600 coyotes were "managed" in these areas. "We have a lot of losses in the sheep pastures, but if the coyote population were any higher we'd have a lot more. We've taken a single coyote that has killed a hundred lambs. I took one myself back in Texas that I called 'Old 52' because he had 52 confirmed kills."

Like almost every other ADC man I spoke with, as well as every rancher—and notwithstanding the fact that he has only been in this district for a relatively brief term—Kilgo was convinced that coyotes were definitely on the increase. I remarked that ADC's scent post indices in New Mexico, as in the West generally, suggested the opposite conclusion. Kilgo was genuinely surprised when he heard this. "Well," he said, "around here they don't seem to be decreasing." He may be right, for, although the ADC has set up about 30 scent post stations in the state to measure the frequency of coyote visits, only four of them are in that part of Kilgo's district which contains most of the sheep in New Mexico,

Kilgo's District

and of these, two are peripheral. None are in the center of the sheep country, where they might settle the argument about coyote numbers one way or the other.

The phone rang. One of Kilgo's trappers—not the missing one—was calling in to tell the supervisor about the depredations of a particular coyote. "A long, lean son-of-a-gun, eh?" said Kilgo with an appreciative grin. For a while he and the trapper discussed what needed to be done. When he hung up, our own conversation turned naturally to the methodology of control.

I learned that here in southeastern New Mexico, as elsewhere, aerial hunting was increasingly in vogue, in spite of the considerable expense. The demand had grown steadily ever since the early forties when it became common practise to shoot eagles from the air. But the prohibition on toxic chemicals in the seventies accelerated the demand, more than doubled it in fact. However, the extent to which ADC uses aerial control still varies widely from state to state. As of 1977, Wyoming expended more than 50 percent of its funds on this method, Texas, surprisingly, only about 20 percent, New Mexico 10 percent, and Arizona, where there is a law against aerial hunting, none at all. Aerial gunning now accounts for 40 percent of ADC's total take of coyotes, or about 35,000 animals a year. It cannot be selective about killing individual offending animals, but it does not exact a toll among non-target species, assuming the aerial gunner wants to be selective. However, given the circumstances brought to light by the eagle case in Texas, conservationists may understandably feel that the Department of Interior's Advisory Committee report of 1978 somewhat overstates the case when it says "A rigid Fish and Wildlife Service aircraft use policy had been developed to insure that aerial programs are conducted in a safe and environmentally sound manner. . . . Pilots and aircraft must be reviewed and approved using established Departmental procedures. Only approved and properly trained Service employees are utilized as gunners."

Barnes? Heintzelman? Allen? The review board of Texas Parks and Wildlife?

Toxicants are still often used in predator control on the Western range, both legally and illegally, but in nothing like the quantities that were being spread around prior to 1972. Indeed, if coyotes, eagles, and other predators—not to mention a long list of non-target species—were magically endowed with the capacity to build monuments to their human benefactors, the mountains and desert valleys of the West would

Incident at Eagle Ranch

be replete with likenesses of Richard Milhous Nixon. The former president's executive order banning the use of poisons in the Great Coyote War was perhaps his greatest, some would say his only, contribution to the environmental cause.

For generations, strychnine had been the usual standby of ranchers and the ADC, and carrion baits liberally laced with it were a standard feature of range country from Texas to Montana. Among environmentalists this poison was particularly notorious for the toll it exacted of non-target species. It was commonplace to find the carcasses of hawks, owls, vultures, eagles, foxes, badgers, even rodents with a carnivorous inclination, in the vicinity of baits. Coyotes, the target species, died by the thousands too, of course; but many of these wily creatures not only learned to recognize the scent of strychnine after a period of high mortality but, by example, would pass on the detection-avoidance pattern to their offspring. Some experienced trappers believe that this control method "broke" generations of coyotes of the habit of eating carrion, thereby increasing their depredations on living sheep.

During the fifties and sixties, strychnine was largely replaced by another toxicant, sodium monofluoroaecetate, better known as 1080, which was odorless; even the most wary coyote could not detect its presence. The poison had been developed during World War II as a rodenticide and it was first used in the West to destroy prairie dogs and ground squirrels. Apart from eliminating the former species from some parts of its range, the secondary effects on the food chain of all those poisoned little corpses lying about were, from the ecological point of view, horrendous. 1080 is held at least partly responsible for the disappearance of the black-footed ferret, the near extinction of California condors and red wolves, drastic declines in various birds of prey and kit and swift foxes; and the indiscriminate killing of many other more common animals, including dogs. Some specialists in control believe that the havoc caused by 1080's use as a rodenticide was more responsible for discrediting it than its subsequent use as a predacide. In any event, as a predacide it proved virulently effective, and throughout vast areas of the West the coyote became a rarity. Particularly in northern states like Montana and Wyoming, where long winters kept the baits fresh, and where coyotes were more dependent on carrion, populations of the little prairie wolf are said to have been halved.[1]

When the poison was finally banned, the ranching community was predictably distressed, and there were many dire warnings that coyotes would soon be as thick as rabbits and would destroy the sheep industry. In fact, for two or three years following the ban, coyote populations did increase somewhat. Yet it is one of the anomalies of the predator controversy that according to Department of Agriculture statistics lamb production was the same after the prohibition of toxicants as it had been before, even in the areas where 1080 had been most effectively used as a control method.

The one major exception to the proscription on poisons has been the M-44, a spring activated tube-shaped device that shoots a charge of sodium cyanide into a curious coyote's mouth when it pulls or bites a baited "trigger." It is much more selective, especially as far as raptors are concerned, than leaving lethal carrion about, although it takes a serious toll of foxes which find the bait as attractive as coyotes do. A number of Environmental Protection Agency restrictions control its use, especially on public lands, where it can only be used selectively to destroy offending predators when there is documented evidence that they are killing livestock. Larry Kilgo said that it was not much used in his district because so many of his trappers work on BLM lands, and the restrictions make it more trouble to fool with than it is worth. Nevertheless, there is enough private land around for New Mexico to exceed the Western average in the percentage of ADC killed coyotes taken by this means (8 percent); and in Texas, where public lands are almost nonexistent, 18 percent of all the coyotes destroyed by the ADC are casualties of M-44's.

Still, the great standby of trappers everywhere is the steel leg-hold trap. Most of ADC's manpower effort is devoted to this control method, although it accounts for only about 37 percent of the coyotes taken by that agency. Traps are notorious for snapping shut on all sorts of things they are not supposed to, including sheep, but officials argue that they can be fairly selective when the trapper knows what he is doing: if the tension device is properly set, for example, species that are significantly smaller than a coyote will not set it off; also, the choice of bait and location have a discriminatory function. But the most carefully managed trapline will often claim non-target species as its victims, and there is no reason to suppose that even among ADC trappers, the lines are always set out to ensure the maximum selectivity. Most ADC supervisors I met with lamented the declining standard of expertise among their trappers now that the older professionals are dying out; and there is considerable eyewitness evidence that on some ADC trap lines the non-target animals caught outnumber those for which the traps were set.[2] Even Larry Kilgo, who professed satisfaction with his trapper force, acknowledged that they do "pick up some foxes, skunks, and badgers." The ADC guesses that about seven thousand "innocent" animals are annually killed in traps;[3] but since neither the individual trappers nor their supervisors can find it much in their interest to report the true extent of non-target casualties, their estimates are undoubtedly very low.

However, ADC officials rightly point out that government trapping activities are a mere nothing compared to those of the fur trapping industry in the West. In 1977, for example, ADC destroyed a total of 70,400 coyotes, 1,226 bobcats, and, reportedly, a few thousands each of assorted smaller carnivores in all of its control programs;[4] whereas, at a minimum estimate, Western fur trappers took 222,400 coyotes, a walloping 50,511 bobcats, and more than a million badgers, foxes, skunks, and raccoons,[5] as well as uncounted thousands of unskinnable non-targets, from dogs to Bob Ramsey's road runner.

The demand for furs has dramatically escalated in the last several years, and the profits to be made have unleashed a horde of amateur trappers onto the Western landscape. Kilgo, like many other ADC officials, took a dim view of this development. "We have a pretty firm agreement with some of our sheepmen that other trappers will stay off. . . . We'd like to see fur prices go down because the fur trappers get in our way." That opinion is not shared by local sheep raisers like Bill Goodrum, who believe that "the thing that's kept the coyote in control is the price of furs."

Interestingly, the sheer numbers of furbearers that die in traps (the national total, including aquatic species like muskrat and nutria, exceeded 15 million in 1977) troubles the general public less, according to a U.S. Department of Agriculture survey, than the suffering associated with these devices. It is chiefly on that account that there is now a sizeable movement afoot to ban traps altogether.

Quite apart from the requirements of predator control on the one hand, and, on the other, the compelling needs of vogue-ish urban women who generally prefer not to think where their "fun furs" are coming from, the defenders of the leg-hold trap have a considerable arsenal of economic arguments for its use. An 800 million dollar industry is at issue: thousands of people depend upon it for a livelihood; it provides many a country boy with the wherewithal to go to college or buy a car; and it is an important monetary shot in the arm for hundreds

Kilgo's District

of small, economically faltering communities, like Leakey and Marfa, in the rural West and elsewhere.

However, none of these arguments quite obscures the fact that, as mechanical killing contraptions go, the trap—even now, with its teeth extracted—is a pretty nasty piece of goods. It is true that, when properly set, it no longer always mutilates irreparably the paw it clamps shut on. But the ensuing struggles of its frightened captive and the cutting-off of circulation often accomplish the damage which the initial snap of the trap did not. ADC regulations require trappers to visit their traps "as often as possible" or in accordance with state requirements, which usually comes to the same thing. As already noted, there is no supervision worthy of the name, and, in practice, "as often as possible" may mean anything from two days to a week.

In the case of the vast army of avocational fur trappers, the latter interval is probably closer to the average, since on weekdays school or full-time jobs get in the way. Consider, for example, "Rowdy" McBride, a fairly representative type of the part-time trapper. He is a sixteen year old high school student, the son of a mountain lion hunter whom we shall soon meet. Notwithstanding his boisterous nickname, he is a polite, well-spoken youth, tall, blonde, nice-looking—in general, an exemplar of the All American Boy. Because of his father's professional influence he is a more successful trapper than many of his peers, and is not indifferent to the "ethics" of the trade. In winter, when he runs his traplines on neighboring ranches, he sometimes checks them out on a Wednesday "if there's a class I can afford to miss." But more often, if any animal has the bad luck to get caught in one of his sets on a Sunday night or Monday, it must wait almost a week to be disposed of. "Oh yeah," Rowdy says, looking vaguely surprised as he responds to the obvious question, "they're almost always still alive." He pauses, a little uneasy, then adds, "I guess it *is* sort of cruel and all, but. . . ." He tries to think of a way to finish the sentence, but there really is none.

Without quite denying the hard-to-deny fact that trapping is an exceptionally ugly way to kill animals, ADC officials and spokesmen for the furriers, western biologists and wildlife managers, all unfailingly scoff at the "sentimental" and "anthropomorphic" concern of those who oppose trapping. Such people, they say, would do better to worry about the welfare of whole species rather than the plight of individual creatures. They point out that among target and non-target species alike, trapped animals are almost invariably expendable; and that in any case

Incident at Eagle Ranch

some other harsh fate would overtake them sooner or later. "They would die in a few months anyway," says Don Balsar, who is in charge of predator research at the Denver Wildlife Research Center, and is himself a former trapper. "And there's always others to take their place."

Balsar has gone to the considerable trouble of calculating that in the nation's large cities, the strongholds of the "sentimentalist" view, many more dogs and cats are annually killed by the "control" operations of the SPCA than are coyotes and bobcats on equivalent land areas of the Western range. It is not quite clear, however, whether this research is meant to demonstrate that "sentimentalists" should not worry about the fate of stray dogs and cats since they too are expendable and will certainly be replaced, or that they should worry exclusively about them, leaving the coyotes, et al., in the custody of less emotional people like Balsar himself.

The thinly veiled exasperation of Balsar, and others like him, is to some extent understandable. Some of the people who oppose trapping are ill-informed amateurs, inconsistent in their views. But for all that, it is not necessary to "anthropomorphize"—a dirty word to almost all wildlife specialists—other mammals in order to feel squeamish about the spectacle of a warm blooded animal with a highly developed nervous system—a coyote or bobcat, or even a badger or skunk—badly frightened, foot mangled, hungry and thirsty, lying in its own excrement for as long as a week, waiting for the club or bullet that will end its misery. To put the trap on the other foot, so to speak, the specialists themselves would presumably not relish seeing their own pet dogs and cats in that sort of a fix.

In short, the proponents of the leg hold trap should probably stick to the argument that the usefulness of the end justifies the cruelty of the means, rather than branding as sentimentalists those who insist, quite rightly, that the means are cruel indeed.

It must be said of traps, however, that if they are not very selective or humane, they at least afford their non-target victims a chance of being rescued if the trapper shows up in time and knows what he is doing. Even so, "rescue" is a relative term. The shattered paws of skunks and ring tailed cats are amputated with a knife; angry badgers are knocked unconscious with a club and henceforth do their digging with a crippled foot. As for the bobcats that are supposed to be released when they are caught in the coyote buffer zones in Larry Kilgo's district, anyone who has tried to extract a panicky house cat from a tree may wonder how the lone trapper manages a trick like that. The trappers I have spoken with say they don't.

In contrast to the leg hold trap, the wire hoop snare offers no hope of release. These nooses are only practical in districts like Kilgo's, where large sheep pastures are enclosed by wire mesh fence. Coyotes (and occasional badgers, dogs, javelinas, foxes, etc.) tunnel under a fence in their infiltrating way and then use the same spot for subsequent entry and egress. Until the snare is set, that is, and the passage becomes one-way only.

In one field test of the snare's effectiveness, researchers discovered that two–fifths of the animals caught were not predators. Virtually all of the local herd of javelina were among the casualties.[6]

Finally, there is "denning," an ungraphic term for killing coyote pups in their lairs either by digging or smoking them out. The destruction of any very young, helpless animal tends to upset many persons who would otherwise be indifferent to predator control issues, a fact of which Larry Kilgo is well aware. He looked a little uncomfortable when the technique was mentioned. "We have some denning," he said, "but I wouldn't say a whole lot." All told, about four thousand pups are killed annually by ADC personnel. Officials point out that the method is "highly selective." And there is no denying that coyotes are particularly destructive to sheep when they are raising young. If the pups are destroyed, even though the parents survive, the depredations frequently come to a sudden halt.

Kilgo was at odds with himself, in a minor way, when he regretted at one point in our conversation that his district did not "have the funds to work the other side of the Pecos River," whereas at another, he remarked that "we have enough trappers." But usually he was consistent and informative. From him I learned of yet another twist in the complicated process whereby ADC programs are financed. His district, unlike those in Texas, is funded on a 50/50 basis, half federal, half cooperative. His list of those contributing to the cooperative share of the funding included a source that was new to me. Along with the contributions of the state, county, and rancher associations, he also mentioned a category called "farm and range funds." This, he explained, is money derived from the fees ranchers pay the U.S. government to graze their livestock on federal lands, which in this district means mostly Bureau of Land Management lands. BLM then rebates some of this income back to the counties, and the counties in turn can appropriate it to pay some of the cooperative share of ADC operations. In other words, the ranchers pay one federal agency, BLM, a grazing fee, some of which is then returned to their county commissioners, who can use it to help pay another federal agency, ADC, to control predators for the ranchers on BLM lands. There is nothing very shocking about this arrangement, and the sums involved are small. Compared to the symbiotic relationships established by government agencies like the Corps of Engineers or the Bureau of Reclamation it is small potatoes indeed. But it does seem a bit like robbing Peter to pay Peter.

It was after 5 P.M. Kilgo was leaning back in his chair, hands behind his head, feet on the desk. He said he did not mind at all staying on. I had not yet mentioned eagles.

"We don't get any complaints," he said, "but I think we would if ranchers thought we could do something. We hear a lot of grumbling but not official complaints. They know our hands are tied. . . . I saw about 50—just a guess—west of Fort Sumner in sheep country. You can jump in an airplane, start 10 miles west of town, and head north for several hundred miles and you'll count eagles all the way.[7] Had he done that? "Well no, I haven't; but I've driven up that way."

I asked if he could document any cases of eagle predation. "Early this year we investigated some east of town," he replied. Did that mean that he had received an official complaint after all? "Well, yes," he said. "We found some early lambs that had been killed by eagles. In our professional opinion they were eagle kills because right across the river a rancher had seen eagles with his sheep." How many lambs were killed? "Four or five. Classic eagle kills, punctures at the back of the head, ribs eaten. They weren't eat up. The session lasted several days. They kept coming in, killed a new one each time." Kilgo was sitting forward now, elbows on the desk. "I've heard tell," he said, "when lambs are plentiful, eagles will kill one in the morning and one in the afternoon. . . ."

He shook his head, flashed me that whipper-snapper grin. "I like eagles. I like to see them. I think they're a beautiful bird. But in sheep country they should be removed. One way or another."

Kilgo left the office with me. There was still no news of the missing trapper and his companion. Later I would learn that, just as Kilgo suspected, their pickup broke down and they had to come out of the rough country on foot.

Kilgo's District

9. McBride's Collar

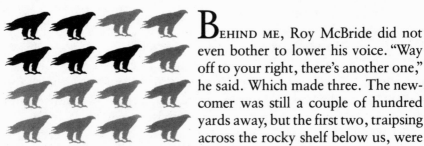

BEHIND ME, Roy McBride did not even bother to lower his voice. "Way off to your right, there's another one," he said. Which made three. The newcomer was still a couple of hundred yards away, but the first two, traipsing across the rocky shelf below us, were so close I could see their lolling tongues and the scruffy summer texture of their fur. McBride's imitation of a jack rabbit's bleating cries, performed on a hand-made caller (he despises tapes), had lasted less than thirty seconds—there was scarcely time to get settled on the lookout bluff he had chosen for this rendition—and here they were, three coyotes, coming into view as though summoned by St. Francis himself. My dog responds less promptly when I call him.

Of course coyotes are not always so accommodating. And McBride later observed that these three, having been tricked once, would not be so easy to fool again. By now the pair just below us were acting cagey, albeit in a useless sort of way, circling around to our left instead of trotting head-on up the slope. But the fact remains that if McBride had taken a gun with him instead of me they would never have had an opportunity to learn from their mistakes.

Even when we stood up, the animals required a long second to realize what was going on. The two below were a breeding pair, the male noticeably larger and bigger-boned than his mate. The female, out in front, was the first to hightail it, scooting back toward a ravine behind

Incident at Eagle Ranch

them. Looking bewildered, the male followed, and in an instant they were gone. When we turned to where the third coyote had been, he too had vanished.

For Roy McBride this was all old hat; for me it was an exciting way to begin a morning. And there was a good bit more to come. We were in the watershed of San Francisco creek, somewhere between Highways 385 and 90, and the coyote-calling was only the first of several occasions when we left McBride's truck behind and explored on foot, mostly along the stony beds of the San Francisco's tributary streams. It was early July, 1979, and this had been a good year for rain in west Texas; there was running water and an occasional deep pool, and the willows and tree-sized mesquite along the banks looked green and cheerful. In the damp sand were the tracks of coyotes, a fox, a bobcat, raccoons, cattle, deer, javelina, and "wetbacks." At one point, while McBride explored one side of a stream and I the other, a pair of javelina chugged out from under a small pressure ridge just as I climbed over it. For several minutes thereafter, they and I played hide-and-seek in the nearby scrub, they peeping worriedly at me, and I happily at them. I will never get used to it, the docility of wild animals in the West. Earlier McBride and I had routed a young mule deer buck with velveted antlers from the thin shade of a spanish dagger. A while later, when we passed that way again, the animal had reclaimed its resting place and this time would not budge as we drove by; just stared at us like someone waiting for a bus.

There were other sights: coveys of scaled quail; flights of doves; a few road-runners; the dried remains of one of several sheep that a mountain lion had killed months earlier, before McBride killed it. And there was the setting itself, red valleys and talus hills from which rose, at fairly close intervals, the stiff eroded peaks and mesas of the Haymond Mountains. Occasionally the track was barred by a stretched wire gate, easy to open but fiendishly designed to make a non-cowboy look like a fool when he tried to tug it closed again. This was all private land. During the seven or eight hours we were out of sight of paved roads or human habitation we covered perhaps fifteen miles on foot and in McBride's pickup without crossing more than three property lines.

McBride is exceptional in that he can traverse these boundaries, as well as almost any others in west Texas, whenever he pleases. Many of the landowners owe him: he has "taken out" more predators for them than he can count. But it is more than that. He is much admired in these parts, even envied. You can see it in the way other men talk to him; they

McBride's Collar

ask him to let them come along on his next hunt the way they might ask the football coach of a winning big-time team for extra tickets. McBride laughs and says he'll take them one of these days, which is what he has been telling them for years. The do not seem to mind being put off. If he were just a coyote trapper it would be different. But McBride is more than that. His real quarry is the "big stuff," the mountain lion and the wolf. He is the best of the last in his trade, and the only one in west Texas who can still make a living at it. He lives the sort of life that many west Texans dreamed of living when they were kids. No one is his boss; he is more at home under open sky than in a house; he can take the modern world or leave it, literally leave it, at will. He is the Marlboro man who would not be caught dead with his taut western face on a poster. At forty-two he can follow his dogs for half a day through country so steep and rough that it would put most men half his age out of commission in one half hour. His relaxed open style works too: grin at-the-ready, voice boyish, tone easy to read. Even the catch-all appelatives McBride uses—"guy," "fella," "man," occasionally "sir"—come off sounding weirdly personal. The friendliness is real, but detached. He is an authentic loner, though not the self-obsessed, self-protecting type that is supposed to be the model of Modern Man; rather, a throwback to the classic on-his-own westerner who can ride off into unfilmed sunsets whenever he wants to. He takes risks: he has been nearly drowned in a flash flood; been wedged upside-down in a crevice, eyeball-to-eyeball with a cornered lioness; has walked away without a scratch from the twisted wreckage of a helicopter. No doubt oil-rig workers and miners put their lives equally at hazard, but there is not the same cachet of adventurousness. McBride better fits the self-reliant mould. He is physically tough but good-natured, candid but hard to reach. He needs mountain lions more than he needs people.

He needs them in order to hunt them. So it would stand to reason that his local role as hero must end wherever environmentalists begin. It is not that simple, though. The ironic fact is that the people who care most about the well-being of predators, and therefore have least reason to like McBride, may end by being in his debt.

By late afternoon I was played out. It was not the exertion. I had been fool enough to undertake the blazing day without a hat, plus the fact that we had put nothing in our stomachs except river water since gulping down a cup of incredibly weak Texas coffee at dawn. McBride cultivates a spartan abstinence as a matter of course. It is essential to his profession and his idea of himself, which both require that life be traversed with as little baggage as possible. Even a full stomach is so much extra weight. Myself, I could have done with a little weighing-down just then, but in spite of that, the day was a great success. McBride, however, was disappointed. He had wanted to make a point for my benefit, and circumstances had foiled him.

He contends that during the last ten years mountain lions have not just increased in Texas, which I was willing to believe, but that their population has exploded. The hours of exploring stony creek beds were meant to prove that the animals are so abundant he could turn up fresh lion tracks and scrapes anytime he wanted to. But the demonstration was a flop. We discovered a turd or two, but they were months old, white and hard as chalk. He had been so sure he could do better than that. "I wanted to find us a perfect print, Guy, so fresh you could make a cast from it." He blamed the recent rains for turning the creeks into torrents, washing away all but the most recent sign along the banks. Nevertheless, he felt put down, as though the lions had made a liar of him.

I was neutral about the situation since I did not know enough to be anything else. Maybe, as in Jim Espy's part of the Davis Mountains, the lion population south of us had run out of exploratory animals; certainly, those that had previously come up this way from the Big Bend country were headed into trouble. Perhaps the high water was a sufficient explanation, or would have been if the recent flash floods had also washed away those months-old scats. Or possibly the lions, like many other wildlife species, were less restless in the heat of summer; although in that case it was surprising that McBride, who knows more about mountain lions that they know about themselves, did not anticipate that they might be lying low.

No matter; I was still impressed by McBride's certainty even if this time it had not paid off. There was no doubt that until recently the lions had been using San Francisco Creek and its tributaries in their far-ranging travels. What amazed me was that McBride knew exactly where they were, or where they ought to have been, in a landscape that is both difficult and immense. The logic behind his knowing makes perfect sense: He pointed to a mountain that dropped off just south of us, then to another great stony outcrop to the north, and explained that the cats, in moving from one high range to another, inevitably choose the watercourses that lie between as the most convenient routes to follow, usually passing through dead-end "header" canyons as they descend. When they reach the streams, they follow the shady shelves above the banks rather than the open beds below. The predictability of their movements surprised me. The lions may have fooled McBride this time, but more often than not he knows where they are, where they are heading, what path they will take.

An older generation of lion hunters knew too. "Do you see that break in the rimrock way up there?" McBride asked. I tried to see what he was pointing at. We were in an area known as Hell's Half Acre, and ahead of us loomed a loaf-shaped mountain, ringed just under its crest by a continuous palisade more than a hundred feet high, vertically striated, horizontally layered. Below these cliffs, the bulk of the mountain, a mass of tumbled rocks, sloped sharply to the desert floor. It is the sort of country that McBride takes literally in his stride when his dogs hit a hot trail. Earlier I had entertained the notion of going with him on a hunt, but I had the scale of this country now and I knew I would not be able to keep up.

At this distance, the "break" McBride spoke of was nothing but a darker shadow in the rimrock's wall, but through the binoculars it became a tall canyon cutting deep into the mountain. "Well," he continued, "at the back of the break is a big shallow cave. For as long as there were sheep around here, ranchers and trappers set blind traps in that cave, and sooner or later just about every lion that passed through the Haymond Mountains would step into one of them. That place was a real death trap." Blind traps are unbaited, since lions do not respond to carrion. Lightly covered with dirt, they are set out at funneling points in the lion roadway. They take a fearful toll of other wildlife too, which often use the lion trails. McBride has found the discarded remains of scores of deer and javelina at such sites.

I stared up at that high, distant cleft in the rock wall. It looked so hard to get to; so serenely out-of-reach of almost any human activity. Somewhat gloomily, I was moved to remark that "way up there, at least, I would have thought the lions would be safe." I did not expect McBride to be in tune with such a sentiment, but he surprised me. "I understand what you mean," he said. "I see that too." Then he added more cheerfully, "But most of the sheep are gone now and so are the traps. The ranchers aren't going to climb up there if they don't have to. And as they move out, or die out, they take the knowledge with them."

Incident at Eagle Ranch

In most Western states (but not in Texas) the mountain lion has
been recently elevated to the status of game animal, and there is considerable evidence, none of it coordinated, that the species is in better shape
now than it has been in thirty years. One reason, according to some
authorities, is that the imposition of bag limits and seasons put many of
the old lion hunters and their dogs out of business. However, McBride
believes that the fortunes of the mountain lion in Texas are solely, and
inversely, related to those of the sheep industry, a contention that is
borne out here in the Trans Pecos where the lion, officially still a varmint, is reoccupying former sheep country from which it was driven
decades ago.

The sheep operations act as roadblocks to expansion of the lions'
range. "You see that bunch of mountains south of us?" McBride asked
as we headed back to Alpine that evening. "Well, the ones closest to us
are owned by the last sheep rancher in this area. There are lions in all
the range south of him, and when they move up and start killing his
sheep, I take them out. But that fella is fixing to sell out soon, and the
place will go to cattle. When that happens there won't be any more complaints, no need for me, and the lions can move on up into that range"—
he pointed past my nose at another islanded clump of peaks to the north
—"without any trouble at all." McBride knows every bluff and canyon
in this country so well that their proportions have a way of shrinking as
he refers to this or that part of them; when he talks about the expansion
of mountain lions in the Trans Pecos he sounds like an urban planner
describing block-busting in a northern suburb.

The lone sheep operation that McBride mentioned stretches from
the mountains immediately to the south, to the flat lands flanking the
highway. Sheep were feeding here; and, at one spot, so were many turkey buzzards. McBride decided to investigate. We pulled over to the
shoulder of the road, climbed the fence, and advanced on the vultures,
which reluctantly hopped up on the nearby mesquite. There was, as
usual with McBride, no problem about trespass. Apart from the fact
that he held a general passport to all the ranches hereabouts, he had
"taken out" even more lions from this particular spread than Jim Espy
had from his.

The object of the vultures' attention was a ewe, not too long dead.
One eye was missing, the rib cage was opened, the udder was gone, and

McBride's Collar

the intestinal cavity had been opened from the rear. "All right," said McBride, "tell me what you see. What's been feeding on that sheep besides buzzards? How did it die?"

There was a real challenge in his voice. I was, after all, the Environmentalist to him; he was the ultimate Predator Hunter to me. For two crowded days we had not been out of each other's sight. Neither one of us had ever had such a prolonged exposure to a representative specimen of the other's subspecies. In spite of this we got along well; McBride is an easy man to like. But he is nothing if not the soul of candor, and at one point earlier in the day he had exclaimed, "I'm enjoying this; it's really interesting. But you know what, guy? Way down deep there's this basic mistrust. At some point you don't really believe what I say." I had replied that that might work both ways.

Now here I was with nothing very intelligent to say about this mangled ewe's demise except that it was obvious a mountain lion or coyote did not do her in. McBride, ordinarily the most amiable of men, scornfully refused to share his own thoughts on the subject. But after we went back to the truck he exclaimed, "You see how it is! Environmentalists are always saying the ranchers exaggerate, but they don't really know what's going on themselves. You tell us we don't know when something is killing sheep, but you can't even tell me what happened to that ewe!"

Roy McBride does not like sheep, or, more exactly, he does not like what they have done to much of the western range. On the other hand he is intensely interested in, even fond of, predators, especially the "big stuff," the lions and wolves. Yet if he is conscious of the paradox of saving sheep while killing the animals that kill them, he wears it lightly. When asked if he considered himself a conservationist, he laughed and said "Hell no." The fact is that he shares with other predator hunters an addiction to the work itself. During most of his career, the end which his work served was not a matter of concern. The only "end" that mattered was the moment when the lion or wolf or coyote was at bay or in the trap. The work was really an exciting game in which the predator becomes the prey. "Which is neater," asked McBride, "a deer or a lion? A lion, right?" By which he means that the lion is more worthy of his deadly interest. The issue of animal suffering and death, which often looms large in the consciousness of urban environmentalists is irrelevant in the rural and small-town West, where McBride and his neighbors

Incident at Eagle Ranch

often do their own butchering, where household pets are regularly flattened on the highway, where a man is thought a little odd if he does not like to hunt.

The game is a demanding one, and McBride is a master player. He has accounted for numberless coyotes since his boyhood, but his specialties are the wolves and lions. During his younger days he had more to do with bringing the mountain lion to the verge of extinction in Texas than any other single person. Given his remarkable stamina and the quality of his pack of hounds, a lion "almost never gets away" once McBride goes after it. He estimates that not more than twenty-five of great cats survived in the state by the early 1960s. If the sheep industry had not also declined in numbers during this period he would probably have hunted down every last one.

But even as the demand for his lion-hunting services waned in Texas, Mexican ranchers were becoming familiar with his work. Throughout the Big Bend country, on both sides of the border, it became axiomatic to "Let McBride do it," when local control efforts failed. In northern Mexico not only lions but wolves—lobos—have been his quarry, though he has quit killing them since 1973. In this case too, his deadly expertise helped push the wolves to the very brink of extinction. If McBride's "wild guess" is right, there may be only ten or fifteen lobos remaining in all of Mexico. Given the immensity of the the terrain and its ruggedness, the uninitiated might hope that he is wrong; but probably he is not. Wolves in Mexico are like tigers in India, especially now that the Mexican government is trying to alleviate its hopeless population problem by breaking up the large ranches and dispersing people all over the landscape on minuscule farms. The base of natural prey is all but gone; the wolf feeds habitually on livestock, and it kills a lot more than it eats; so every peasant knows if one of the animals is within a fifty-mile radius of his village, and sooner or later it is hunted down. And nowadays there are no wolves to replace the ones that die.

In recent years McBride's skills have been sometimes turned to environmental ends. As a member of several scientific study teams he has captured lions alive and turned them loose in new ranges with radio collars around their necks; supplied coyotes for predation studies at the Denver Wildlife Research Center; surveyed the population of Florida panthers for the World Wildlife Fund; and, most recently, live-trapped some of the last of the Mexican wolves for the Sonora Desert Museum at Tucson, where efforts are being made, thus far unsuccessfully, to

McBride's Collar

breed them. McBride, who is more knowledgeable about wildlife than some of the scientists he has worked for, is also unusual among the trapping brotherhood in being an educated man. In his spare time he earned an M.A. in wildlife management, which enables him to combine the "scientific perspective" and the jargon of the biologist with the down-home knowledge of the trapper in the field. He has even acquired, belatedly, a moderately protective interest in the "big stuff" that he hunts. He would willingly capture alive some of the trouble-making lions he now kills if only there were a place to which he could deport them, but neither state wildlife departments nor zoos will take them. Some of the animals, he believes, could be released in mountain ranges of the eastern states. He doubts that federal efforts to determine whether the eastern panther survives outside of Florida will be successful and, as evidence, he flourishes a photograph from *The Smithsonian* of a cast of a "panther's" track which, he says, is obviously that of a large dog. "There's no real taxonomic difference between the subspecies anyway," he argues. As for the Mexican wolves, he plans to capture alive the two remaining pairs he knows about, adding them to the breeding stock at Tucson—although he has misgivings about the results of the project thus far.

In spite of these preservationist impulses, McBride does not lie awake at night thinking about the beasts of prey he has literally hounded to death. His conscious view is fatalistic; he sees himself as an instrument in an inevitable process: where there are sheep there can be no lions; where there are cattle, there can be no wolves—at least not in a world where the ranges of most sizeable species except man have become increasingly restricted. Unlike the adaptable coyote, lions and wolves are too limited in their numbers, too extravagant in their depredations, too demanding in their territorial needs, and too easily hunted down to survive when their interests and man's conflict. "When they cause trouble the ranchers are going to get them sooner or later, with or without me."

For McBride, however, such considerations are of secondary interest. The more compelling reason why he would never consider giving up the pursuit of lions and coyotes and wolves as long as any of them remained is because it would mean giving up himself. The pursuit is the only thing that really matters. He compares serious trappers to "carneys"—that is, people whose line of work is a true addiction that they cannot abandon for better wages, living conditions, anything, even though the rewards are not all that apparent. In describing the "carneys," McBride describes himself. At one point during the drive that evening, he recalled a TV documentary he had seen about the lifestyle of primitive Eskimos. "Those people live without guile or deceit; they don't know how to be anything but independent and honest. You should have seen them come up on this polar bear with just their spears! They're too busy staying alive to worry about big government or ask for handouts or anything like that. You know what, fella? That was mankind's highest point."

This is essence-of-McBride. Except for close personal attachments, all forms of dependence are suspect. As for independence, it is a physical state of being that can be had only by existing in the natural world on very simplified terms, travelling light, being on your own, concentrating on elemental matters like the weather, the fire you cook at, the quarry you hunt or trap. It is a world where one inexhaustibly hunts the polar bear/mountain lion, and where there is always an inexhaustible supply of polar bears or mountain lions to hunt. McBride is Texas' answer to Peter Beard.

In pinpointing the blame for the dependent, fallen state of modern man, Big Government is McBride's pet *bete noir*. But he is too sharp not to know that the problem has a more fundamental—a more ecological —origin. As we neared Alpine, he deplored an immense new ranchette-cum-trailer-park development that had been spawned at the very boundary of Big Bend National Park. ("All those people trying to make pots or raise chickens.") Suddenly, he remarked, "This friend of mine told me that if he could reduce the world's population to one tenth what it is now, he would do it, even though he'd have only a one-in-ten chance of surviving himself. I believe I feel the same way." He glanced at me, curious. "What do you think, guy?" It was all make-believe, of course; perhaps even McBride's friend was hypothetical. Nevertheless, I hedged the odds. "Make it one-in-five" I said, "and I'll go along." He grinned. At this amiably misanthropic moment the "basic mistrust" between the lion hunter and myself had disappeared.

Left to himself, McBride would follow the great predators into their last strongholds. He hankers after Belize, that small country next door to, and coveted by, Guatemala, where, he assures me, mountain lions and jaguars are still in plentiful supply. Besides, he likes Mexican and Latin American people. Not their governments, cities, or even their attempts at progress; just the people themselves. "They're real poor, and they have way too many children. But they support their own families and they don't expect favors, you know? They know how to live; they don't need a whole lot of things to be happy."

McBride has a family of his own, a strikingly handsome one, which he must still support. However, his two strapping sons—the oldest is already an experienced lion hunter—and his beautiful daughter are now almost grown, and his bright, attractive wife, Jere, is staking out a career of her own as a special education counselor for much of west Texas. In her spare time she has learned to fly, the better to cover her own territory and taxi her husband to distant assignments. McBride's passion for his work is his passion, not hers, but she knows that he would "never be happy if he had to give it up." Nevertheless, she takes a dim view of his talk about Belize. "Roy was a government trapper when I married him. Our first home was a tiny little shack. When you woke up in the morning, you could tell where your head had been because the rest of the pillow was covered with dust." She glanced around at their present home on the outskirts of Alpine. "We've been here about ten years. It's the only home we've ever really *lived* in." Her husband had no comment.

In expressing his distrust of Big Government and its "give-away" programs, McBride is fond of citing the relationship between ADC and the ranchers. McBride began working for ADC in 1957 at the age of twenty. In the early sixties he was the government's official lion hunter in Texas. In this period, he pioneered the aerial gunning of coyotes in the state. In 1967, the ADC director in Texas, Milton Caroline, made him a district supervisor, but after a year and a half he quit the job. Administrative work, he decided, was not his line; and besides, he was disenchanted by Caroline's view that the trappers in the field were "a sub-type of human who didn't deserve to earn a decent living." (He is very partisan about trappers. Regarding the eagle case, for example, he feels that Jim Beavers, whom he knows and likes, should not have been suspended. "And if they were going to put that trapper, Allen, on trial, why didn't they put some of the big shots on trial too?") He argues that trappers should have salaries that are comparable to supervisors'. "Supervisors under civil service make a hell of a lot more money and they have an easier job. The trappers have no incentive!"

During the last ten years, McBride has occasionally worked for the ADC as a lion hunter but usually he hires out directly to the rancher associations to kill offending animals, thereby cutting out the government as middle man. "Maybe," he said, "I'm just an unsupervisable sort of person." When he speaks of the ADC, he can be downright heretical: "Everybody is aware a lot of coyote control is unnecessary . . . In cattle country there's a tremendous amount of preventive control that isn't needed. But the ADC says, 'Look, I've got this amount of money to spend,' so the rancher says, 'Okay.' If he were funding the control himself, he'd say, 'Get lost' . . . I'm not saying predator control isn't necessary; it's vitally necessary. But it's the rancher's responsibility. There would be a lot less control if it cost the rancher more money. Now the most he pays is half . . . I ask these ADC guys 'How do you justify what you're doing?' I've yet to get an answer! If they ask me why I hunt lions I tell them because I like it and the rancher pays me . . . If we're going to the moon, we need a government effort, but why do we need the government for something as simple as coyote control? It takes away all initiative. Where does it end? Why not have the government spray the weeds around my house? . . . If ADC is paying the bill to kill a lion, hell, the rancher will want to get rid of that lion even if it's just killing deer. If he doesn't have ADC he won't bother . . . The real issue to me, maybe I'm too simple, is that the guy who needs control should do it himself or pay for it himself. Make ADC cost effective. Make it operate strictly on a fee basis."

At first hearing, these criticisms of ADC, delivered, as it were, from within the enemy's lines, may sound like music to environmental ears. But defenders of ADC argue (a) that many ranchers cannot handle their own predator problems, (b) that if ranchers initiated their own control programs the ecological consequences would be far more disastrous than if control were in the hands of professionals, and (c) that if the ADC were not involved in control work, there would be no way of monitoring the effects of control on predator populations.

For all of these arguments, McBride has ready answers: "If a rancher can't swing his own control, he should get out. The most successful operators do their own control anyway. I can show you any number of ranchers who do their own, or hire their own trappers. They're not doing it for the fun of it; it's another job, like mending fences. They do it only when it's necessary. . . . If ADC was the only one doing predator work maybe I could go along with it. But, hell, fella, the ranchers are doing it anyway! The ADC is just additional, supplementary. And how can ADC be more professional? There's a certain type of guy who likes

McBride's Collar

to do control work; it's always the same bunch of guys, good and bad, who trap predators, whether they're being hired by the ADC or the ranchers. I'm an example! . . . As for ADC keeping track of what's going on, do *you* believe that? What have they kept track of?. . . Of course, my experience was with the way Caroline ran it."

McBride has quit ADC, but ADC is not quit of him; he has devised a new and ingenious means of killing coyotes, a toxic collar, which may effect a small revolution in the methodology of predator control. "New" is used relatively here, since he invented the prototype of the present model in the early sixties. He was on a "private job" at the time, trying to kill a female coyote that had been exacting a heavy toll of lambs on a sheep ranch near Iron Mountain, just west of Marathon. For once, McBride seemed to have met his match.

Coyotes, it is true, are remarkable for the alacrity with which they learn from experience, especially bad experience. But for all that, their wariness is usually overstated. Unlike the three animals McBride had summoned up for me, most coyotes do not get a second chance when they are matched against a trapper who knows what he is doing. Nevertheless, there are "super-coyotes," those rare exceptions who, because of their high canine IQ and sheer luck, manage to evade every effort to do them in. The Iron Mountain coyote was such a one. She avoided traps, ignored poisoned bait. On one occasion she wrecked the rancher's pickup when he tried to run her down. On another, McBride, spotting her while in his own pickup, pursued her over a divide, only to find she had dematerialized in the wide open flat that lay beyond. She was out there, he knew, pressed flat against the ground, aware that if she moved he would pick her off; but although he drove the flat for an hour, he was not able to break her nerve. On another occasion he dragged the fence line she customarily crossed with rubber tires. "After I was done you could see the tracks of a centipede in the sand." But not hers. That night she crossed the fence coming and going, leaving no sign behind except the three sheep she had killed.

In this case at least, necessity was the mother of invention. McBride decided that since his nemesis was biting sheep in the throat in the conventional coyote fashion, he could kill her if he covered the vulnerable area with 1080, the merest taste of which is fatal to canids. The use of the poison was still legal at the time, so McBride swabbed it liberally on the necks of several lambs after removing the rest of the flock from the area. Unfortunately for McBride, and the rancher, enough of the 1080 seeped into the lambs' mouths when they grazed to kill them within hours. But McBride was at least as ready to learn from experience as the coyote. On the second try, he hand-stitched several rubber pouches, filled them with 1080 and water, swathed them in wool, and tied them around the necks of a dozen lambs. Next morning, one of the lambs was dead; so was the Iron Mountain coyote.

McBride was so effective as a coyote trapper, and was so often otherwise occupied in hunting mountain lions, that for some time he had almost no need for the device he had invented. Several years passed, during which he used it not more than a dozen times, before he began to realize its potential. In the late sixties he applied for a patent. By the time it was granted in 1973, Nixon's executive order banning toxicants was in effect. In terms of commercial exploitation, the collar was now off-limits.

Not long after this, U.S. Fish and Wildlife's Research Center at Denver got wind of McBride's invention. This agency was largely concerned with research on predator control, and one of its most important mandates was, still is, to devise new methods of discouraging predators from killing livestock. Soon after McBride received his patent he was contacted by Denver Wildlife Research and asked to send a few samples of his collar up to Denver for study.

Since that time, the history of the collar has been an up-and-down affair. For two years Denver Wildlife Research experimented with the collar on its own, at a cost of nearly $750,000. Plastic chokers were developed which, according to McBride, looked like "Mae West flotation devices." Because of the ban on 1080, packets were injected with cyanide and, later, a chemical called diaphasanon. Lambs were staked out as bait rather than turned loose. The results were disappointing; the coyotes were not interested. Finally McBride was summoned to Denver, and for six months acted as a consultant in field testing the collar, which under his direction was made smaller and more pliable. However, the results were still unsatisfactory until, in 1976, the Environmental Protection Agency granted the Denver agency a permit to use 1080 on an experimental basis.

Thus, after three years of experimentation and at formidable expense, the Denver Wildlife Research people were using the same collar which McBride had designed more than a decade earlier at a cost of a few dollars—a bandaid-like contraption consisting of two small rubber

McBride's Collar

pouches containing a miniscule quantity of 1080 diluted in water, attached to a pair of elastic straps.

Since 1976, the effectiveness of McBride's collar has been tested in more than sixty supervised in-the-field experiments, some of them conducted by McBride in Texas, others in Montana by Denver Research's predator specialist, Guy Connolly. Volunteer ranchers with serious predation problems are instructed to withdraw most of their sheep or goats from pastures where coyotes have been causing trouble, leaving a small group of collared lambs or kids behind. When an offending coyote bites one of these animals at the throat it is finished. Sometimes the predator's body is found, sometimes not; but either way, depredation almost always comes to a sudden halt.

On the occasion of one such recent test, McBride invited me to do a little unofficial supervising of my own. A goat raiser in Bosque County was regularly losing nannies and kids to a denning pair of coyotes, and had asked McBride for help. In this case, Denver Wildlife Research had appointed a wildlife biologist at Texas A & M to be its official observer. McBride and I rendezvoused with this man in Brownwood. During the subsequent conversation over coffee it became evident that he was a strong supporter of Milton Caroline—he was already aware that I was not—and it was also soon evident that my unauthorized presence would not be welcomed during the test, not even at the collaring of the "target" goats, although, as it turned out, the rancher himself would have been glad to have me on hand. Not wanting to halt the experiment, I made myself scarce for the rest of the day. It was no great matter. The moment that counted came a few nights later when the rancher called McBride to tell him that the collar had done its work. Two coyotes were dead.

The tests continue. The pattern is almost always the same: a rancher's stock is being regularly attacked by one or more coyotes. Sometimes dozens of lambs or kids are killed in a matter of weeks. In some cases the rancher is inexperienced as a trapper, or the ADC man he calls in is inexpert; in other cases the coyote is lucky or smart. McBride recalls one instance in which ADC spent tens of thousands of dollars in trapper man hours and aerial flight time to catch one coyote, all to no avail, before he was called in and his toxic collar put an end to the problem. Once the collars are affixed and the target lambs set out in an otherwise empty pasture, a marauding coyote is doomed if it strikes again. "Everybody knows the collar works," says McBride, and the record bears him out.

Incident at Eagle Ranch

Up at Denver Wildlife Research, Don Balsar, the Chief of Predator Mitigation Research, cautions that "the collar is not a panacea. It's just one more tool." The first part of that statement is accurate enough but the second part is probably not. Depending on how it is used, McBride's deadly little choker could well be a major breakthrough in the methodology of predator control, a device that would satisfy both the ranchers and their environmental opponents, and would probably have the long term effect of saving the lives of more coyotes than it would kill.

No expertise is required in handling the collar; any rancher can do the job himself. More important, it is by far the most selective coyote killer that has ever been devised. Not just non-target species but unoffending coyotes are safe from it. "The terrific thing is that you get the right *individual* animal! You don't have to clean sweep the area of coyotes the way they try to do now."

There are limitations to the collar's use. Since most ranchers will not disturb sheep during the lambing season, those few weeks are out-of-bounds. And since ranchers cannot keep their flocks rounded up and out of the way indefinitely, the "target" lamb technique can only work when coyotes are raiding on a regular basis; but, as McBride points out, that is when control is most urgently needed. (In Mexico, where there are no restrictions on the use of 1080, some of McBride's clients keep a hundred or more lambs collared at all times as a continuing safeguard against predation, thus eliminating the need to sequester their flocks whenever a coyote makes a kill.)

The use of 1080 is the chief roadblock to the collar's more general application. Because of taste or odor or lethal limitations, other poisons do not work as well. For the same reasons, non-lethal substances that are designed to deter coyotes without killing them are of no use either; the coyotes learn to avoid the collar, not the sheep. Understandably, the environmental community is suspicious about any exception to the EPA ban on 1080, although several organizations are beginning to recognize that the collar may be the selective tool they have been asking for. McBride is more worried about the government than the environmentalists. He suspects that the ADC is not too enthusiastic about the collar's possibilities. If it works too well, it might put a lot of ADC trappers and aerial gunners out of work. And if the ADC does endorse it, McBride fears that so many restrictions will be imposed, so much supervision required, that its effectiveness will be much diminished. "I hope

McBride's Collar

the ADC doesn't take it over. What's the point of hiring a government guy to drive way out to a ranch and put it on when a rancher could buy the thing and do it himself? Of course, from ADC's point of view that might be a boon. They could get collar men, clean-up men, training men, more secretaries and office space." He insists that the collar is no more a health risk, and much less of an environmental hazard, than pesticides that are sold over the counter. "And how can the ranchers misuse it? The only way it can kill is if something is biting on a sheep's throat."

Apart from not quite knowing what to do with McBride's collar, the federal government does not quite know what to do with McBride. He is genuinely "without deceit or guile" and tends to speak his mind, no matter whose company he is in. He has criticized ADC and Denver Wildlife Research—the agencies that will have most to say about his collar's future—to their official faces. Bureaucratic egos can be very sensitive about such things. And there is also the difficult truth that McBride, the incorrigible free agent, has created with a lot of imagination and a very few dollars a more effective and selective control device than the federal experts have come up with after years of trying, at a cost of millions.

When McBride and I were preparing to go our separate ways, his face took on an I've-got-a-secret look. "Say, guy," he asked, "how would the environmentalists feel if there was a way of keeping coyotes off sheep that didn't kill the coyote, and that was environmentally safe?" I replied that that would be too good to be true. The government had been trying to come up with something like that for years without any luck.

"Wait," he laughed. "Just wait until this *next* patent comes through!"

Incident at Eagle Ranch

10. ADC

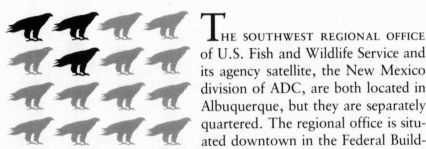THE SOUTHWEST REGIONAL OFFICE of U.S. Fish and Wildlife Service and its agency satellite, the New Mexico division of ADC, are both located in Albuquerque, but they are separately quartered. The regional office is situated downtown in the Federal Building; ADC is located in an innocuous-looking structure high up on a subdivided slope called the Heights, far from the parent agency. Fish and Wildlife, in the way of bureaucracies, would never willingly disown one of its offspring, least of all one that has so many powerful political friends. But the ADC frequently attracts unpleasant attention in the environmental press, and there are probably moments when regional supervisors of Fish and Wildlife wish that it had not been born. The Southwest's regional director, Bill Nelson, "came up through the ADC," but for that very reason, he says, he "probably bends too far the other way" in not seeming partial to ADC interests. He estimates that the agency gets less than five percent of his time. Meanwhile, the unloved child goes pretty much its own way. There is, it is true, a "restructuring" of the administrative chain of command in the works, partly the result of the eagle fracas in Texas which left Nelson in the bullet-biting position of ordering an investigation of his old friend and colleague in ADC, Milton Caroline—a duty, it should be noted, which Nelson did not shirk.

During the restructuring period, I drove up to the Heights to visit the director of ADC in New Mexico, Vernon Cunningham, who was also serving at the time as the acting supervisor of all ADC operations in the Southwest. His predecessor in that role, George Rost—to whom Milton Caroline had frequently appealed in his efforts to impede Stinebaugh's investigation—had just retired in time for this administrative reorganization to occur.

Unlike Caroline, Cunningham did not seem to regard the ADC as the chief reason for his existence. In fact, contrasts between New Mexico's ADC supervisor and his Texas counterpart abound, beginning with the way they got started in their profession. Caroline first joined Fish and Wildlife's refuge division and then transferred to ADC early in his career, whereas Cunningham, who began with a job in ADC because "a lot of people like me weren't getting any kind of wildlife jobs with just a Bachelor of Science degree," has since wished that he could switch to one of the ecological services "to get a broader view." All the same, he explained, "this job doesn't bother me because it's such a complex program, politically and biologically. A day never goes by when all hell doesn't break loose. It's interesting. Anyway," he added, "I think I can do a better job than someone who might be more biased. If you deal mostly with livestock people you get to see only one side. You need to back up and ask, 'Is that what's really going on?'"

If style reflects essence, Cunningham was dispassion itself: the voice reflective but bland, the facial expression calmly neutral, the pale blue gaze fixed noncommittally on the office wall behind me. His observations on the ADC program were appropriately objective, even clinical. "I can assure you," he said, "we do have problems here—none real flagrant —but New Mexico's ADC is far from being a really sound program." One problem, he explained was the lack of supervision: "We have three district supervisors in New Mexico and about forty trappers. One man supervises as many as eighteen trappers. He can't possibly control them. The supervisors are going night and day, but still the supervision is not good." (Just a few hours earlier I had left the cubbyhole office of Tom Fowler, Caroline's onetime right hand man. He had said, "We both know there's little real inspection in the program.")

Cunningham attributed many of ADC's problems to its dependence on the support of local ranchers' associations. "The trapper knows that part of his salary comes from the local ranchers. The association says, 'You're working too hard on the other side of the county; how much is it going to cost to get our own man over here?' The trapper ends up, human nature being what it is, feeling tied to the ranchers."

Incident at Eagle Ranch

Six years ago, when Cunningham was new to his job, he had dreamed of "doing away with the rancher associations." Now, he admitted he still hadn't "gotten on top of the problem." He recalled a particular example: "I had a trapper in southeastern New Mexico. I looked in his area and saw there were no loss reports of livestock, although he was occasionally catching a transient coyote. So I moved him out. It stirred up a lot of local reaction. The ranchers argued that they didn't have losses because the trapper was there."

Cunningham's anecdote reminded me of an earlier one that had been more cheerfully related by the district supervisor in West Texas, a fellow named Jodie Webb. A few minutes after declaring that he was besieged by ranchers' calls for assistance, he remarked that most of his trappers were permanently ensconced in their territories and would rather quit than move. "Say a man is working a ranch that isn't having any losses. Well then, I'll have this man work further out" [in a non-sheep raising buffer zone]. How much further out? "Oh, anywheres up to six or seven miles away." After a pause, Webb had added, "If I have a man who keeps my cooperators [the local ranchers' association] happy, I damn sure want to keep him where he is."

Although Cunningham's and Webb's attitudes might differ when it came to "keeping the cooperators happy," it was evident that in both cases the cooperators got their way. I confronted Cunningham with a situation in Southwest New Mexico that I had heard about. Almost all of that corner of the state is given over to ranching cattle, not sheep. Now, if there was one certainty that had emerged from my explorations in the West, it was that coyotes are rarely a serious problem in cattle country. Certainly there are incidents, sometimes of a sort that, as one cowboy put it, "makes for feelings." Coyotes have been known to devour not only a calf as it was being born, but also the hindquarters of the prostrate cow. But such occurrences are uncommon; they clearly call for "corrective" rather than "preventive" control. Among the scores of cattlemen I spoke with in Texas, New Mexico, and Colorado, not one complained of a serious problem with predators. Several felt that coyotes, as rodent controllers, did more good than harm. Others like Beau White and Clay Miller were less tolerant, but only because they suspected coyotes were killing too many of their antelope and deer. The relative unconcern of the cattlemen was confirmed by the sheep raisers, who often complained that their cattle-raising neighbors were indifferent to their predator problems. Federal statistics also support this conclusion. According to rancher-reported losses, which are hardly likely to be understated, only seven-tenths of one percent of calves born on the Western range are done-in by predators.

Cunningham's territory is no exception to the rule. Recently, an ADC sponsored project involved the killing of one hundred and twenty five coyotes in the cattle country of Southwestern New Mexico for research purposes. The chief aim of the operation was to determine the population dynamics of a heavily hunted coyote population. The conclusion of this study, which any amateur could have predicted even if there had not been previous studies to confirm it, was that the age structure of coyote society in that part of the state was pyramidical, with a disproportionately high percentage of one-and-two-year olds composing the base. From the viewpoint of local ranchers the "research" had the virtue of eliminating a sizeable number of coyotes from the range. But it did have one additional effect: it revealed, almost incidentally, that of the one hundred and twenty five coyote stomachs examined, only one contained "fresh veal"—which may or may not have been carrion.

"Well," Cunningham acknowledged, "we do fly the cattle country down there. Why? Because it's historically done, and it makes the ranchers happy. It's 'selective' only in that you get target species, not offending individuals. And if you figured out the cost/benefit ratio—" He shook his head doubtfully, then started over: "Here's the problem: Southwest New Mexico isn't sheep country. But the County Commissioners and the Farm and Range representative, they say 'Look, we want a helicopter. You put up five thousand dollars, we'll put up five thousand dollars. So we fly. I don't have data to say we do or don't do much good. Personally, I think too much taxpayer money goes into it. I worry about that. But the ranchers are happy. And the coyote is expendable." He paused. "I don't know," he sighed, staring at the wall. "You inherit these things. They can't be all wrong or they wouldn't have been done in the past. At least the ranchers put their money where their mouth is."

For a while we spoke of other matters: About the black market in poisons, especially 1080 ("A minor amount"); about ADC trappers selling bobcat furs illegally ("We have two cases that we've turned over to the enforcement division"); about eagles ("I have a gut feeling the ranchers are doing their own control; there are rumors they shoot them off the power lines"); about the revitalization of the sheep industry now that the price of wool is going up ("Ranchers in southeast New Mexico are buying up land like you wouldn't believe").

Incident at Eagle Ranch

In response to most questions, Cunningham's answers were admirably forthright. But when our conversation drifted back to the structure and aims of ADC, the supervisor's replies became equivocal. I had met with this ambivalence in well-intentioned administrators before; it denoted a sort of bureaucratic malaise, born of the dichotomy between individual conviction and official policy. In being honest, Cunningham sometimes sounded as though his public and private selves were trying, without great success, to come to terms:

"Depending on the public's whims, we do or don't get money. This year there was a big add-on to our budget; we got three hundred thousand. The woolgrowers had been getting back to their congressmen. But I don't think Interior wanted the money; I get the impression they don't really think we should be in this. Yet when a congressman goes to Interior and says 'You better get a man out there'"—He shrugged. "I wish U.S. Fish and Wildlife would get off the pot and make up its mind whether it wants this job or not. If someone up there would say this is a needed program, no matter what Defenders of Wildlife says, we could do something to protect livestock with minimum wildlife loss. I'm in this program. I try to do my job. We get a lot of non-target species, but the rancher would catch a lot more than we do. And you do get coyotes that are awfully wise. You do need some expert trapping. If we surrendered our authority to the states the program would be going from the frying pan into the fire. Of course, *if* the states could deal with it politically, I'd say the feds should get out . . . I just don't know. If this was my own money—I'm kind of tight anyway—I'm not sure I'd spend a million dollars a year controlling predators in New Mexico."

It was getting dark when Cunningham and I parted company. In the valley below the lights were coming on. Albuquerque is not a very large metropolis as American cities go; there are about one hundred others that outrank it. Yet now an electrical constellation was extending almost as far as one could see along the banks of the Rio Grande River. On the Heights, the wind that coasts along the slopes of the Sandias Mountains had begun vibrating against aluminum window casements and make-believe shutters, producing a banshee moaning that contradicted the subdivision look of things. Some of the New People on the Heights complain that the sound gets on their nerves.

All things considered, the testimony of Messrs. Caroline, Beavers, Fowler, Webb, Kilgo, McBride, and Cunningham, among others, is not calculated to reassure those who view the U.S. Animal Damage Control Division with something less than enthusiasm. In fairness, the agency's operations are tidier now than they were a decade ago. Some, though by no means all, of the recommendations proposed by the Leopold Report in 1964 and the equally consequential Cain Report in 1972—both the products of advisory committees appointed by former Secretaries of the Interior—have influenced ADC policy.[1] Of these changes, far and away the most important has been the ban on the use of toxicants—excepting the M-44 ejector—on the Western range. Among other changes: most personnel at the supervisory level of ADC are now expected to hold degrees in wildlife management; endangered predator species are officially protected; some advances have been made in the study of predator ecology; the aerial hunting of predators now requires, in theory, the supervision of state and federal authorities; and the ecological and esthetic value of predator species has been acknowledged as an aspect of ADC's "philosophy."

However, in spite of these changes, and always excepting the prohibition on poisons, the in-the-field operations of ADC are pretty much a case of business as usual: (1) ADC control is conducted with virtually no meaningful supervision of trappers and aerial gunners; in fact, the only effective surveillance is done by the ranchers, who protest only when too few, not too many, predators are killed; (2) ADC is still very much the creature of the ranching community, bound to it by political, economic, and, frequently, personal ties; (3) notwithstanding official statements to the contrary, most ADC control continues to be "preventive;" that is, it involves the more-or-less random killing of target (and sometimes non-target) species rather than the "corrective" killing of individual offending animals; (4) neither the ADC nor anyone else can produce a realistic estimate of the agency's usefulness to the livestock industry or the West's economy—or, for that matter, its costs in terms of ecological imbalances—because adequate documentation does not exist.

In response to the ongoing sound and fury that ADC has generated, President Carter's Secretary of the Interior, Cecil Andrus, promised that in 1979 he would announce a new set of guidelines for that agency, later to be known as the "Revised Federal Policy on Predator Control."[2] This policy statement was to be based on three federal documents, all of them published during the preceding months. One of these was an independent study of ADC's financial and administrative structure by Interior's

Incident at Eagle Ranch

Office of Audit and Investigation, noncommittally entitled *A Review of the Animal Damage Control Program.*[3] Another was the ADC's Environmental Impact Statement, a self-assessment compiled at the request of the Council on Environmental Quality.[4] The third, *Predator Damage in the West,*[5] billed as a successor to the Leopold and Cain reports, was the work of an advisory team appointed by Andrus and composed of representatives of livestock, environmental, and governmental factions. None of these productions makes for exhilarating reading, but they do contain important information.

First, the Audit and Investigation Office's *Review:* This relatively brief critique is concerned with the administrative and bookkeeping practices of ADC. The audit people investigated the agency's operations in six Western states. In five of these, Utah, Wyoming, California, Texas, and New Mexico, ADC runs the control program itself. In the sixth, Washington, the operation has been leased to the state on a do-it-yourself-with-federal-money basis. The opening pages of the *Review* sum up the investigators' findings—a sort of report card with grades that no one would want to bring home to the folks:

1. ADC's records contain "incomplete financial data" concerning cooperative funding, and "inaccurate and non-comparable program data."

2. Concerning ADC supervision, there is a "lack of field inspection or in-depth year end evaluations" of individual programs.

3. In allocating funds, ADC depends on "the use of historical funding patterns rather than documented analyses . . . concerning such matters as the number of livestock protected, livestock losses, etc. . . ."

4. In a more general sense, ADC is functioning with "inadequate operational information (i.e., livestock protected, total livestock losses due to predation)."

5. In violation of federal policy, which requires the written consent of landowners when ADC control programs are conducted on private land, there is an "absence of some private property agreements."

6. The ADC's Policy Handbook is "outdated."

7. In its contract with the state of Washington, which permits that state to operate its own program under federal supervision, the ADC is guilty of "inadequate contract monitoring and enforcement of contract terms"—so inadequate, in fact, that the auditors recommend that the contract be terminated unless the whole arrangement is tightened up.

The reader will note that all of these criticisms except the first and last have cropped up in one form or another during the interviews reported in these pages. For example, the "lack of field inspection." But even though ADC has promised to mend its ways by conducting more inspections, its good intentions will not amount to much as long as other conditions remain the same. Perhaps the ADC trapper Andrew Allen would not have flagrantly slaughtered eagles in Real County if he had been supervised by an ambitious young fellow like Larry Kilgo instead of the incompetent Beavers. And no doubt South Texas Helicopter Company and, as I would later learn, district supervisors like Jodie Webb, would not have ignored repeatedly the necessity of acquiring signed agreement forms if the state director had been Vernon Cunningham rather than Milton Caroline. But the fact remains that even under the best of circumstances the day-to-day activities of trappers or district supervisors are not subject to "real inspection." Even Kilgo relies heavily on his faith in his men's characters—and on rancher complaints—to evaluate their work.

As for the "use of historical funding patterns," the evidence of this is everywhere apparent in ADC districts. If a trapper "keeps the cooperators happy" he may remain in the same territory year after year, whether or not there are any livestock losses, or even any coyotes. As long as the ranchers provide a large percentage of the funding on a local basis, arguing that they don't have any losses "because the trapper is there," there is no likelihood that the pattern will change.

Another reason it will not change is because the ADC has "inadequate operational information" at its disposal. Here again, the prospects for reformation are not too bright. As we have discovered in this journey through the Southwest, there is an extraordinary dearth of hard evidence about the extent of predator damage or even the specific areas where it most persistently occurs. District supervisors admit they cannot hazard accurate estimates of livestock losses in their own areas, and few attempts are made to confirm the validity of rancher complaints. Furthermore, the director of predator research at Denver Wildlife Research has told me that the Center has abandoned all hope of supplementing its meagre supply of in-the-field studies of predator damage because of problems with funding and research methodology.

The *Review*'s conclusion that some district supervisors are not requiring ranchers to sign "private property agreements" confirms, in the larger arena of ADC operations, my own experience—particularly in

Texas. Jim Beavers, Andrew Allen, and the South Texas Helicopter Company were not the only ones to take a cavalier attitude towards these permits. For example, even after the fuss stirred up by the eagle trial, Jodie Webb in west Texas routinely ignored this requirement, according to the inadvertent testimony of some of his cooperators. He would cheerfully admit to me later that he did not much like paperwork because it "took up too much time." (Since Webb had assigned himself a virtual monopoly as ADC's aerial gunner in his own district—a non-supervisory activity—it is not too surprising that he was sometimes too busy to get to the paperwork.) However, no doubt Webb also felt, rightly, that these agreement permits are usually *pro forma* anyway, except, perhaps, when a federal investigation is underway. For here again, better kept records will not greatly affect the in-the-field operations of ADC personnel. Whether or not any forms are signed, if a trapper kills a lot of non-target animals, or takes a shot at an eagle, or picks up a few bobcats on his lines and sells their pelts illegally (a practise that I believe is widespread, as I shall argue later), that is for him and perhaps his cooperators to know, and for the enforcement division to find out if it can.

Concerning the financial operations of ADC, the *Review* restricts itself to criticizing the fact that much of the money provided by state and local rancher associations is unaccounted for. This is almost certainly due to deplorable bookkeeping rather than, as suspicious environmentalists might suppose, to chicanery, pay-offs, etc. Regrettably, the auditors do not attempt to arrive at some sort of cost/benefit estimate of ADC operations. Perhaps this is because, as they themselves point out, the operational information is "inadequate." I am not bold enough to rush in where accountants fear to tread, but there are a couple of figures that can be ascertained from the ADC's own statistics with no more expertise than a bit of grade school math. For example, in 1977, ADC spent almost 10.2 million protecting livestock. During the 1976–77 trapping season, the agency killed more than 71,000 coyotes and bobcats. That figures out to about $145 per corpse. This assumes, naturally, that ADC's estimates of its expenditures are accurate. But as we have just noted, the auditors' *Review* discovered gross underestimates in the amount of state, county, and rancher association funds expended. Since these cooperators contributed more than fifty percent to the total ADC budget in 1977, that means they may have been paying anywhere from $75 to $100 per dead predator, while the taxpayers' share came to more than $70. In 1977 the value of a lamb was about $50; which means that each of those 71,000 predators had to kill three lambs on the average just to enable ADC to break even on a cost/benefit basis. It is improbable that this could have happened, however, because most of those dead predators were killed in preventive control programs, many of them miles away from the nearest sheep ranch.[6]

The counter argument is that ADC reduces the total number of predators in sheep areas, as well as sometimes killing offending animals; therefore it is only fair to figure in the number of sheep saved as well as those that are lost. Unfortunately the number of sheep saved cannot be hypothesized because of insufficient data,[7] although Department of Agriculture statistics seem to indicate that, overall, sheep mortality in the West is about the same whether predators are on the premises or not. None of this challenges ADC's claim that it helps many individual ranchers. But in terms of the balance sheet, and putting ecological considerations aside, the evidence suggests that ADC—like a lot of other government programs—is operating in the red.

About the ADC's Final Version of its Environmental Impact Statement (EIS) there is less to say. In its final form, it is a considerable improvement over the penultimate draft, which was generally and deservedly criticized for its insufficient or inaccurate data and self-serving bias. In the final production some of the erring passages have been tidied up, more information about predators other than coyotes has been supplied, and the ADC's ambitiousness in projecting its own future has been toned-down. There is a useful bibliography, much interesting information about the "harvest" of predators, the ways they are taken, their estimated populations, costs of control, and so forth. Alas, however: The EIS is still a rank garden overgrown with weeds. For instance, the ADC claims that "approximately three-fourths of predator removals... is corrective; that is, control measures are applied only after predation loss has occured [sic]." As the glossary confirms, "corrective" means "removal of offending animals." Given that definition, ADC's claim is pure hokum.[8] Even if my own explorations had not provided more than enough evidence that ADC control is usually unselective, the agency's EIS statistics suffice to make the same point inadvertently. According to these figures, aerial shooting and denning—neither of which is selective except for species—accounted for forty percent of deaths among coyotes, the ADC's chief target. Trapping, which disposed of most of the rest, does not even pretend to be selective for "offending animals" in most situations where it is regularly used. (As we shall see later on, this non-selective approach even carries over into the current live trapping program for eagles, where one would expect the ADC, already burned, to avoid further controversy.) All things considered, the ADC's claims for a corrective approach to control sound a bit like some general's argument that bombing villages is simply a corrective measure for controlling snipers.

The EIS contains other incongruities. ADC relies on its handful of studies and various rancher surveys to promote a somewhat exaggerated picture of predation loss—an estimated minimum of 350,000 sheep, mostly lambs (4 percent of the total annual Western crop) destroyed in 1977 alone.[9] This figure is at least more modest than the Department of Agriculture's which, according to a front page story in a February 1980 issue of the *Wall Street Journal,* claims that one of every ten sheep in the United States is lost to predators. Even so, ADC's 4 percent must be weighed against Interior's estimate of an annual adult coyote population for the entire West at lambing time (after the fur harvest's winter toll) of about 800,000 animals—a fairly generous ratio of one coyote for every two square miles of useable coyote habitat. ADC only works about 11 percent of that total area, about 200,000 square miles, which includes all the major sheep ranges. Yet even if we grant an exceptionally high coyote density on ADC's territory—say, an average of one adult coyote per square mile—that would add up to a maximum of 200,000 coyotes within reach of ADC's operations. This means that every adult coyote on ADC lands, which include thousands of square miles containing no sheep and other thousands that are more-or-less coyote-free, would have to kill, on the average, almost two sheep apiece annually in order to accomplish the mayhem suggested by ADC's estimate of livestock loss. Obviously a couple of "bad" coyotes with a score of twenty or thirty dead lambs to their credit can cancel out the unoffending behavior of several "good" coyotes that conscientiously restrict themselves to a diet of rodents; but even so ... The truth is that all estimates of livestock predation loss are a guessing game, but as noted earlier in these pages, the limited evidence suggests that about half of ADC's minimum guess (2–2.5 percent) would be closer to the mark. That still adds up to a lot of dead sheep (175–200,000), but it seems a more believable figure when compared with a maximum estimate of coyotes on hand.

There are other problems with the EIS. The description of environmental impacts on predator and non-target species is superficial and in the latter case inevitably inaccurate; the discussion of research on new control methods is scant (the toxic collar gets eight or ten lines); and there is no discussion of cost/benefit ratios because the benefits have never been assessed. Most importantly, the proposed alternatives to the present program are presented in a peculiarly simplistic and yet bewildering way, with no clear distinction between "Components" (which refers to methods of control) and "Alternatives" (which deals with the various possible goals of hypothetical control programs). One thing is certain: the more one considers the alternatives as they are presented in this document (e.g., initiating a rancher compensation program, reducing the overall coyote population by forty percent) the more one concludes that almost all of them would be furiously opposed by environmental or livestock interests, and, in some cases, both. As we shall see, alternatives that could work are not mentioned. The effect of the EIS is to promote this thesis: that only minor changes in ADC policy are feasible, and business as usual is the sensible course to follow.

The opus produced by the Secretary of Interior's Advisory Committee, *Predator Damage in the West,* necessarily depends on the ADC for most of its statistics; its bibliography is inadequate; and it deals exclusively with coyote predation. Nevertheless, it is a better written, better researched, better organized document than the EIS. It contains a great deal of useful information about the sheep industry, as well as about the biology and predatory habits—what is known of them—of the coyote. It differs most strikingly from the EIS, however, in its more thorough discussion of the environmental impacts of the present ADC program and the alternative "options" that ought to be considered. The alternatives, at least the most "acceptable" of them, are summarized in the last three pages of the text. Here, hedged in by language so ambiguous that the intent is sometimes all but lost, the Committee discusses possible new "Strategies and Options" for ADC policy. A summary of the most important of these "options" follows, with accompanying remarks:

1. **Alternate Funding Levels for ADC.** Of the four possibilities considered, the Committee seems most in favor of a whopping fifty percent increase in ADC funding. It suggests that this increase would reduce losses to livestock producers and consumers while increasing "the take

of target species." The Committee anticipates that producers, in response to the increased federal effort, would reduce their own presumably more sloppy efforts at control. (Comment: This provision probably reflects some hard bargaining between livestock and environmental factions on the Committee, with the environmentalists going along on this one in order to get some of their own pet alternatives placed on the "acceptable" list. Ironically, while the Committee was formulating this option, Congress, in response to pressure from the livestock lobby, was quietly increasing ADC's budget by nearly one hundred percent.)

2. Realigning Predator Control Responsibilities. To no one's great surprise, the recommendation here is that the ADC should remain an agency in U.S. Fish and Wildlife, rather than being transferred to the Department of Agriculture or, under a contractual arrangement, to the states. (Comment: Notwithstanding Vernon Cunningham's forebodings, there never has been any doubt that ADC would continue on as Fish and Wildlife's unloved child.)

3. Policies for Predator Control on Public Lands. The Committee is noncommittal under this heading; it simply lists the options: reducing control, making it more selective of target species, using it only in loss situations, increasing the use of non-lethal techniques on publicly owned lands in the West—without much weighing the prose in favor of any of them. (Comment: The Report's final summary and its earlier discussion of predator control on public lands are particularly unimaginative, chiefly because they do not even raise the issue of whether ADC policies should be different on lands controlled by the federal government and dedicated to the principle of multiple use than they are, say, on the Edwards Plateau. Moreover, the Committee does not mention, in its final pages, the most intriguing of the alternatives discussed earlier under this heading, the idea of restricting predator control on public lands exclusively to sheepgrazing areas. About which, more presently.)

4. The Use of Poisons. The Committee seems to advocate an increase in the use of M-44 ejectors, but otherwise anticipates no change in the current ban on poisons. (Comment: Although testing of the toxic collar was well advanced during the period of the Committe's deliberations, the Report fails to discuss the possibilities of this important and selective control device, either because adequate information was not forthcoming from the ADC or because the controversial and now banned 1080 is the only poison that seems to work in the collar.)

5. Modifying ADC's Funding Mechanism. Here, the Report more promisingly offers up a choose-one-out-of-three list of improvements on ADC's present funding set-up: (a) It apparently approves the idea of requiring individual ranchers to pay a service fee to ADC for specific aid, ensuring that the program's beneficiaries are the ones who pay the bill. (b) It strongly endorses the consolidation of state, county, and rancher association contributions into a single kitty, to be distributed by ADC at the state level according to real need, thereby reducing the influence of local rancher interests in the allocation of control efforts. (c) As a less likely alternative to the preceding two, it suggests that the feds might foot the entire ADC bill, thereby rendering the agency immune, if it wants to be, from state and local pressures. (Comment: It is worth remembering that even if one of these schemes was implemented, ADC budgets would be greatly influenced, as they are now, by Western congressmen who are politically committed to the interests of the livestock lobby. Even so, anything that would limit the power of rancher associations to dictate ADC policy at the local level would be a worthwhile innovation.)

6. Expanding the Extension Program. The intent of this option would be to expand the current federal Extension Service Program, which provides guidance on better agricultural and range practices, soil conservation, etc., so that it can supply ranchers with do-it-yourself advice on how to control predators. (Comment: In theory, this option sounds promising. Since ranchers are in any case entitled to kill predators—except for endangered species like the eagle—on their own land, it might not be a bad idea to educate them in the most ecologically sane methods of control. However, it is unlikely that the Extension people presently available would be qualified to do the teaching without going through an expensive training program themselves. The alternative would be to hire trappers to instruct the ranchers, which would be even more costly.)

7. Compensation for Predator Losses. The Report's phrasing suggests clearly that it would be impractical to compensate ranchers through some sort of federal insurance program for losses due to predators. (Comment: Many environmentalists find the compensation idea very fetching, but it is manifestly unworkable. It would require droves of investigators to determine where and if an actual loss to predators had occurred; moreover, the results would satisfy no one since even under research conditions

Incident at Eagle Ranch

many livestock deaths on the open range are classified in the "undetermined" category.)

8. Increase Predation Research. Unsurprisingly, the Report suggests the need for more research on both lethal and non-lethal control techniques, though it notes that the potential for the latter is not very promising. Curiously, the Committee does not mention other research options, such as further studies of the extent of predation or the value of corrective as opposed to preventive controls, even though the Report itself repeatedly refers to the lack of information on such subjects. (Comment: Sad to say, when it comes to discovering new control methods that are more humane and/or selective, the track record of government researchers is minus two on a scale of ten. As earlier noted, after a couple of decades and millions of dollars worth of trying, Denver Wildlife Research is not even close to a major breakthrough. The one relatively new device that is now widely used, the M-44 ejector, was designed by a trapper on his own time; and as we have seen, the only potentially effective contraption that is in the offing—also a backyard invention—is Roy McBride's toxic collar, which exists in a bureaucratic limbo. As for non-lethal methods of control, Don Balsar at Denver Research still speaks encouragingly of "combinations" of techniques that may prove effective. But the odds are against him. The Center has long since given up the idea of controlling coyote birth rates, a remedy much favored by well-meaning but uninformed environmentalists. [Most people can't be induced to spay their pets; how then does one sterilize thousands of coyotes ranging over millions of acres of rangeland? And even if one could do the job, would one want to? The effect would be the extirpation of the coyote in more areas of the West than is now possible with the help of all lethal methods combined.] Viewed objectively, most other non-lethal controls are almost as unpromising. Electrically wired fencing will work on small pastures; it is even possible that some sort of portable electric fence can be devised for penning range sheep at night. But in most range operations, where predation is especially likely to occur, such fences would be prohibitively expensive. Moreover, they would pose more environmental problems that they would solve. If they can stop a coyote they will also stop any other wild animal larger than a cottontail. Antelope, in particular, are already bedevilled enough by ordinary mesh fencing without being exposed to electric shock treatments as well. As for scare devices, research in this area will almost certainly come to a dead end. Blatting horns, flares, flashing lights—all of them seem to have the potential of disturbing the human inhabitants in test areas more than they disturb the coyotes. In the case of one such sound and light show which was being tested while I was in Denver, it took the coyotes only a couple of nights to wise-up to what was going on. [Using scare techniques on wintering concentrations of eagles has not worked out either.] The most heralded of all non-lethal control techniques involves the use of aversive chemicals, notably lithium chloride, to discourage coyotes from killing livestock. The intent is to make the coyote sick when it bites into a sheep, thereby discouraging a further interest in lamb and mutton. Thus far, the results of several in-the-field experiments with this approach have received mixed or wholly negative reviews. The usually sanguine Balsar acknowledges that coyotes will go to considerable lengths to avoid the aversive agent without also avoiding the sheep—even flipping the animals onto their backs if necessary.

9. **Better Husbandry.** In a final comment the committee seems to support, in a vague sort of way, the idea that sound management might be required of sheep raisers, or at least suggested to them, in exchange for ADC services. Under the same heading, the Committee mentions that "various steps could be taken to improve the quantity and quality of sheepherders." (Comment: The Report cautions that "the effectiveness of husbandry practices for reducing losses is uncertain." This may be true in the case of coyotes, which are the Report's exclusive concern, but as we have seen, there is no question that better husbandry, particularly the adjustment of lambing dates and the relocating of lambing pastures, would oftentimes reduce the threat of predation by eagles.)

The more one thinks about the Committee's Report, the more evident it becomes that *Predator Damage in the West* is not in the same league as the Leopold or Cain Reports. Three of its "acceptable" options merely support the *status quo* (2, 4, and 7). Another option (1) is a sop to the livestock industry. Four others have consequences that, as posited by the Committee, are vague, (3, 6, 8, and 9). Only the alternatives concerning the reorganization of ADC funding (5) which the 1972 Cain Report had previously urged without success, come across as bold, if not new, initiatives.

After considerable delay, Secretary Andrus' "Revised Federal Policy on Predator Control" was at last released to the public on November 9, 1979. Some wildlife enthusiasts greeted it with acclaim, and livestock interests with predictable expressions of outrage. But the document,

which has no more weight than an official memorandum, shows little
substantive change in policy.

Consider: The provisions include (1) an assurance that ADC will continue as a division of U.S. Fish and Wildlife; and (2) its research budget for both lethal and non-lethal controls will be increased significantly. (3) Ranchers will receive federal extension service aid in learning to do their own control. (4) All the control methods that are currently in use will continue to be used except the practise of denning, which ADC personnel must now forego. (5) Also banned will be "further research or development of potential uses of Compound 1080." (6) Two inter-denominational committees will be set up, one to oversee research efforts, one to implement the new policy on public lands. And finally and most interestingly (7), preventive control—that is, the random killing of target species within a given area—"would be limited to specific situations where unacceptably high losses have been documented during the preceding 12 months."

What does all this add up to? Very little. The first three items, all of them extracted from *Predator Damage in the West*, are chiefly notable for being non-controversial. There was never any serious question that ADC would be separated from Fish and Wildlife; the extension program for ranchers will, as already noted, probably cost more money than it is worth, with no significant reduction in the number of predators killed or the number of ADC trappers in the field; and the additional research money, while all to the good, will not produce any important short-term results. As for the fourth provision, what it means in practise is that trapping and snaring will continue unabated; the use of M-44 ejectors will certainly increase; aerial gunning, which was also scheduled for a big increase, will probably be slightly reduced.

The prohibition against denning is a humane and welcome rule to have on the books. It has understandably evoked cries of jubilation from Defenders of Wildlife and other organizations which have fought long and hard to make ADC stop killing helpless coyote pups. However, its chief effect will be to spare the sensibilities of animal lovers, not the lives of coyotes. When an ADC trapper discovers a coyote den in the future, he can either advise the rancher to brain or gas the occupants himself—or, more simply, let them starve to death if and when the adults are trapped.

Andrus' fifth provision, putting 1080 off-limits, is weirdly superfluous. The compound, bane to environmentalists, boon to ranchers, is already banned in all ADC range operations. The one perceivable consequence of this "revision" is to prevent the future use of McBride's toxic collar—perhaps the only truly selective control method ever devised —unless some new odorless, tasteless poison can be found that will work as well as 1080.[10] According to reports of the latest experiments at Denver Research, that is not likely to happen soon.

As for the two committees—provision six—one of them, a Research Advisory Group composed of the usual mix of environmental, livestock, and government interests, will be nominated by the advised —Denver's much harried Predator Research Department. It is hard to imagine policy shifts coming from such a structure. The effectiveness of the other committee, consisting of representatives of the various public lands agencies, will depend on how strictly it interprets Andrus' seventh provision.

At first and second glance, the seventh provision seems more substantive than any of the others. Its intent to reduce preventive control in favor of more selective programs is clear. Preventive—wholesale— killing of target species would occur only "when other techniques have been found to be ineffective or impractical." There is even a specific condition imposed: twelve months of high losses must occur in an area before preventive killing can begin. Promising as all this sounds, however, a third look at the provision begins to make one wonder. When I spoke with Inez Connor, the Secretary's spokeswoman, she acknowledged that the actual implementation of the regulation had not been worked out. And when I asked for a more detailed explication of what the Secretary had in mind, Connor twice promised to oblige and twice failed to follow through. This was no doubt due to bureaucratic oversight. But there are also oversights built into the memorandum itself. To begin with, the general thrust of Andrus' ruling is not new. For example, it is already clearly stated in the ADC's official statement of "Policy and Philosophy" that control programs "will emphasize removal of the offending individual animal wherever and whenever possible." We have seen in the course of the previously described journeys through the West just how, in its Environmental Impact Statement, the ADC simply misrepresents the matter, claiming that seventy five percent of its control work is corrective, only twenty-five percent preventive; the reverse would be closer to the truth.

To what extent, then, may we hope that the Secretary's new mandate will be applied? It will be up to the ADC, of course, to determine

Incident at Eagle Ranch

when selective techniques "have been found to be ineffective or impractical." And it will be up to ADC to decide where "unacceptably high
losses have been documented during the preceding 12 months." As long
as the ADC remains wedded to the livestock industry, its response to
the new ruling is predictable. Can anyone doubt that on the great sheep
ranges of the West, one district supervisor after another will "document"
the fact that during the preceding year livestock losses have been "unacceptably high" in precisely those areas where preventive control is
already in effect? And what, by the way, is an "unacceptably high" loss?
How will the "documentation" be determined when, as we have seen,
no adequate means of documentation exists? The inescapable inference
is that the trappers, their district supervisors, and the ranchers will come
up with the answers themselves. There is always the hope that on the
public lands, at least, the Secretary's newly appointed inter-agency committee may take a stricter view of the ruling than is likely to be the case
elsewhere, even though none of these agencies—they include ADC—
have shown much inclination to buck the livestock interests and their
political proponents in the past. If that hope goes a-glimmering, then
this wonderful-sounding regulation, like most of the "new" ADC policy,
will not amount to much.

Having churlishly found fault with ADC's practices and Interior's
revised policies, it is only fair, as they say, to take a turn in the barrel myself. If an entrepreneur trapper like McBride can develop his own selective control device for a few dollars while the experts spin their wheels,
then perhaps an interested observer of the ADC can develop his own
revised policy statement about how that agency should do its job. Most
of the following proposals do not, of course, originate with me. All of
them have in common the fact that they are workable. All are motivated
by the statement of intent which ADC's Vernon Cunningham neatly
expressed: to "protect livestock at minimum wildlife cost." Although the
bias is environmental, none of these proposals would seriously hurt the
livestock industry, and most would help ranchers who have real predator problems.

The proposal headings, with discussion to follow, are these:
1. ADC funding; 2. ADC field personnel; 3. Predator control techniques; 4. ADC policy in cattle country; 5. Research Policy.

1. Reorganizing ADC's System of Funding. No issue is more
fraught with environmental consequence than ADC's subjection, at

the local level, to the ranchers themselves. Local rancher associations, county commissioners, and individual sheepmen contribute fifty percent or more of the ADC's budget in many districts, with consequences that have already been indicated in the interviews with ADC personnel. As with so many give-away programs, it is the big operator who gets the largest handout. The only way to break, or at least loosen, this hammer lock on district supervisors and trappers is to revise the funding structure.

Of several possible alternatives, the only one with a chance of being implemented would be the consolidation of state, county, and local cooperator funding into a single state fund, administered by ADC at the state or regional level according to real need. Still, this plan would face an uphill battle. As Interior's Advisory Committee observes, a single state fund "would not be agreeable to many producers who would anticipate the possibility of losing control of the allocation of control efforts, with some receiving more assistance and some less." Moreover, some producers may "eventually reduce their contributions as individuals and through local associations if they feel the program with a single fund is less responsive to their needs." Truer words were never uttered. When the Texas Sheep and Goat Raisers Association tried, in the early seventies, to convince its constituents that they should accept a levy on their flocks of a few cents per head to increase general funding for predator control, the ranchers soundly defeated the proposal. Apparently predator control became a less urgent priority when they were faced with the prospect of paying for more of it themselves. In any case, ranchers are an independent and anarchic lot, even less inclined to be satisfied with government programs than most people. They complain about the present ADC program and they would undoubtedly complain about the new set-up too. Nevertheless, it should work to the advantage of most of them. Control efforts would be concentrated in the areas where the need for them was greatest rather than, as now, in counties where "historic funding patterns" are in force because a few well-off ranchers and their associations contribute much of the money. In the real trouble spots, sheepmen with predator problems would presumably contribute more in exchange for better control, thus compensating for some operators who would drop the program because it was "less responsive to their needs." Fewer trappers would spend all their time working the lands of a single influential rancher like ex-governor Dolph Briscoe, who could easily afford his own control work.

Incident at Eagle Ranch

From an environmental point of view, the new arrangement would go far towards releasing ADC trappers and their supervisors from the beck and call of a handful of local sheepmen. There would be less reason to perpetuate preventive control in areas where livestock loss is minimal; or to maintain trappers in the same territories for years and decades "as long as they keep the cooperators happy;" or to extend trap lines further and further out into buffer zones, miles from the nearest sheep, simply to assuage a rancher's fears of a coyote invasion. In short, having "one fund per state" as the Advisory Committee's report comments, "would allow the flexibility needed to direct control efforts only towards offending coyotes. This would reduce the chance of non-target species being taken. There would be an associated increase in both safety and humaneness."

Congressional legislation would be required to change the present system of ADC funding, and there is no doubt that livestock interests would put up a fight. But there is some reason to believe that environmentalists could win this one if they made a concerted lobbying effort, particularly if they agreed to support other policy changes, notably 3 and 4 below, which woolgrowers would more readily accept.

2. Reorganizing ADC's Field Personnel. The success of this proposal depends on the acceptance of the preceding one. Common sense indicates that, in contrast to the present set-up, ADC trappers ought to be deployed as a strike force—"trouble shooters"—plying their trade where they are most needed, rather than as garrisoned squadrons doing patrol duty. They should be concentrated in those areas where predator problems are chronic; not, as now, where rancher associations have the most money to spend. In practice, it is true, this rearrangement would not be as radical as it might seem on paper. In areas where high densities of sheep are recurrently attacked by predators, ADC personnel might find themselves working the same territory, if not the same ranches, for years at a stretch. But at least they would do so only as long as predation continued to be a real problem. When and if rancher reports of losses ceased, they would move on to other trouble spots. Certainly, more ADC people would be truly mobile than is the case now. The increased maneuverability of the trapper force would affect control policy in the field more than any pronouncement by officials in Washington. Greater emphasis on corrective control would evolve because "keeping the cooperators happy" (the ranchers would no longer be cooperators at the local level) would now depend on how effectively ADC trappers reacted to situations of actual loss rather than how well they guarded ranch frontiers that coyotes only occasionally, if ever, cross.

A shift to a genuinely corrective control policy would enable the higher-ups in ADC to better allocate the agency's resources on a basis of need instead of depending on the "historical funding patterns" of which Interior's auditors complained. (It is interesting to note in this connection that ADC Supervisor Jodie Webb recently hired two or three additional trappers to supplement those already employed in his west Texas district—thanks to the recent Congressional appropriation which ADC must spend whether it wants to or not. Webb says he needs these men because he is swamped by rancher complaints of predator damage. Yet this is the same supervisor who advised one of his trappers to move his lines "anywhere from six to seven miles" from the nearest sheep ranch just to keep the man busy. If ADC were restructured on a less "historical" and territorial basis, Webb himself might have to consider changing his address. The area around Marfa where he is presently entrenched has few remaining sheep.)

Finally, the shift to a corrective policy might allow for a somewhat smaller cadre of trappers, better paid and better trained.

The wholesale use of the "trouble-shooter" concept, coupled with the reorganization of ADC's funding, would not suddenly usher in a golden age of enlightened federal predator control. Although trappers tend to be loners, and not necessarily admirers of the ranchers they serve, they and their supervisors would continue to be aware that their jobs and sheep ranching go together. The balance of political and economic power may be gradually shifting in county seats like Leakey and Marfa and Roswell, but meantime the big operators, often fellows who are too old or affluent or otherwise occupied to run their spreads themselves, will continue to get more than their share of federal control whether their need is urgent or not. And much of that control, by any other name, will still be "preventive." But even these influential ranchers will have to depend more on their own efforts, or at least their own money, if they want to keep predators out of buffer zones "six or seven miles" from their fences. Whereas the ADC—at least to a greater extent than is now possible—will be able to respond to specific cases of need on a genuinely corrective basis.

Incident at Eagle Ranch

3. Predator Control Techniques. Even in sport hunting, the killing of wild animals is only sometimes a "clean" and relatively painless operation. In control work, it never is. Aerial gunning is intrinsically "unsporting" and the shots are hard to place. Snares, poisons, traps all involve protracted struggle and suffering. This grim truth has inspired great numbers of gentle-hearted folk, in and out of the environmental movement, to denounce various control devices on humane grounds. And, no matter how reluctant the controllers and managers may be to admit it, this position does make sense. Anyone would be furious if the SPCA started killing unwanted dogs and cats by methods that prolonged their suffering for hours and even days. So why should that attitude change when the animals involved are coyotes and bobcats, the biological co-equals of their domestic cousins?

Regrettably, however, those who argue against predator control on ethical grounds tend to ignore an indisputable fact: if sheepmen are entitled to protect their stock against the attacks of predators, some sort of pragmatic lethal control is necessary. As we have seen, the large scale use of a non-lethal methodology is not in the cards for some time to come. Meanwhile, it is in the best interests of everyone, especially the predators and the non-target species that are often the incidental victims of control techniques, if the ADC and the ranchers apply the most selective control method available. Which, as my reader will anticipate by now, is a roundabout way of endorsing, after much thought, the use of McBride's toxic collar—even though the device contains a miniscule dose of 1080. (That endorsement, by the way, is strictly my own; neither here nor anywhere else in this book do I speak for any group.) 1080 is deadly, all right, and environmentalists have been right to oppose the reckless way it was used in the past. But no substitute has been found that works as well; and its use in the collar would not have harmful ecological consequences. No poisoned baits would litter the rangeland, and even if the ranchers or the ADC wished to misuse the collar, the very nature of the device would prevent them from doing so. If, for example, a rancher wanted to transfer 1080 from the collars to baited carcasses, he would soon discover that dozens of collars were needed to lace the body of a single dead horse. (The poison cannot be effectively used in smaller "dropbaits.") And if some sheep lose their collars, the collar without the sheep would be no more likely to attract wild creatures than any other bit of plastic lying in a pasture. Secretary Andrus' ban on 1080 should be modified to allow for the experimental application of the device in large, representative areas of sheep country throughout the West. Notwithstanding Roy McBride's arguments, the federal government should retain control of the collar's distribution and keep careful records of which ranchers have how many; but the ranchers, once instructed, should put it to use themselves. The most immediate application of the collar is in fenced range pastures where coyotes are attacking sheep on a fairly regular basis. But there is now some evidence from Mexico that the collar can also be used effectively and safely on open range simply by sending an "advance guard" of collared lambs into a new grazing area before the majority of the sheep are moved in. According to McBride, Mexican ranchers who are using this strategy have given up the wholesale killing of predators, and are experiencing almost no loss of stock even though only a few coyotes—all of them "offending" animals—are slain. I am convinced that the use of the collar would do more to eliminate ADC's widespread dependence on less selective and often more cruel devices than all other proposed control methods put together. It would also, I suspect, go a long way towards reducing the number of ADC trappers in the field (a development that ADC might not welcome). As for the concern that any use of 1080, no matter how selective, might legitimize its more general application, I hardly think that will happen as long as environmentalists are ready to make a fuss, as they would, for example, if sodium cyanide, now used in the M-44, were more generally employed in control programs. Government officials have been too badly burned by the 1080 issue in the past to want to start that fight all over again. Finally, Interior could make effective diplomatic use of the collar in its dealings with the livestock lobby. The sheepmen are now eager to have the device; and its approval for general use could be made contingent on their acceptance of reforms in ADC's funding.

4. **ADC Policy in Cattle Country.** There is one dramatic change in ADC policy that would require no battle in Congress, that would certainly make environmentalists happy without unduly alarming sheepmen; that would eliminate considerable expense for the taxpayer; and that would reduce the numbers of predators killed by ADC without any significant effect on livestock losses. All this, if ADC would eliminate preventive control of predators in cattle country. Given the intent of ADC's current "philosophy," that ban should already be in effect. Very few cattlemen have a serious predator problem. For those that

Incident at Eagle Ranch

do, corrective control is almost always the answer. Yet in vast areas of the West where not a sheep can be found, ADC's aerial gunning and trapping campaigns are routine operations. As already noted apropos of the interview with Vernon Cunningham, ADC statistics confirm a disproportionate amount of control work that is dedicated to "protecting" cattle. Oklahoma leads the list, with nearly sixty percent of its budget set aside for this purpose. California is next, with forty one percent of its ADC funds—about eight hundred thousand dollars (in 1977)—devoted to the protection of cows. Arizona, New Mexico, Texas, Oregon, Montana, and North Dakota each contribute thirty percent or more. Clearly there is a large discrepancy between the amount of ADC service provided and the real need for it. It is surprising that sheepmen, if not conservationists, have failed to complain about the inequity in this distribution of funds.

In fact, no one has complained. The one place this issue is even referred to is a small sub-section of *Predator Damage in the West* where it is discussed only in terms of public lands policy. Amazingly, the report concludes that there would be no change in environmental impacts if this policy were implemented and it states that "environmental groups would be indifferent to this option." The Committee was apparently operating on the totally unwarranted assumption that if ADC's control effort were redirected from cattle to sheep country, the number of predators killed would increase in the latter areas in exact proportion to the decline in the former. At best, that is questionable arithmetic. Even more to the point, there is no reason why the discontinuance of preventive control in cattle country should necessarily involve an equivalent funding increase for preventive control in the sheep pastures. If the other proposals mentioned above could be put into effect, little or no transference would be necessary. It should be remembered that only about three percent of the West is now intensively used by the sheep industry, whereas ADC operations are conducted on eleven percent. Much of the land comprising the eight percent difference is cattle country. Yet throughout most of the West cattle and coyotes coexist without benefit of the ADC's ministrations. There is no good reason why some cattleraising areas should be exceptions to that rule. And if ADC did pull back into sheep country, the environmental consequences would soon be evident. On thousands of square miles where predators are now controlled for no real reason (e.g., southwestern New Mexico) they would be left alone, at least by the ADC. And unlike sheep raisers, few cattlemen would dig very deep into their pockets if they had to pay for trappers and aerial gunners entirely with their own money. If Interior were willing to withstand a howl of protest from some elements in the Cattlemen's Association, it could implement this change itself. Clearly, it is an option to which environmentalists should no longer remain "indifferent."

5. **Research Policy.** Enough has already been said about federal research into new lethal and non-lethal controls. The reader will have gathered that except for the toxic collar, no important breakthroughs are imminent. My own feeling is that too much money is going into control methodology, and not nearly enough into other areas of needed research. There are still no answers to the most important questions of all: Just how much damage are predators really doing to the Western livestock industry? And how much of that damage does the ADC prevent? In an earlier section of this book I summarized most of the very limited information—surveys, a handful of in-the-field studies—that might be of some use in trying for the answers, but clearly these are not enough. ADC's "minimum" guess that three hundred and fifty thousand sheep are lost annually is unconvincing. Denver Wildlife Research Center has simply given up on the subject: not enough funds, inadequate "controls," general discouragement, etc. Yet there are means available for arriving at a damage estimate that would be a lot more accurate than any we have now. One approach would be to steal a leaf from Neilsen: select about three hundred wool growers from ten or twelve representative sheep raising districts in the West where predation is said to range from heavy to light to none at all, and require them, in exchange for a small honorarium, to report any predator kills the moment they are found. U.S. Fish and Wildlife personnel or trained biologists at wildlife management schools in the districts could be appointed to spotcheck claims of losses as soon as they came in. Since it would not be necessary to pay the cooperating sheepmen damages for any livestock mortality that occurred, as in the case of "controlled" experiments, the whole operation, over a period of a few years, would probably cost less than most of the studies that have already been tried, and the findings would be far more comprehensive. It should be noted that Denver Wildlife Research Center was considering a more modest system of telephone monitoring, but gave it up because of "lack of funds."[11]

There are other important questions that need answering too: What percentage of an adult coyote population in a given sheep raising

Incident at Eagle Ranch

area is actually engaged in killing sheep? Exactly how much time and effort and money must sheepmen spend, on ranches of various sizes and in areas where predation is reportedly heavy, medium, light, in order to do their own control work? And how does that effort compare with the manpower and money spent by ADC? In short, to what extent is the ADC doing control work which, according to McBride and others, is merely supplemental to what the ranchers do or could do themselves? Would the latter's efforts significantly increase if ADC help was withdrawn? And while we are at it, why not a really comprehensive study comparing lamb crops in areas where predators are and are not a reported problem? The U.S. Department of Agriculture's statistics on sheep production are readily available, and ADC ought to know where the coyotes and eagles are being pesky; working up a comparison would not be difficult or expensive. Another way of asking that question is: what percentage of a rancher's lamb mortality would have been caused by something else if the predators had not been an intervening factor? . . . One gets the idea. There are a great many unanswered questions about predators. And some of them are just as important as how to build a better coyote trap.

If the above proposals were put into effect, they would unquestionably shift ADC's emphasis from preventive control to corrective control, with a consequent decrease in predator deaths. The ADC operation would perhaps be somewhat smaller and less costly than is presently the case, but it would be more flexible and efficient. Nor would the livestock industry be hurt by these changes; in the case of those sheepmen who experience serious predation problems, these revisions would work to their benefit. Of course, government agencies being what they are, and bureaucratic inertia being what it is, no one need expect entrenched habits, attitudes, or functionaries to disappear overnight even if all of these proposals were adopted. But they would make a big difference. They constitute a program of action which, thus far, most environmentalists have scarcely considered; and in the case of the last three points, there would probably not even be any serious opposition from the sheepmen.

One final comment about Animal Damage Control: that agency is the first to point out that in recent years, at least, its activities have accounted for a relatively small percentage of the predators killed in the West. In 1977, for example, ADC destroyed some 71,400 coyotes and

1,226 bobcats. Whereas the fur industry, during the 1976–77 season, accounted for 222,400 coyotes and more than 50,500 bobcats—those are the official figures; an accurate count would be considerably higher —not to mention some sixteen million other wild animals ranging from foxes and otters to muskrat and skunks—all in the name of high fashion and fun furs. Then, of course, there are the uncounted thousands of predators that are killed by the ranchers themselves, and a weekend host of gun-toting Westerners who shoot varmints for the hell of it.

Nevertheless, government must set a standard for the people it serves; and for that reason among others, it is vital that the ADC, so rigorously intent on controlling predators, should itself be rigorously controlled.

Part Four

The
Larger Issues

11. Managers

ANYONE CONCERNED with the future of the West's major predators soon learns that ADC is only one part of the picture. The search for answers eventually leads into the even more labyrinthian domain of wildlife management and research. Although it might be possible for the controllers—the ADC and its adherents—to drive the eagle, the lion, the bobcat, even perhaps the coyote to the wall if they had the unlimited authority and the means to do it, it is not in their power, even on their best behavior, to save them. In order to do that, the Western predators must be managed. But that can not be done unless we know more both about them and ourselves. We still hem and haw, trying to answer the most fundamental questions: not just what these animals are supposed to mean to us, but how many of them do we want around?

In the field of predator management and research, as in the case of wildlife generally, there is no alternative to bureaucratic dominance, whether state or federal—a hulking fact, immovable as a wall, against which environmentalists and their opponents, and sometimes the bureaucrats themselves, take turns bloodying their heads. To contemplate the functioning of government officialdom for any length of time is to end by sounding like the suicidal Hamlet staring at his bare bodkin. The law's delay and the insolence of office are the least of it. There are also the immutable norms of agency empire-building; of success measured in terms of seniority and conformity; of procedural inertia; of policies

Incident at Eagle Ranch

shaped solely by the forces of political expediency and the pressures of special interests; of cost/benefit computations that would appall a sophomore business major; of duplication, inefficiency, and red tape on an epidemic scale; of short-term planning, short-term funding, short-term thinking. Above all, perhaps, there is hugeness, impure and unsimple, casting its leviathan shadow upon every good idea that tries to grow.

We bear this bureaucratic state of affairs better in some agencies than in others. Though we still complain, most of us in our secret hearts have been defeated by the Postal Service, the various tentacular arms of HEW, the Securities and Exchange Commission, and our state departments of education. But we are less browbeaten in the case of the conservation and environmental agencies. Our concern, as a people, for the nation's natural resources is such a comparatively recent phenomenon, a mere generation or so in the building, that we can not reconcile ourselves to the ossificaitons of governmental policy that, even here, are increasingly the rule. Hence, the attitude, half disenchanted, half still hopeful, with which we regard the U.S. Fish and Wildlife Service and its counterparts in state government—an attitude shared, as I rediscovered in my recent travels, by many functionaries in the agencies themselves.

The bureaucratic rigidity in the wildlife services needs a closer look, because the future of predator populations, not to mention other wildlife species, depends on whether the condition worsens or improves. To begin with, it is important to realize that during most of the years of their governmental existence, the state and federal wildlife departments have enjoyed a white hat reputation rare among public agencies. Even those political and economic interests that have kept them half-starved for funds have viewed them as an unessential good rather than, like the IRS or Welfare, a necessary evil. In my greener years, the many wildlife management people I knew were a dedicated, optimistic lot, burning the midnight oil, forever talking shop even in their leisure hours. Those were the years when the Leopoldian ethic was beginning to make itself widely felt, when the significance of wildlife habitat was becoming excitingly understood, when the prospect of an endlessly renewable supply of harvestable game species was becoming a reality. During the forties and fifties, important initiatives were taken, important laws were passed, and, best of all, important results were perceivable on every hand. Populations of deer, antelope, elk were dramatically increasing; waterfowl, in some places at least, were again darkening the skies; wild turkey were reappearing in woodlands from which they had been absent for a century. The wildlife management (and research) class received the credit, often deservedly, for these happy changes. For the biologist, the crusading bureau chief, even the enforcement agent, it was, as one of the poets who started it all declaimed in a different context, in that dawn bliss to be alive. However, it was also during this period that federal and state wildlife officials[1] became indissolubly committed to the interests of the nation's army of hunters and fishermen (as well as the West's ranchers)—through management, research, restocking, and control programs. From these groups the professionals drew their ideological and financial support.

Since those heady days the wildlife managers and researchers have come upon less smiling times. There are still plenty of idealistic people on hand, but many of them find it increasingly difficult to escape not only a pervasive hardening of administrative arteries but an existential pessimism about the meaning and worth of their own efforts. In contrast to the period of their great advances, many of the professionals now seem uncertain of the objectives and priorities they ought to have.

Perhaps a single representative occurrence will illustrate this rather uneasy state-of-the-art. During the late sixties and early seventies, the mule deer—the most popular, most abundant, most hunted, above all, the most studied and managed big game animal in the West—experienced a steep decline in population after decades of explosive growth. Hunters and ranchers—and some bureaucrats—blamed (and continue to blame) coyotes and mountain lions for this decline. In April 1976, the elite among state and federal authorities on the mule deer gathered at Logan, Utah, to read papers, compare notes, and discover, if they could, what was going on.[2] The papers that were read at the conference disclosed a variety of information about the animal's eating habits, the possible changes in its habitat, the influence of predation, the reliability of censusing techniques, and so forth. They make interesting reading; and some of them are very informative. In particular, the concluding statement by a biologist at the University of Montana, W. Leslie Pengelly, is a masterpiece. Indeed, if I were the President of the U.S., and he were a somewhat less fatalistic man, I might appoint him my Secretary of Interior on the evidence of this paper alone. It is a wise, witty, and intermittently sardonic commentary on the preceding reports, and should be required reading for all wildlife management students. Pengelly's point

Incident at Eagle Ranch

was that the conference had not even begun to answer the crucial question: Why is the mule deer in trouble? After years of protecting them, overseeing their harvest, counting their teeth, checking their eating habits, their parasites and diseases, their love life and reproductive cycles—in short, after conducting literally thousands of studies, the experts could not say what was happening to them, why it was happening, or even if anything really *was* happening, much less what should now be done. All those knowledgeable people. All that information. And yet nothing was coming together. Why not?

The problem of leadership is one part of the answer to that question. It is not exactly a secret that the higher echelons of federal and especially state wildlife services are in some instances manned by people who long ago closed their doors to the promise of new ideas, new alliances, new priorities. One can hardly blame them. Life used to be much simpler. In the golden age, the only thing a manager really needed to worry about was the availability of wildlife habitat, and until lately there was still quite a lot of it around. All he had to do was restock, enforce game laws, manage resident or migratory species depending on whether he was a state or federal official, and set the kinds of seasons on commercially exploitable wildlife that were generous enough to ensure "optimum sustainable yields." As long as the huntable species were increasing, even overpopulating their range, he was happy; the hunters were happy; everyone was happy. Now, however, all that is changed.

The managers' difficulty in adapting to new circumstances was best exemplified at the mule deer conference by what was not included on the agenda: Among sixteen papers presented, not one dealt with the question of whether the mule deer herd had been overhunted. This, in spite of the fact that (as Pengelly pointed out) an estimated six to eight million deer had been legally harvested in the previous ten years, not to mention an almost equal number that had probably been killed by poachers or fatally crippled by incompetent hunters.

Considering those awesome statistics, it might be considered "odd" —Pengelly's word—that no speaker addressed the subject. But it wasn't really. Many of the assembled experts had been committed throughout their professional lives to the credo that as long as the habitat remained intact, human predation would not significantly affect wildlife populations. Even more to the point, during the last many years these experts had been determining, rather liberally, how much human predation was

Managers

allowable. All things considered, it would probably have been "odd" if someone had spoken on this subject—in spite of the fact that hunting pressure had radically escalated during the last decade even in the remotest corners of the West; and in spite of the fact that overhunting is the one common denominator that conforms in regional scope with the decrease of the mule deer herd.

The point here is not whether overhunting might be a major factor contributing to that decline. That question still goes begging.[3] The point is that the people who set the agenda for the conference apparently could not adjust to the possibility that the question should be discussed.

Another symptom of the managerial malaise is the breakdown of cooperation, or even communication, between government wildlife agencies. At the meeting in Logan several speakers alluded to such failures in terms of their special fields of interest. For example: the methods of tabulating harvests and censusing deer herds, such as they are, vary from state to state and year to year. Because of the "dampening effect of state boundaries," each fish and game department pursues its own projects on limited funds even though the same research may be duplicated in an adjoining state. Moreover, there is "no truly effective forum for critical reviews of new ideas or techniques in wildlife ecology."[4] In the larger arena of wildlife services, the same evidence of non-cooperation is evident on every hand: Federal and state commissions quarrel about migratory and threatened species; different federal departments will not work together on projects that have a shared subject; state departments of recreation, fish and wildlife, and natural resources squabble amongst themselves and with the federal government about land acquisition; etcetera, ad nauseum. Often the welfare of a wildlife species runs a poor second to the bureaucratic—and human—imperative to stake out one's own turf. At one point, Pengelly, with perhaps too much of the burnt-out in his own voice, observed that cooperation would be nice, but because of "human inertia . . . we probably just won't get around to it."

The papers presented at the mule deer conference illustrate yet another problem: the chaotic state of wildlife research. At both the state and federal level, projects are chronically underfunded (although as a matter of fact the overall amount of money that has gone into wildlife research is quite large—many, many millions of dollars in the case of the mule deer). Equally troublesome, research projects tend to be short-lived. After a year or two, just when the biologists are beginning to learn

something, there is a cut in state or federal allocations and the money
runs out. And if they do learn something, chances are it will be out of
date in a few years because the study should be on-going but is not.
Also on hand is that unappeasable dragon, expediency. Is there a public
hue and cry about eagles? Then the eagles will get a study. Does a congressman want to please the sunflower seed growers in his state? Then
there is a four-hundred thousand dollar study of seed-eating blackbirds.
Granting all these problems, however, what hits the observer most is a
crushing awareness of the randomness, the duplication, the lack of any
coordinated aims, that sabotage the selection of research subjects in the
first place. The main reason for this haphazard approach at the state,
federal and university levels is that there are no research priorities and
there are no long range plans. Federal "master plans" do exist but there is
little discussion, much less agreement, about what the priorities should
be. In the U.S. Fish and Wildlife Service the various regional divisions
have in recent years become more autonomous than ever in contracting
research. At the state level, it is almost unheard of for staff biologists to
coordinate their studies with those going on in neighboring states. And
unless a grant is involved, utility plays no perceivable part in the selection of research projects at the universities. Significantly, at the Logan
conference there was no follow-up to the one call for cooperative research (on habitat); and the only clearly stated aim of either research or
management was to meet the "demand for huntable deer." Compared
to the logic with which some projects are chosen, even research based on
public and political arm twisting begins to sound pretty good.

In the April–May 1979 issue of *Fish and Wildlife News,* a trade
publication for wildlife managers, the Chairman of the Council on Environmental Quality, Charles Warren, suggested that the wildlife profession might consider managing the areas it administers for the purpose
of "species diversity," rather than intensively manipulating them "to
favor fewer desired game species." In response, the spokesmen of three
more-or-less professional organizations (two of them headed by
speakers at the mule deer conference) plus the National Wildlife Federation, co-signed a stinging letter-to-the-editor which, without really
addressing Warren's suggestion, complained that it "appears to arise
from a vacuum" and "ignores social, economic, and political forces that
have shaped and continue to shape wildlife management in this country."
Moreover, "statements of this kind shake public confidence in the positive values that are and can be gained from wildlife management" and

"CEQ's current tack only serves to make the wildlife profession's already difficult mission even more arduous." In short, mind your own shop, Mr. Warren, and stay out of ours.

The letter illustrates some of the points already made, chiefly the professionals' resistance to new approaches and prevailing distrust that exists between different private and government entities that should be working with each other. But the most interesting thing about it is its almost paranoid tone. Here are some of the biggest big shots in the wildlife business reacting to another big shot's idea, published in a very unpublic journal, as though he had given them a kick in the pants—which, judging only on the basis of the original article, was not what he had in mind.

Now it is a truism that all government agencies are sitting ducks; it is as easy to criticize them as it is hard to get them to change. My own generalizations are necessarily sweeping and one could hardly blame many a dedicated professional if he complained about such blanket charges. He could point out, fairly enough, that an outsider can not possibly appreciate the byzantine intricacies of decision making and funding processes; that for every two merely expedient or redundant research projects there is at least one that makes total sense; that in any case, the real problems facing wildlife have more to do with "social, economic, and political forces" than with the managers themselves.

Certainly it is true that many of the dilemmas besetting state and federal wildlife agencies are ones over which those agencies have little control. But the particular ones cited are to some extent interrelated and have a common source, and are at least partially subject to correction by the professionals themselves. All of them have something to do with the fact that the wildlife managerial class is no longer very certain of its own mission. If that is lacking, all the rest has got to follow. Why should agencies work together when they are no longer sure what long range purpose their work is supposed to serve? Why should they contrive the means of outmaneuvering special interests, politicians, even the public and its trendy concerns, when they no longer know what their own priorities should be?

It is a wondrous, though hitherto unnoted irony that the coming of age of the environmental movement has probably done more to undermine the morale and the sense of purpose of government wildlife officials than all the developers, politicians, poachers, and budget cutters combined. Any one who doubts this should frequent the offices of

Incident at Eagle Ranch

federal and state management people in the West for a few weeks. Neither strip miners nor meddling legislators will spark the same injured and impassioned tone that enters a wildlife administrator's voice when he speaks of the "protectionists," the "preservationists," the "armchair environmentalists" and what they do not know about wildlife conservation. There is even the conviction that the influence of these outsiders is insidiously infecting the wildlife management establishment itself. "Do you know," one outraged official observed, "that at some of the Eastern wildlife schools a lot of students read Sierra Club stuff, even Defenders of Wildlife, as much as they do the management journals!"

Some of this antipathy is inevitable, since several citizen environmental groups have at least a covert bias against hunting and trapping, and many of their members are apt to care more about the individual members of a wildlife species than they do about the species as a whole. On the other hand they may not care much about how many sheep a coyote kills, or the economic aspects of wildlife management. Some of them oppose leghold traps, and the extremists would like to see all hunting banned. To many old-line managers, who have devoted all of their professional lives to multiplying supplies of huntable, trappable, fishable wildlife and who perforce regard wild animals much as a stockman views his cows or sheep, these new attitudes signify the spread of an idolatrous heresy. On both sides, of course, there are many ecumenical people—a majority according to the polls—who rightly believe that the disputed points of dogma matter less than the shared belief in the importance of wildlife as a national heritage.

Yet the differences between the traditionalists and the reformers are real enough, and one might as well be frank about them. The "new" environmentalist, if he is the genuine article, may support recreational needs as a means to an end, but his fundamental commitment is to protect wildlife species, regardless of their utilitarian value, *from* people. In the opposite corner, the wildlife management class and its adherents, though usually (but not always) granting the need to preserve endangered species, are still primarily committed to the maximum exploitation of useful wildlife *for* people—especially the hunters, fishermen, etc. who pay the management bill for their recreational needs with licensing fees. As with all faiths, inconsistencies and variations abound, but between from and for is where the line is being drawn. Not incidentally, the controversy concerning predators has probably done more to draw that line than any other issue.

As usual, there is much to be said for and against both views, and as usual compromises are available. Certainly the time has come when the preservationists must and will pay more of the management costs. The intent of defining the conflict here, however, is to suggest that the professionals, especially at the state level, have not exactly led the way in closing the gap. The sense of being no longer appreciated—worse, of being told what to do by laymen—has made them touchy and defensive. Certainly they make some efforts to placate the new reformers, but these are almost always in the form of reaction rather than initiative; and therein lies the basic problem: whether they admit it to themselves or not, the managers have lost their sense of leadership in their own field.

If they are ever to get it back again, they must come up with the kind of genuinely comprehensive master plan for future wildlife management which the times require, one that incorporates both utilitarian and preservationist philosophies, though perhaps more of the latter than many old line professionals are willing to concede. Such a plan must establish goals on a priority basis, and incorporate a reasonably uniform methodology to accomplish them.

It would seem almost too obvious to mention—if the conference at Logan and others like it did not indicate the contrary—that the first priority of any long-term planning has got to be keeping better track of the population status and trends of the nation's major wildlife species. As matters now stand, whether the subject is mule deer or bobcats or pelicans or you name it, there is usually a large managerial lapse between the official assurance that they are doing fine and the general perception that they are not doing very well at all.

A comprehensive and continuing wildlife inventory on an interstate level has never been tried, unless one counts the half-hearted effort of the federal government years ago to tabulate the states' annual estimates of their game populations, an effort abandoned when it became clear that the figures were meaningless. There are, of course, surveys of a few species. Federal officials check the nesting success of migrant waterfowl and whooping cranes; government "recovery teams" are supposed to be doing something about several species that are almost done-for; the states continue to come up with guesses about populations of deer and fur bearers based mostly on the "harvest" and a smattering of browse and pellet surveys. But their emphasis is on a handful of "huntable" species; and even there, as one noted researcher observed,

"We haven't had to worry much about accuracy until lately because there were plenty of deer to go around."

"Until lately" is right now. And what we need now is a reliable monitoring system for representative species of all the nation's wildlife. This list must include not only game and fur animals, and those that are rare or threatened, but also the chief predators and a large assortment of "indicator" species that are ecologically significant because they are either important to the prey base of a region or unusually susceptible to environmental changes.

One thing is certain: the managers will never get a handle on what they are supposed to be doing until they have a better idea of the stocks of wildlife on hand, and whether those stocks are increasing or diminishing, and at what rate. A strategy for accomplishing a general wildlife inventory should have been in the works by now. If the challenge of that kind of survey goes on being ignored it will not be due to inadequate methodology or lack of funds. The responsibility will rest with the professional class itself, with its inability to establish cooperative systems within its own ranks. Given a spirit of cooperation, a systematic tabulation of wildlife population trends could probably be more efficiently carried out than the haphazard spot checks that are now the rule.

Concerning methodology, the following modest proposals are hardly meant to be the final word, but they indicate some of the available possibilities. To begin with, the states should agree on the way information is to be acquired and tabulated, taking into account the inequalities in state budgets. Inevitably the accuracy of any survey would be relative; wildlife does not come forward to be counted. However, an accurate census is not necessary in establishing the status of a species; it is enough to have some idea of its abundance and to know whether its numbers have increased or decreased by a measurable percentage from one year and one decade to the next.

One way of acquiring this kind of information would be to make better use of the most ubiquitous force of wildlife personnel already on hand, namely the conservation officers in the field. Research biologists distrust the testimony of non-specialists for good reasons; shrewd observation and folklore have a way of getting all mixed up. On the other hand, enforcement people often resent the experts' sometimes condescending indifference to their first hand knowledge of their own particular bailiwicks. Naturally, the conservation officers may not be in a position to estimate wildlife numbers, much less infer the reasons for annual fluctuations; but they are better able than anyone else to detect population trends on a county-by-county basis. Some of these people told me they had warned their supervisors about the drop in mule deer populations years before the biologists were prepared to admit that a serious decline was underway. Certainly, if a conservation officer is doing his job at all, he can tell pretty accurately whether the huntable and/or observable species in his territory are down or up from the preceding year. His observations would become even more exact if they were systemized under the guidance of the research biologists themselves. In some states, conservation officers do take part in transect deer surveys, but the effort is a limited one. With planning, these people could conduct periodic tract surveys and road checks of several species, from jackrabbits and quail to roadrunners and porcupines, as well as deer or antelope. They might also keep weekly or monthly records of the confirmed appearances of less common wildlife in their districts. Of course, local variables, the weather and what-not, would influence precision. But as general indicators there is no question that such counts would pay off—the research biologists I questioned have admitted as much—especially since the conservation officers, long at the bottom of the management hierarchy, would feel that their practical knowledge was finally being used. If this kind of survey were coordinated with the officers' slack seasons and regular patrols, it should not greatly increase their workload. In any case, except for their enforcement duties, it is the most important job they could be doing. They would function much as county agents do when reporting the current census of livestock in their districts—with the obvious difference that no actual census would be involved.

This system of reporting could then be combined, at the state level, with other sources of information, including more accurate tallies of animals killed by hunters and trappers, the spot censuses run by the research biologists themselves, as well as incidental state or federal research projects—which would in time, perhaps, be directed at determining the accuracy of other trend data. In the case of regionally rare and endangered species, "natural heritage programs," already set up in many states with the help of the privately funded Nature Conservancy, would be an important additional source of information. There would need to be some consistency in the way major sources of data were gathered and collated, but there are models for that type of computerization, including the one set up by the Nature Conservancy. In any case, that is what systems analysts are for; and for that part of the operation at least, the federal government could foot the bill. Indeed, state wildlife departments would not necessarily incur any major expense other than the cost of an additional biologist or two to help set the system up according to interstate guidelines.

The important point is that such a survey can be made to work. It will be imperfect, but at least ten times better than anything we have going now. Again, however, it will require that the states work with each other and with the feds, instead of feuding, as they often do now, like 15th century Scottish clans. On the other hand, not all the states would have to sign a truce before the project got moving.

Assuming that a cooperative survey did get underway, the second priority follows of itself, namely, the task of trying to account for fluctuations, particularly long-term declines, in wildlife numbers. The specialists will again remind the layman that this is more easily said than done; and there is no denying that factors influencing population densities of a species are often intricate and subtle. But it is also true that such explanations can be overused, especially when one is dealing with species that are experiencing declines over an extensive area. In such cases, it is a fairly safe bet that the reason has to do with bad weather conditions, deteriorating habitat and/or human activities. But the list can actually be narrowed further—since habitat is usually most affected by weather conditions or human interference. Bad weather usually means one of two things: a severe winter or droughty spring and summer, both of which reduce available food supplies, which in turn reduces fertility, increases susceptibility to disease, predation, etc. Adverse human activity, on the other hand, can include everything from clear-cutting forests or not cutting them at all (depending on the wildlife species), to increased agricultural or residential development, to environmental pollution, to, yes, overhunting. Even so, however, the list is finite; when the prolonged decline of a wildlife species is perceived over a large geographic area, it makes sense to find out first of all if there are some really big changes—in human population and land use patterns especially—going on. The important thing to note here is that information pertaining to most such human activities, as well as anything one wants to know about weather, is available ready-made from one

Managers

government source or another. The wildlife professionals occasionally use such data—the severity of preceding winters is noted (sometimes) in figuring the length of the next hunting season; reports of large irrigation projects are understood to be bad news for desert game, etc. Yet this kind of information is never used in a systematic or comprehensive way.

Consider how it could be applied: At the Logan conference one of the speakers theorized that the decline of mule deer in the West seemed to coincide with the decline of sheep. Since sheep keep vegetation at a low successional stage, the way deer like it, might there not be a cause and effect relationship between fewer sheep and fewer deer? Actually, deer are down in areas where sheep never ranged as well as in areas where they still do; but even so, the speculation would be worth checking out. Under the present set-up, however, this could only be done by means of several prohibitively expensive projects involving study areas that contained various combinations of deer and sheep. Whereas, if game managers had a reasonably accurate county-by-county, year-by-year tabulation of deer populations based on the computerized records of harvests, reports of conservation officers, *and* if these were correlated with U.S. Department of Agriculture figures on sheep population trends in the same counties, it would be possible to come up with some valid conclusions on the "sheep connection" at little cost. Same with human population trends, changes in agricultural practices, and so forth.

In fact, there is no reason why analysts could not only standardize the means of keeping track of wildlife population trends, but also correlate them with each other, and with already available statistics on human demographics, weather conditions, agricultural or forestry practices, hunting and trapping activity, and so on. Naturally the findings from these correlations would be mostly negative; that is, they would identify the influences that were not causing problems more exactly than those that were.[5] But the process of elimination is not a bad way to find out where the pipe is leaking.

I am not knocking the traditional methodologies of research. But it is a not-so-simple truth that biological investigation into the complex private lives of wild creatures usually uncovers more questions in the short term than answers. Such studies can only be helped, not hindered, if they are accompanied and directed by the broad-brush approach that is being urged here. There is not enough time left for the "democratic process of hit-or-miss," as one biologist calls it, to continue at its present moseying pace.

Incident at Eagle Ranch

One thing is certain. Until some kind of large scale monitoring of wildlife populations has gotten underway, the professionals will never be able to cope with other vital questions that are being thrown at them; for example, how many deer or eagles do we actually want? And if we must choose maximum populations vis-a-vis optimum harvests, which is our preference? I will try to address those issues a little later on. But it will be with the tacit understanding that the whole discussion is academic until the managers do a better job of telling us how many predators and other wildlife we have.

Almost to a man, the bureaucrats and biologists I questioned admitted they could monitor wildlife populations more accurately than they are doing now. One of the most eminent of them observed, "It would be nice if we could get a truly cooperative thing going, but I don't think we will." Then, after a moment, he added, "But if we ever *do* get our act together, it will probably be because we have to come up with the numbers to show the preservationists and anti-hunters that there's still enough wildlife to hunt and trap."

If the professionals want to regain the leadership they have lost, they would do well to realize that they must start coming up with the numbers soon.

12. Predators

WHEN WESTERNERS TALK about eagles as predators, the golden eagle is the bird they have in mind. But it should be mentioned in passing that bald eagles get in the act too. During winter migrations they often follow the same flyways as the goldens and turn up in places where you would not expect to find them, places like the Auld Ranch where I spotted four of them myself. Jerry Heintzelman, the helicopter pilot who testified for the government at the San Antonio trial, remembered that several bald eagles were killed during the hunts he flew. And on a badly managed ranch near Auld's where natural lamb mortality was high, ADC's Sam Crowe observed several balds feeding on dead lambs. In areas like this where both species of eagles are on hand, the locals kill more bald eagles than they themselves realize, since immature birds lack the white head feathers that most obviously distinguish them from their golden cousins.

Still, it is the golden eagle that bears the brunt of the sheepmen's anger because it is the more numerous and wide ranging species, and because it has a reputation for being more aggressive and ambitious in its choice of prey. There are a number of reports, some of them respectable, which describe golden eagle attacks on adult deer, antelope, even coyotes —though usually not with fatal results. That the eagles sometimes have better luck with the young of these species can not be doubted, although one reliable observer told me of an incident in which a mule deer doe effectively protected her fawn from a hovering eagle by rearing on her hind legs and pawing the air. The eagle, it seems, "wasn't very serious; it was more or less playing with her."

When they are being serious, golden eagles usually hunt the animals they are best adapted to kill. Their taste runs to jackrabbits, cottontails, prairie dogs, and rock and ground squirrels, in that order of preference; and they are very fond of carrion. The analysis of droppings from scores of eyries throughout the West indicates that between 75 and 90 percent of the eagle diet consists of rabbits. Availability is apparently not the only factor that enters in: Observers have watched goldens preying on jacks in areas where the animals were quite scarce, even though other prey animals, notably an abundance of prairie dogs and lambs, were on hand.

Environmentalists are understandably eager to point out that, far from being a liability, eagles actually improve the stockmen's range by controlling rodent populations. Even some sheepmen have revised their thinking after examining the contents of eagles' nests. However, there is some uncertainty in the scientific community about whether the birds significantly suppress rodent populations, and the final verdict will probably be a long time coming in. The important point is that nesting eagles do not as a rule "suppress" lambs, although some researchers point out that the rule may get a little bent in years when natural prey is exceptionally scarce.

The research on nesting eagles is important because it is almost the only hard data on their eating habits that we have. It is also significant because in most of the West, adult eagles are rearing their young at the same time that lambing is underway. It therefore follows that if the grown-ups are not killing lambs then, they have missed their chance.

As it happens, most of the ruckus about eagle predation involves immature birds. At trouble spots in Montana and Texas, anywhere from eighty to one hundred percent of the eagles that have been live-trapped turned out to be juveniles and subadults. It takes fledgling eagles five long, dangerous years to reach the age when they are ready to stake out a territory and set up housekeeping. Meantime they do a lot of wandering. The supposition is that they are displaced from the territories of mated pairs and, at least on the eastern side of the Great Divide, many of them follow the river valleys out into the foothills and high plains fronting the Rockies. There they dawdle about as winter comes on, some of them gradually moving south into Texas and Mexico in a restless search for areas where prey species and carrion are in good supply. Over most of this immense terrain, they rarely average more than ten birds to a hundred square miles except in eastern Wyoming where the tally gets up to thirty five.[1] However, topography, wind currents, and prey availability make some areas more popular with eagles than others, so they do occasionally crowd up. When that happens, the slim evidence suggests that something special is going on—an abundance of winter-killed cattle, deer, or sheep in a rabbit-poor year; that sort of thing. Only in Texas' Real County, at the edge of the Balcones Escarpment, have I been able to discover evidence of a "historical" winter concentration: In a memorandum written in 1962, a Fish and Wildlife investigator mentions sighting almost as many eagles on the Auld Ranch as I saw sixteen years later. A likely explanation is that any eagles that get that far are discouraged from going further by the limitless scrub covered plains of south Texas, which begin where the escarpment ends.

The one thing that is certain is that if eagles constitute a significant threat to livestock, specifically lambs, it has to be at those relatively few times and places where there are a lot of them around. In most of the Western rangelands, the sheepmen themselves admit that eagles, in contrast to coyotes, are not exactly ruining them. And when ranchers do insist they are sustaining heavy losses, they are unable to produce the corpus delicti—as they easily can when a coyote is giving them a bad time. Even Bill Sims of the Texas Sheep and Goat Raisers Association has come around to admitting that "eagles are a pretty local problem." The only question is just how local "local" really is.

Some part of that answer can be gleaned from the reports of the in-the-field study teams researching the extent of coyote predation on various Western ranches. Just about all of the studies were conducted in eagle country; and in each case hundreds, sometimes thousands of necropsies on dead lambs were performed. Only two of these projects have turned up any evidence of eagle predation at all. One case concerned a ranch in western Montana.[2] Out of four hundred and fifty dead lambs and ewes examined, just two deaths were attributed to eagles—and these had occurred under rather special circumstances: it seems the eagles had become used to feeding on coyote leftovers, and when the coyotes quit killing sheep for several days, the birds tried their own hand at it. As soon as the coyotes started in again, they went back to carrion.

In the other case, a three year project in a part of southern Wyoming where migrant eagles reach their highest average densities, the study team discovered that on five large ranches, supporting about forty thousand ewes and lambs, the average annual toll of all predators, mostly coyotes, during a three year period was about 2 percent of the lamb crop.[3] 9 percent of these predator-caused deaths—less than .2 percent of the total crop—was attributed to eagles. But the report, sad to say, makes frustrating reading—like trying to understand the circumstances of a murder by perusing the police docket. From a few scattered sentences, it is possible to infer that most of the eagle predation occurred during one bad weather spring, on a single ranch, Ranch "B,"—the only one where lambing was unsupervised and where lamb mortality from all causes was very high. A more detailed account of this particular range operation, the weather, the topography and ground cover, the prevalence of eagles, of carrion, of natural prey, the condition of the lambs, etc., might have told us something important about the circumstances under which eagle predation occurs, but as best I can discover that sort of useful information about the case has not been published.

Which leaves us with the only two known localities that are notorious for confrontations between men and eagles: west Texas, especially Real County, and the southwestern corner of Montana, near Dillon, the locale of the Helle-Rebish ranches and the scene of the only serious case of eagle depredation ever documented. Government researchers have estimated that during 1974 and 1975 about 75 percent of all lamb mortality on the Helle-Rebish was due to eagles.[4] True, that overall estimate is based on skimpy data, but the fact remains that during a two hour period in June 1974, a single researcher picked up sixteen lambs killed by eagles; and in May 1975, another scientist removed fifteen kills in a six hour period.

In 1975, the Fish and Wildlife Service began a research and live-trapping program at the Helle-Rebish ranches which continued through the spring of 1978. From the start, the project was plagued by difficulties. There were not enough funds, although operating costs ran to $25,000 annually (the ranchers received $2,200 for confirmed losses); there was no use of telemetry to track transient eagles; eagle censusing was an on-and-off affair; the ranchers would not allow researchers on the lambing grounds; reports were poorly done; and the collection and examination of dead lambs was inadequate. The only really successful aspect of the project was the live-trapping of eagles. In 1975, a remarkable one hundred and forty seven birds were caught and deported. After that, the numbers dropped in keeping with the reduced population of eagles on hand, although the figures were still impressive: sixty nine in 1976, thirty five in 1977, forty eight in 1978. Ironically, the worst predation occurred in 1975, when the greatest numbers of eagles were being caught.

But in spite of the project's shortcomings, some important facts do emerge, most of them summarized by Bart O'Gara, the head of the Cooperative Wildlife Research Unit:[5] (1) The study area is apparently a natural funneling point for migrant eagles, some of them enroute from Canada. (2) It is also furnished with a great many rock and lava promontories, ideal roosts for tired eagles. (3) Almost all of the trouble-making birds were juveniles and subadults. (4) Few resident pairs of eagles were available to disperse the transients from their territories. (5) The years 1974 and 1975, when eagle predation was at its worst, coincided with a decline in jackrabbit populations both locally and throughout the West. (6) The Helle-Rebish ranches were about the only sheep operations in the area. (7) The spring of 1974 and the winter of 1975 were very severe, not only inhibiting the emergence of ground squirrels and other rodent prey, but inducing high natural mortality among lambs, which may have drawn carrion hunting eagles to the area.

In short, every imaginable factor that might create a serious eagle predation problem was present at the Helle-Rebish ranches in 1975.

There is an important sequel, however, which is not stressed in the later project reports. This concerns the inexact correlation between eagle densities and lamb mortality during the subsequent years, 1976 through 1978, when weather conditions improved and the supply of natural prey, both ground squirrels and jackrabbits, increased. The eagle population in the area was more widely dispersed, and also less numerous, in part, perhaps, because of the first year's heavy traffic in translocated birds. (Almost none of the trapped and marked eagles returned; most of them simply disappeared, although three bodies were recovered near release sites.) Nonetheless, judging from sightings and numbers of birds caught, there were still a large number of eagles on the Helle-Rebish ranches during this later period, probably one half to one third as many as during the "invasion" years of 1974 and 1975. Yet necropsies revealed that almost all of the identifiable lamb mortality was due to stillbirths and starvation; eagle predation ceased to be a critical factor on either ranch, dropping from the estimated 75 percent of all lamb mortality in 1975 to about 5 or 6 percent in 1977–78 (or about 1.5 percent of the total lamb crop). Yet despite this disproportionate decrease in predation compared to eagles on hand, and in spite of ideal weather conditions attending both lambing seasons, 87 percent of the lambs on one of the ranches survived—nothing to brag about—and only a disastrously low 67 percent crop on the other. Even under the best of circumstances, one of the ranches was a losing proposition. It it reasonable to conclude that during the bad weather years of 1974 and 1975, lamb mortality would have been extremely high, contrary to the claims of the ranchers, even if there had not been an abnormal concentration of eagles in the area. Furthermore, the evidence indicates that during some years when sizeable numbers of eagles were still on hand, and still being live trapped, the birds were not causing anything like the damage that the researchers themselves had anticipated.[6]

One conclusion of the Helle-Rebish report was that live trapping is not a very practical way to control eagle predation. This assessment has had no perceivable effect, however, on ADC operations in that other eagle hot-spot, west Texas. In the year since I accompanied Sam Crowe, ADC's "eagle man" in the Southwest, on a wintry jaunt across a part of southeastern New Mexico, he and/or his supervisors had evidently decided that *preventive* eagle control is what the ranchers ordered. During 1979 and the first weeks of 1980, Crowe and his assistants had already trapped three eagles on one ranch in New Mexico, and seventy on four ranches in Texas, with the number steadily increasing as this book goes to press.

Several interesting facts emerge, sometimes inadvertently, from Crowe's account of his recent activities:[7] (1) Although his availability has been widely publicized in the Southwest during the last several years, these five operations were the only ones that have recently called on him for help. (2) In each of these cases, the live-trapping of eagles was begun without any serious attempt to find out if the ranchers' complaints were justified—in clear violation of the intent of the Eagle Act, as well as of ADC's stated policy of "corrective" control. (3) Almost all of the live-trapped eagles were immature, and a number of them were underweight and undernourished (evidently because they had not yet acquired adequate hunting skills) even though a veritable smorgasbord of lamb was spread out on the hills around them. (4) Two of the eagles were so weak from starvation that Crowe's team had to force feed them, lest they die while held captive—which raises the question of what happens to already weakened birds after they undergo the trauma of being trapped, transported, and released in unfamiliar territory. Some of them would not have passed nature's stern survival test in any case; but it seems likely that others that might have made the grade also fail.

From a personal viewpoint, none of this information fascinated me as much as the identities of the four Texas ranchers who had sought Crowe's aid. One of them turned out to be Buster Holland's boss, who was also the husband of W. F. Love's widow and a successful rancher in his own right. He had arranged with Crowe to have seven eagles trapped on one of his ranches near Alpine apparently for no better reason than that quite a few of the birds were in the neighborhood. The other three operators were Real County men. Perhaps my reader can guess their names: There was Dan Auld, the multimillionaire and eagle hater, on whose property sixty five eagles have already been caught. There was Bob Ramsey, the eagle baiter, at whose request Crowe and team have trapped seven birds even though Ramsey was still unable to document a single eagle kill on his own land. And there was Buddy Pape, Auld's foreman and a convicted eagle killer, who could only turn up one eagle for Crowe to trap on the leased ranch he operates in his spare time.

There is something of Alice in Wonderland about all of this. The government, formerly the prosecutor, has now begun working for the defense in the eagle case. And to what purpose? When all the dust has settled and the cries of outrage have subsided, what evidence of serious eagle predation has been produced in west Texas by the ranchers? by a government team of four men? by at least three federal and private research investigators? by yours truly, visiting the reported scenes of the crime with a fairly open mind? The answer is: none. After four years of trying, Pape, Crowe and others have turned up only about a half a dozen eagle kills on the Auld ranch, the center of controversy (and one of these was presumably Ramsey's baited lamb). Ramsey himself has been shown to misrepresent his losses. Furthermore, if the eagles were really causing a lot of trouble, both he and Auld could have changed lambing dates long ago without terrific financial loss.

The truth of the matter is that some eagles do indeed prey on lambs in Real County and west Texas, with an intensity that is inversely pro-

Incident at Eagle Ranch

portionate to the supply of natural prey on hand. But even in the areas where they tend to congregate, they are almost never a severe problem compared to other causes of lamb mortality. If Crowe and his team spent more of their time investigating eagle predation and less time setting traps, they might discover this for themselves.

Confirmed eagle haters among the sheepmen will never believe eagles are not voracious lamb-eaters. (With more logic they can point out, as Reba Pape once did to me, that even the loss of one lamb to eagles is one too many.) In the long run, few of them will be satisfied with anything the government does in the way of corrective control that falls short of granting them permits to kill as many eagles as they want to kill. This view is supported by the comments of Bart O'Gara, head of the research unit involved in the Helle-Rebish case. After remarking on the ineffectiveness of live-trapping as a control measure, he states, "Knowing that no one has received a kill permit since 1970, many ranchers will continue to take the law into their own hands. The ethics of forcing a rancher to break the law or go out of business must be considered." That seems to be a telling point. But then one asks, who are these "many ranchers" who must take the law into their own hands? Auld? Pape? Ramsey? Leinweber? Buster Holland? O'Gara himself can only cite the Helle-Rebish ranchers as proof of serious hardship, and the more one searches for evidence, the more unusual that case becomes. There may yet be others like it, but it is certain they will always be few and far between.

In a "Conceptual Plan" for the management of golden eagles, published in 1978, the Fish and Wildlife Service indicates that it is not likely to grant kill permits anytime soon.[8] This is both a politically astute and ecologically sane decision. There can be little doubt that over the long haul, the golden eagle is a threatened species. Current best guesses place the wintering population of eagles at about forty thousand, an estimate based on aerial transects flown on sample tracts in six Western states. That sounds like a good many eagles. However, an unknown but presumably large percentage of these birds are migrants from Canada. The majority of them, perhaps 70 or 80 percent, are immature birds ranging from ten months to five years of age. Of that total number, say thirty thousand, only an average of one-fifth, six or seven thousand birds, are likely to be fledglings of the crop produced in any one year. Even if three-fourths of them were raised in the Western United States —probably an overestimate—and if all the native pairs of breeding birds were successful in fledging an average of one eaglet per nest annually, then it is likely that not more than four or five thousand breeding pairs of golden eagles currently reside in the American West.

Moreover, there is little doubt that golden eagle numbers are declining. The "Conceptual Plan" describes this decline as "a slight downward trend." In fact it is more than "slight"—from a weighted average of 16.6 eagles per one hundred square miles in 1973 when aerial surveys began, to 12.9 in 1978. The decline is not evenly distributed—in some survey areas eagle numbers have slightly increased; also, biologists suspect that part of the overall decrease may have been due to a cyclic low in jackrabbit populations during much of the survey period. But jackrabbits in the West have been on the increase lately, yet the overall wintering population of eagles continues to slide. A long term sampling of eagle nests, which began in 1965, suggests some correlation with the rabbit cycle; but it also clearly indicates an absolute reduction in the number of active eagle nests since the study began fifteen years ago. Observers in the field tend to confirm these findings.[9]

When this real and not so gradual decline is matched against the slim evidence of serious eagle predation, it seems a little premature for wildlife managers like O'Gara to be pushing for kill permits, especially since he admits it would be impossible for ADC to adequately document loss claims before handing out such licenses. Interestingly, O'Gara quotes a distinguished Montana biologist as "volunteering" that "if all of the immature birds causing damage at Dillon [the Helle-Rebish area] were killed, scant effect on the [eagle] population would result." Since there was no way of knowing which eagles were causing damage, and since the live-trapping of one hundred and forty five eagles in 1975 did not quell predation, we can only conclude the O'Gara and his colleague are talking about the death of several hundred eagles on the Helle-Rebish ranches alone, out of an estimated nine thousand eagles wintering in Montana. This kind of comment reflects a grievously mistaken view of wildlife productivity, widely held in management circles, to the effect that almost any species will quickly rebound even though large numbers of that species are killed above and beyond the percentage that would perish in the natural course of things. It is true that a one-time slaughter of eagles at the Helle-Rebish operation might not have too lasting an impact on overall eagle populations. But O'Gara himself obviously does not suppose the killing would end there. If kill permits

are made available, every sheepman in the West who sees a half dozen
eagles on his property will be clamoring for one. And judging from the
non-lethal performance of ADC's Sam Crowe in Texas, one can guess
how much "documentation" will be required before the permits are
handed out.

O'Gara's argument, of course, is that without the legal permits,
ranchers "will continue to take the law into their own hands." That is
true. Some ranchers who are not in the least danger of going out of business because of eagles, as well as God-knows-how-many thrill seekers,
will continue to shoot these birds whenever they dare. But it is also true
that many ranchers and other rural Westerners have been badly shaken
by the verdict in the San Antonio trial. They are now a lot more careful
that no one is looking when they pull the trigger. Which tends to curtail
their activities. Among the private aircraft companies that service the
ranchers, the reverberations of the trial have been particularly important. The fate of South Texas Helicopter Company has not gone unno-
ticed. Aerial gunning is potentially a much more serious threat to eagles
that ground shooting; but as long as federal investigators make their
presence known at all those small airfields near Marfa and Roswell and
Billings and Laramie, repetitions of the large scale slaughter that took
place in Real County are not likely to recur. It would also help if the
federal system of providing rewards for government witnesses in eagle-
killing trials were speeded up. And environmental organizations must
continue to publicize cases in which Western judges let off eagle killers
with token fines. Environmentalists might also set up their own reward
system, as the National Wildlife Federation has done with some success
in the case of the bald eagle.

Apart from illegal shooting, the most direct man-related cause of
eagle deaths is powerline electrocution. There has been a widespread
assumption that this problem was largely solved, but the recent study at
Brigham Young University, mentioned earlier, suggests the opposite.
Thousands of eagles are still dying high voltage deaths each year. It is
unlikely that the problem will ever be wholly corrected, but the power
companies are sensitive to bad publicity; they have cooperated in the
Brigham Young project, and a renewal of government and environmentalist pressure, which has dwindled to nothing in the last few years,
would ensure corrective modifications on the major lines where eagle
mortality is most severe.

Predators

As for eagle control, the Fish and Wildlife "Conceptual Plan" calls for a force of forty people to be eventually engaged in live-trapping eagles. Given what is known of eagle predation, and especially given the performance of the ADC team in the Southwest, that proposal is absurd. One part-time team would be enough to deal with very rare situations like the Helle-Rebish ranch. However, given also the world of *realpolitik,* a single full-time "eagle man" in each of the ADC's western divisions seems a more plausible compromise, the visible proof that "ADC cares." Such trappers should be required to prove that significant eagle predation is occurring before they catch the first live eagle. After all, it took O'Gara only a half day to find fifteen eagle kills on the Rebish ranch, so it should not be as difficult as O'Gara himself suggests to document really serious claims.

In the longer term, the preservation of golden eagle nesting habitat will have to be considered. In the case of some human activites, notably timber-cutting, the protection of eyries and the rerouting of logging roads should suffice if—a big "if"—the nesting sites are pre-identified. In the case of others, particularly strip mining, the solution may be harder to find since the destruction of a breeding pair's foraging territory may be involved.[10]

Underlying all of these considerations, however, is the urgent need for a more adequate survey of resident golden eagle populations. In this respect, the golden eagle is a bit luckier than most wildlife species. The same spectacular qualities that make it so eminently shootable have also captured the public's sympathy and interest. As a result, the federal government has made some attempts to determine its status, both by flying winter transects and by conducting an annual spot check of about one hundred and fifty active and inactive nests along the front range of the Rockies—which presumably represent most of the eyries that have been found in that vast area. Although the transect flights should also be expanded, it is this nesting survey that needs the most attention.

The identification and annual surveillance of a much larger sampling of nests in representative areas throughout the West has got to be the most important priority of any eagle management plan. Apart from the obvious usefulness of being able to monitor the breeding success of native goldens, a more inclusive search for nesting sites should uncover some localities that are optimum, rather that merely representative, nesting habitats. Such areas could then be singled out for future protection if and when it is needed. Also, before-and-after checks of active eyries in the vicinity of mining operations, new housing developments, and new roads would eventually indicate the effect of such activities on nesting birds. Finally, if a nesting inventory could become part of a more general monitoring program of wildlife populations, weather conditions, and human demographic changes—the sort of survey discussed earlier— the professionals would be able to make highly probable correlations between, for example, jackrabbit populations and the number of eaglets fledged in a given year.

In the same more imaginative way, aerial transects of wintering eagle populations should be aimed at identifying small local areas, if there are any, where eagles regularly congregate year after year, as well as simply computing average densities in one hundred square mile blocks. If, for example, it could be demonstrated that the area of the Helle-Rebish ranches consistently hosts abnormally high spring concentrations of transient eagles, and that the predation problem that occurred in 1974 and 1975 is likely to recur at intervals in the future, then it may be that the ranches would serve their best use as a staging ground for young eagles rather than young lambs. In that case, federal or state officials could consider leasing or even purchasing the land. It is already clear that no better fate could befall the Auld Ranch. Indeed, if some government or non-profit private agency could acquire the property from Auld or his heirs, offering the sort of tax advantages which such a public-interest sale would involve, the resulting sanctuary could become a splendid, if somewhat ironic, monument to the crusty old hunter's memory. Unfortunately, Dan Auld is not likely to see it that way.

One thing is certain. The massive and ecologically harmful live trapping that is currently going on at Auld's ranch should stop at once. It is not another Helle-Rebish situation. For its wealthy owner, the ranch may well be little more than an expensive hobby. In any case, the financial loss that Auld might suffer by postponing his lambing season, to avoid real or imagined depredation, is likely to be outweighed by the taxpayer cost of keeping four men busy for months at a time capturing eagles on his land.

The professionals should recognize that their mandate concerning the golden eagle—which they were pretty slow to accept until the public forced it on them—is now very clear: It is their business to protect eagles, not lambs. Excepting a few isolated cases where live captures may be honestly justified, law enforcement, not trapping or kill permits, is in order when ranchers "take the law into their own hands." Ranchers' losses to eagles are almost invariably negligible even in local situations and must be accepted as a small price for keeping a vital part of the nation's heritage intact.

As for the general public, it should be made aware that there is no inevitable reason why eagle populations must continue to decline. With the exception of a relatively few birds now threatened by strip mining activities, most breeding pairs of golden eagles in the West have their nests in rather remote wild areas. The habitat is still there. If the goldens do continue their long slide towards a rare or endangered status, it will be because the professionals have failed to do their job.

THE COYOTES

After sorting through the available evidence, including interviews with many of the ranchers themselves, I am confident that during the seventies, when 1080 had been banned as a coyote killer and the supply of jackrabbits was low, coyotes could not have destroyed more than 2.5 or 2.6 percent of the annual lamb crop in the West. The data for 1978 and 1979 indicate that in most areas of the West coyote predation on sheep has declined significantly, so the current percentage of loss is certain to be even less.[11] Nevertheless, it is important to remember that averages do not tell the whole story. Although most ranchers lose few sheep or none to coyotes, a minority do have serious predation problems.

A few other generalizations are in order. Unlike the lion or eagle or even the bobcat, the coyote is not a potentially threatened species. Environmentalists undermine their credibility when they warn, as some do, that this most adaptable and exuberantly reproductive of all the major predators "may go the way of the wolf." It has been wiped out in limited areas, of course, and there is no doubt that if all the nation's citizenry backed an immensely expensive campaign to eradicate it, it actually could be eliminated from most regions of the West. It is not *that* adaptable. But nothing of the sort is happening now, and there is no reason to suppose a massive putsch is in the offing. In suitable habitat, which now includes most of the U.S., the little critter is in good supply. James Goodrum, the New Mexico sheep raiser and warehouse owner, may be right when he says that a coyote will howl over the grave of the last man—though if that happens it will be less a judgment on the coyotes' adaptability than on ours.

Incident at Eagle Ranch

The real questions concerning coyote management have more to do with where and how the coyote survives than whether it survives at all. How many of these animals do we actually want, assuming we have a choice? Under what circumstances should they be permitted to exist without control? How much control is needed, and where? And who should do it? I have suggested answers to some of these questions in preceeding chapters. The reader will be convinced, I trust, that in major sheep raising areas where coyotes are numerous, confrontation is inevitable. Contrary to a widely held urban view, it is simply not true that coyote predation on sheep is an incidental matter, with an occasional rancher losing an occasional lamb. If an Easterner were to permit a flock of chickens to scrabble for any length of time in the brushy clearings of a cut-over woodland he would soon discover that the local foxes were taking a more than occasional interest in his flock. It stands to reason that the same principle holds true for coyotes and sheep. In sheep-raising areas there must be control, and I have already expressed my views on how, in an imperfect world, it should be handled.

But that still leaves most of the West, and most of the coyote population, undiscussed. In sheep-less areas no clear concept of coyote management exists. Ambivalence and contradictions abound. One cattleman swears by the coyote as a sort of built-in rodent control; but the cattleman next door had a calf killed a while back and wants the varmints exterminated. Still another makes more than a little pocket money doing his own fur trapping and hopes both the supply and the demand keep up; a fourth suspects the critters of killing off his deer or antelope. Meanwhile, one biologist finds that coyotes do, in fact, suppress jackrabbit populations, at least when they are on the rebound. Whereas another does not see that they have much effect one way or another. In the exurbs, Mrs. Pro waxes lyrical about the coyotes yodeling in the neighborhood, while her neighbor, Mrs. Con, mutters darkly about rabies and missing cats.

The wildlife managers themselves are schizophrenic. The coyote is too controversial, disorderly, and inedible to be treated as a game species although many hunters enjoy varmint calling. There is its fur which has lately become an exploitable resource and some people are actually favoring trapping seasons and quotas. There are the declining deer herds—and a strong inclination in some professional circles to lay the blame at the coyote's door. There are all those environmentalists and humanitarians denouncing the cruelty of leg-hold traps, upholding the transcendental values of God's dog, and citing examples of the coyote's cleverness and exemplary family life. There is the vague and hard-to-answer question of the coyote's role in the little understood ecological scheme of things. And there is the unstated doubt that, apart from ADC control efforts, a creature as prolific, ubiquitous, and contrary as the coyote is worth managing at all.

From this welter of conflicting possibilities, some ordering of priorities can be extracted. It is clear that the main objection to the coyote, apart from its taste for lamb and, occasionally, veal, is its supposedly adverse effect as a predator on valuable wildlife. On the other hand, its one tentative claim to practical usefulness, apart from its passing vogue as a fur bearer, is its capacity to devour economically harmful wildlife, that is, rabbits and rodents, in great numbers. It follows, therefore, that in most of its range the coyote's potential for both economic and ecological good or ill depends on its relationships with other wildlife species. So it would seem to be in the interests of everyone concerned, ranchers, hunters, and environmentalists, if the wildlife managers found out a lot more about those relationships than they know now.

Right now, they know hardly anything at all. There have been many studies of the coyote's eating habits; and it is a certified fact that the animal will eat almost anything it can get its furry paws on. During summers in south Texas, as much as eighty percent of its diet consists of wild fruits and bugs.[12] In the same area as well as many others it makes its living during part of the winter eating some of the hundreds of thousands of deer that hunters fatally cripple. In spring, depending on the locality, examination of coyote scats or stomachs may turn up the remains of an unnerving number of deer and antelope fawns, not to mention the occasional bobcat kitten or fox pup. But in most places, most of the time, the basic diet consists of the West's wonderful variety of rodents—rats, mice, voles, rock and ground squirrels, prairie dogs, cottontails, and of course that rangeland staff of life, the jackrabbit.

Yet knowing what coyotes eat is not at all the same as knowing the effects of their eating habits on prey species. On that more tricky subject, general ignorance is the rule. The conventional wisdom, once widely accepted by wildlife specialists, and still regarded as an article of faith by most environmentalists, was that coyotes, as well as other predators, culled the weak and old from prey species, thus keeping them within the bounds of their food supply, and preventing large scale deterioration of the habitat. Up to a point, this view still makes sense. In a world where

Incident at Eagle Ranch

few things are self-evident, it is self-evident that sick or orphaned
animals are likely targets for predation. And there have been a number
of speculative correlations made between declines in various predator
species, ranging from domestic cats in Indonesia to raptorial birds and
mountain lions in the American West, and subsequent explosions in
populations of mice, rats, deer, whatever.

Nevertheless, these correspondences are now being viewed by
many biologists with increasing skepticism. For example, although it
makes sense to assume that weakened animals are susceptible to predation, it hardly follows that predators subsist chiefly on them. The likelihood—supported by some studies—is that the majority of prey
animals, especially young prey animals, which end up in predator
stomachs are as healthy as the ones that get away. The law of random
chance, as well as of natural selection, is out there working too.

Hundreds of studies of coyote ecology and behavior have been
completed or are ongoing, some important, some not. Yet only one of
them, as best I can discover, has come up with some answers to the vital
question sof whether or not coyote predation actually controls rodent
and lagomorph species. Since most claims for the coyote's usefulness
depend on the assumption that it helps ranchers by reducing rodent
competition with lifestock for available forage, the question clamors for
some sort of answer.

The one notable study which addresses this issue is a long term
project in the Curlew Valley of northern Utah, where jackrabbit/coyote
population densities have been monitored for more than a decade.[13] So
far, the findings indicate that coyotes do influence the bust part of the
jackrabbit's boom-and-bust cycle. Even more strikingly, theoretical
analysis suggests that coyote predation, by itself, is enough to start those
cycles on their downward course. Which means, at least in northern
Utah, that the coyote population is not just dependent on the ups and
downs in the jackrabbit cycle; it directly influences them, perhaps
breaking (and braking) the boom, and almost certainly prolonging and
intensifying the bust. This, of course, is encouraging news for coyotes
and their human well-wishers. But research has a long way to go on this
important issue and it is disappointing that more has not been done.

If the coyote's practical usefulness is still an unsettled issue, there is
no question about the value of the game species on which it sometimes
dines. Evidence abounds that in some localities coyotes kill a great many
deer and antelope fawns. But it is one thing to know that much—all one

has to do is check scats and coyote stomachs—and another to know whether predation hurts the overall populations of big game ungulates or not. As long as deer and antelope were abundant in the West, there was no special urgency about getting the answers. Now, however, the game managers' interest in the issue has increased in inverse ratio to the rate at which the deer herds have declined.

In a contribution to a recently published text, *Big Game Ecology and Management,* G.E. Connolly, a biologist with Fish and Wildlife, expresses this changing attitude. He emphasizes that the use of predator control in game management is a worthwhile option, but that it must be predicated on a number of considerations: whether the game is more valuable than the predators that are to be controlled, whether predators are the primary factor in the depletion of game populations, etc. Most importantly, he emphasizes that a general control policy is inadvisable; every situation should be evaluated separately in terms of the best available data. Unfortunately, available data is scarce. In 1976, Frederick F. Knowlton, U.S. Fish and Wildlife's authority on coyotes, amusingly but not very reassuringly assessed the research situation by declaring that his "final, definitive and irrevocable judgment" on whether or not coyote predation affected mule deer populations was: "maybe."

About four relevant studies, varying in depth and quality, have been published since then.[14] At most, they might change Knowlton's irrevocable "maybe" to an irrevocable "sometimes." Research in Utah and Nevada indicated that fawn crops increased by as much as seventeen percent after coyotes were thinned out, but in a Nevada study area the same approach registered no gain at all. Of course, all sorts of contributory factors influence the intensity of coyote predation—the availability of alternate prey, weather conditions, the condition of the habitat (which was the determining factor in the Nevada case), and the effects of hunting, legal and otherwise.

For certain, coyotes are not *the* cause of the hard times on which the mule deer has fallen. After all, the deer herd was already increasing before the great coyote pogroms of the fifties and sixties got underway. Nevertheless, the coyote has probably not helped matters any. As Connolly, among others, points out, it is an inexorable law of predator-prey relationships that when the number of prey animals decreases, without a corresponding drop in the number of predators, the percentage of predation loss goes up.[15] If, for example, a pair of coyotes takes a dozen fawns from a deer herd numbering in the hundreds, no harm is done; but if they kill that many in a herd of fifty, the viability of the herd itself is threatened. It is the same principle which (apparently) enables coyotes to suppress jackrabbit populations most drastically when they are already on the decline.

There is another consideration which must be taken into account —one that the biologists themselves have not much stressed—namely, that coyote numbers are not tied to rises and falls in deer populations as they undoubtedly are to the jackrabbit cycle; with the result that their numbers, and consequently their impact as predators, may remain stable or even increase during periods when deer populations are going downhill. Under such circumstances, although coyotes do not initiate a drop in deer numbers, they no doubt hasten it along. However, if the initial causes of the decline in mule deer—which are probably man-related—are not overcome, a reduction in coyotes will at best provide only a temporary respite before the downward trend resumes.

Mule deer may not be the only "useful" species affected by coyote predation. It is widely believed by ranchers, hunters, and managers alike that in areas where they are not controlled they can have a devastating effect on antelope herds. Only two detailed studies of coyote predation on pronghorns have been published recently. In both cases, the verdict goes against the coyote. In west Texas, the antelope in an area where coyotes were controlled produced almost one-and-a-half times as many fawns as those in a nearby tract where predation was not inhibited.[16] In Oregon, efforts to establish a nucleus herd of antelope were unsuccessful until the local coyote population was reduced.[17]

The environmentalist, as well as the wildlife manager, must live with the fact that these curious imbalances are man-made and not, on a large scale, alterable. Two hundred years ago the pronghorn in its millions, along with the buffalo in its millions, occupied immense reaches of prairie grasslands. In that expanse, Indians and wolves, not coyotes, were the dominant predators, and the wolves evidently did not have much tolerance for their little cousins. It would have been nice if we had left some of all that, but we did not. Indian hunters, buffalo, wolves, and the prairies of native grasses are now gone. The coyote has inherited much of that changed space along with sheep, cattle, and jackrabbits. The antelope, though it has made an impressive comeback, is hemmed-in by fences over much of its range. Especially in those fenced-in areas, where the herds are localized and relatively small in numbers, it needs all the help it can get to thrive.[18] Under these artificial circumstances, even the most ardent enemy of predator control may eventually be forced to swallow some bitter medicine: fewer coyotes and more antelope, or the reverse? He cannot always have it both ways.

If there are a hundred questions, and a few answers, about the coyote's relationship to the wildlife that it preys upon—rodents, lagomorphs, deer, antelope—there is no doubt at all about its effect on fellow predators. Eagles may occasionally benefit from carrion provided by coyotes, but the terrestial predators are at a disadvantage. In particular, bobcats and foxes become underprivileged minorities. Coyotes are simply bigger, smarter, more adaptable and prolific in competing for prey; and quite often, the foxes and bobcats become prey themselves. The degree of conflict depends on the habitat. Bobcats can hold their own better in rocky country than on the open desert, but research studies, the testimony of trappers, and records of fur harvests confirm that wherever coyotes are reduced by control, local populations of bobcats, foxes—even badgers, skunks, and raccoons—increase.[19]

The preceding paragraphs, worrisome though they are, are not meant to blemish the reputation of the coyote among his many admirers. Overall, the coyote is probably no more responsible for reductions of deer or antelope, or bobcats for that matter, than for the decline in total numbers of sheep. Human activites such as strip mining, the proposed MX missle shuttle in Utah and Nevada, the new subdivisions and irrigation projects taking shape everywhere in the West, not to mention trapping and hunting, all account for the destruction of more "useful" wildlife than the coyote could dream of killing. But there is no getting around the fact that wherever prey populations are already declining, coyote predation can accelerate the downward trend. How much, and in how many areas of the West, is still anybody's guess.

Environmentalists have good reason to be annoyed that this state of ignorance continues. Four years after the mule deer conference at Logan, Utah, the answer to the question of whether coyotes significantly affect deer (or antelopes) is still Knowlton's "maybe."[20] If perhaps a dozen state, federal, and university specialists had agreed to work together back in 1976, they would probably have a better answer than that by now.

On the other hand, it is fair to note that the federal government has made some effort to keep track of trends in coyote populations during the last several years. The methodology, mentioned earlier, involves the use of scent stations at which visiting coyotes leave their footprints in circles of scraped sand. In theory, a periodic check of these sites will indicate whether coyotes in the area are increasing or decreasing. Critics of the system point out that the information provided by the scent post index does not always correlate with other known data. For instance, an intensive control effort in a particular area may be followed by an increase, rather than the expected decrease, in coyote visits to the local scent posts. Proponents of the index survey argue that this seeming inconsistency is probably explained by the flux and flow of transient populations of coyotes within a given district, which well may be the case. The important thing is that a methodology to measure population trends *is* being worked out, and it will presumably become more accurate in due course unless, as so often happens, the funding for the project is suddenly discontinued.

To return again to a favorite theme: even though an index of coyote population trends is valuable in itself, it would be a great deal more useful if it could be related to comparable indexes of other species, as well as to weather conditions, assorted human activities, etc. If, let us say, the professionals could demonstrate that the coyote population in a given county was holding stable or perhaps even increasing while the antelope or deer herd (or for that matter, the sheep herd) in the same locality was on an upward swing after a period of decline, they could negatively infer that coyotes had been an insignificant factor in suppressing those animals in the first place. Unless, of course, other indexes indicated an increase in alternate prey species, jackrabbits, for example. In that case the implication might be that the well-being of the ungulates in coyote country is more dependent on the abundance of jackrabbits than on the prevalence of the coyotes themselves, with the additional inference that coyotes need to be controlled, if at all, only during periods when the jacks are scarce. On the other hand, if both coyotes and jackrabbits are in good supply, but the ungulate herds are decreasing . . . Well, one gets the idea. It is a general idea, of course. The data, when not clearly negative, would have to be checked out. But as a starting point, inferences with some supportable evidence to back them up are a lot better than inferences with no evidence at all.

To sum up: Some progress is being made in one of the two areas of coyote research where information now matters most, namely, the general survey of population trends; but in the other area—an evalua-

Predators

tion of the coyote's impact on wild and domestic prey species—there is a dismaying lack of data. Limitations in cooperation and imagination, more than in funding, are the reason.

A survey of a representative number of sheep raisers throughout the West, backed by spot checks of claims of predation loss, would be more economically feasible and would produce a more accurate picture of what coyotes are really doing to sheep production than any alternate method that has been tried. As for the beneficial influence of the coyote in controlling rodent populations, and its harmful influence in depressing big game populations, a half dozen coordinated research projects are in order. In the not-so-long run, these studies should be tied-in with a more efficient means of monitoring population trends in various wildlife species—lest it become a managerial habit to control coyotes in deer or antelope areas whether the deer or antelope happen to be decreasing or not. Until the professionals get on with the job of acquiring this data, there can be no rational approach to managing the little prairie wolf in most of its range.

THE BOBCATS

In many ways, the shy, elusive *lynx rufus* is an ideal in-between sort of animal to use for illustrative purposes in discussing the management of predators. It is democratically representative, occurring at least locally in most areas of the United States. It is admirably adaptable in its eating habits and habitat requirements. Its numbers have declined in recent years because of trapping pressure, but it is far more numerous than the mountain lion or the eagle—although, in the West, much less abundant than the coyote. Because of its wide range and pervasive presence, it has the theoretical opportunity to prey upon livestock more insistently than either the lion or the eagle; yet in terms of actual troublemaking it cannot compare with the coyote. Less is known of its ecology than of the eagle's or the coyote's, but compared to the mountain lion it is an open book. Unlike the lion and the eagle, it does not require vast areas of wild space in order to survive; but it is more vulnerable than the coyote to the effects of control and commercial exploitation. At least in recent years, the value of its fur has made it probably the most valuable of the larger predators in economic terms; yet in spite of recent expressions of public concern about its future, it has never attached to its unobtrusive self those accretions of folklore, or esthetic and symbolic

Incident at Eagle Ranch

meaning, that illuminate and becloud human perceptions of the other Western predators.

The bobcat's knack for keeping a low profile has undoubtedly been the chief ingredient in its recipe for survival. Certainly it is a versatile creature, at home in deserts, swamps, and rugged mountains. But its birth-rate and population densities are pretty low, and for such a careful, stealthy little animal, it is astonishingly easy to trap. For generations, the ADC has been killing bobcats in its preventive control programs, though as we shall see, the cats have never ranked high as a serious threat to livestock even among the ranchers themselves. In general, the bobcat has gotten by simply because relatively few people were after its hide. Neither environmentalists nor the wildlife managers have paid it much attention.

In the last decade, however, all that has changed. The various international laws inhibiting trade in endangered feline species, notably the spotted cats, plus the fur dealers' insatiable search for new products, plus the public's growing demand for furs as the environmental consciousness of the sixties waned, all combined to make the little bobcat's not very durable pelt a suddenly hot item. In less than a decade, its value increased by three thousand percent. Skins that were selling in 1970 for ten dollars were bringing three and four hundred dollars in 1979. In the same period, there has been a comparable increase in the national take of bobcats. At the beginning of the seventies, the reported fur harvest was about 10,000 animals according to the International Association of Fish and Wildlife Agencies. During the 1976–77 season, it had reached either 72,000 or 106,358 animals, depending on whether one accepts the Association's figures or the more detailed estimate of the Endangered Species Scientific Authority (which, however, includes a small percentage of bobcats taken in control and hunting activities). In 1977–78 the Association and ESSA figures both showed a marked decline in the harvest, 69,245 and 83,500 respectively, even though prices continued to escalate.[21] Environmentalists see the downturn in the number of bobcats trapped as red-handed proof that bobcat populations are decreasing. A few wildlife managers admit as much; others argue that regulations have been tightened in some states, cutting down the take.

No one really knows the truth of it. At the instigation of Dr. Peter Escherich, staff zoologist with the Endangered Species Scientific Authority, biologists from all parts of the country finally gathered in Front Royal, Virginia, in the fall of 1979, for a "Bobcat Symposium." There, as at the Mule Deer Symposium a couple of years earlier, the conclusion that was reached was succinctly expressed by a participant: "My God," he said, "We're at a pretty primitive stage of management!" In fact, as he and his colleagues discovered, about forty of the states had no management programs at all. Still, as he more cheerfully added, "At least we've got people talking to each other." In wildlife management circles that is always welcome news.

Bobcats are way down on the priority lists of state wildlife agencies, although some research has gotten underway in recent years, largely in reaction to environmentalists' demands for facts. The ESSA may have been galvanized into co-sponsoring the symposium (with the National Wildlife Federation) by the prospect of a Defenders of Wildlife suit to stop the export of bobcat furs, a suit that has since been partially lost. At the meeting, representatives from many states—Wyoming was a notable exception—insisted that the increases of from fifty to two hundred percent in bobcat harvests were somehow not hurting their bobcat populations. For the most part, these optimistic reports were based on the fact that the fur harvest, although sharply reduced, had not yet taken a real nose dive. How the bobcat populations might be faring in comparison to previous decades was anyone's guess, since there were no useful statistics available. Matter of fact, some of the most solid statistics presented did not bear out the generally unworried verdict, at least not in the West. Utah's Fred Knowlton reported that between 1972 and 1978, bobcat visitations in the scent post index survey in Western states "declined systematically by fifty percent or more." And Douglas Crowe, a biologist with Wyoming Fish and Game, and one of the few scientists to have studied the bobcat in the West for an extended period, reported significant declines in the state's bobcat population.[22] Both of these men emphasized that their surveys have been concentrated in the areas most accessible to trappers, and that decreases in back country populations of bobcats are certain to be much less drastic. Indeed, Crowe's argument to this effect was so telling that it had much to do with convincing the judge to rule—with some important qualifications—against the Defenders of Wildlife suit.[23]

Actually there is considerable evidence from the field supporting the idea that bobcat populations are not what they used to be. State restrictions are not likely to account for all of the decline in the fur harvest during 1977–79, when the prices were at an all-time high. It is also true

Incident at Eagle Ranch

that the number of bobcats taken by ADC during the seventies dropped dramatically; although, as we shall see, there may be more to that development than meets the eye. In my own travels, I found many ranchers like Bob Ramsey setting traps for the easily caught animals, and veteran predator hunters like Roy McBride who opined that even in Texas, where bobcats are "thick as fleas," the populations had locally dropped by as much as fifty percent. Apart from all this incidental and inconclusive evidence, there is one irreducible fact that must be dealt with: given the bobcat's not very high reproductive rate and the ease with which it can be caught, it is ridiculous to suppose that it has not lost ground in those huge areas of the West (and elsewhere) where it is readily accessible to trappers.

In the short term, the species may be helped more by a recent downturn in fur prices (by twenty percent in 1979–80) than by any changes in management practices. In the long term, who knows? If the pressure lets up, the professionals may once again revert to the collective unconcern about the animal's status which characterized the period before the late seventies. Or they may keep on "talking to each other," learning as they go.

If the second alternative is followed, the bobcat could become the ideal excuse for discussing an important discrepancy, until now ignored by the professionals themselves, between two favorite managerial terms, optimum wildlife harvests and optimum wildlife populations, which are often used interchangeably. "How many do you want?" the managers ask us, with reference to any of various wildlife species. But in asking, they do not propose a distinction between how many we want to kill and how many we want alive.

The case of the bobcat neatly illustrates the need for this distinction. Like most wild creatures, the animal regulates its own populations according to territorial imperatives and food supply; it does not affect the ecology of its habitat in any long-lasting way, and it rarely makes a serious nuisance of itself. Yet during the decade in which the pressure on these animals has radically increased and during which trapping and hunting regulations have been liberal to non-existent, the professional managers have apparently never wondered if it might be a good idea to underharvest the species, given the increasing preference of most Americans for optimum populations of living wildlife, rather than to yield unconditionally to the rising demands for furs.

Predators

The standard managerial attitude is that most harvested animals would die anyway. "The kill," according to Duane Pursley, chairman of the Fur Resources Committee of the International Association of Fish and Wildlife Agencies, "improves animal health and welfare, cutting down starvation from overpopulation and disease."[24] Other professionals argue that even if overharvesting does occur, the species will recover when reduced limits are eventually imposed. The first of these assertions is demonstrably untrue. Of course there is a fearful mortality among the young of all wild species, bobcats included (as there still is, for that matter, among human offspring in most parts of the world). But once that critical stage is passed, a high percentage of individual animals, especially among the larger predator species, live out their prime under natural conditions.[25] In the case of the bobcat, for example, research studies have indicated that forty one percent of an untrapped population in Kansas was more than three years old, whereas only a wretched nineteen percent reached that age category in an "exploited" population in Wyoming.[26] It is not necessary to be overly sentimental about bobcats to find those Wyoming statistics intrinsically depressing. But subjectivity aside, one wonders how much that kind of exploitation can contribute to the Wyoming bobcats' "health and welfare."[27]

As for the recovery argument, it is true enough in the case of most adaptable species, as far as it goes. The trouble is that it rarely goes far enough. Again, consider the bobcat. Even though the price of its fur may continue to decline, chances are that it will remain a viable item in the marketplace as long as the foreign spotted cats persist in flirting with extinction. If the optimum harvest mentality has its unadaptable way, it is doubtful that the bobcat will ever recover—certainly not in the areas where it has been most seriously depleted—to optimum population levels—even supposing anyone had any idea what those optimum populations were before the current exploitation began.

Obviously the above is not intended as an argument against the concept of harvesting; it *is* meant to question the way the concept is applied. In practice, the present system does not merely remove the surplus, not even in the case of a terrifically managed species like the mule deer, much less the bobcat. It depends mainly on reductions in the harvests to warn, belatedly, of declines in total populations. That approach should be superseded by a new one: Not "what population is required to maintain the maximum yield?" but "What yield is allowable to maintain the maximum population?" It is a matter of emphasis, really; but

Incident at Eagle Ranch

the emphasis is all important. What might have happened, for example, if wildlife management officials had reacted more swiftly in placing limits on the sudden boom in bobcat furs before environmentalists reacted for them; if they had begun shortening seasons sooner, giving themselves a chance to decide what the optimum population of bobcats ought to be; if they had even done the unthinkable and recommended rather than opposed a temporary ban on the export of bobcat furs? What harm would they have done? What trade agreements would be injured by their caution? What merchant furrier would drown in sighs? What fashionable lady's tears would overflow? What part-time trapper would add himself to the welfare bill?

On the other hand, how much widespread support and respect might they have earned by going slowly? How much better off might the furriers be if more limited harvesting had perhaps protracted the demand of bobcat fur instead of accelerating fashion's cycle of boom and bust? Most important of all, how much more "optimum" would the bobcat population now be if it had not been subjected to this sudden drastic pressure?

"We can keep this [trapping] up indefinitely," says Duane Pursley, "as long as the animal population keeps up." That is true enough in the case of muskrat and nutria. But in the case of bobcats, and species like them, how does Mr. Pursley know that the animal's population *is* keeping up? Until it *stops* keeping up? There is always a distinct lag between the time any commercial species, especially a secretive animal like the bobcat, begins to lose ground and the time when the drop is reflected in harvest figures. Since that is the case, how well does the somewhat stale concept of "maximum harvest" actually square with the more enlightened concept of "optimum population?" The answer is, not at all. Only when the age structure of "exploited" bobcat populations reveals that a lot more than a fifth of them are three years of age or older, despite ongoing harvests, can the professionals maintain that they are managing those populations well. Only then will their environmentalist constituents, who theoretically have as much right to that wildlife resource as trappers and furriers and ladies of fashion, be assured that the health and welfare of the bobcat is being satisfactorily maintained. Obviously, a reasonable balance between optimum harvest and optimum population cannot always be achieved. But in an age when the number of live, healthy animals living in the wild is becoming a more important value than the number of dead ones extracted from it, the managers should be

Predators

prepared to err on the side of a less-than-maximum-harvest whenever they are in doubt. And if they had a better idea of how many bobcats they were managing, they would err less.

One additional, less general comment on the issue of bobcat management: as already noted, the take of bobcats in ADC control operations has plunged during the seventies from more than five thousand killed in 1972–73 to about twelve hundred killed in 1976–77.[28] There are three available explanations for the drop. One is that the ADC, without officially changing its policy, has relaxed its attitude towards bobcats. Yet during my explorations of the ADC in Texas and New Mexico, I detected no such change in attitude—preventive control was still very much in effect. Even so, the two states reflected the overall decline in the number of bobcats reportedly killed by ADC trappers; in both New Mexico and Texas, the take dropped by about sixty percent between 1976 and 1978.[29]

Another more likely possibility, favored by environmentalists, is that the reduction in ADC's harvest of bobcats reflects the excessive pressure brought to bear on the species by fur trappers. There are fewer bobcats around for the ADC to catch.

But a third explanation also deserves consideration. The reader may remember that Jerry Heintzelman, the government witness in the eagle trial, admitted that he and his confederate, the convicted eagle-killer, Andrew Allen, often took off on aerial hunts at government expense during which they gunned-down bobcats and then sold the pelts illegally. Heintzelman later told me that he knew of other trappers similarly occupied. In New Mexico, Vernon Cunningham also mentioned a couple of cases that had been turned over to the enforcement division for investigation. During my own travels, I interviewed several knowledgeable people who simply took it for granted that some ADC trappers trafficked in illegal bobcat furs. If that is the case, no one should be surprised. ADC trappers are poorly paid. A single bobcat's skin can be worth more than they make in a week. And opportunities for both trapping the animals and selling their hides under the table are easy to come by. Some ADC personnel must find this clandestine activity awfully hard to resist.

The ADC trappers' illicit sideline is not likely to have a measurable impact on bobcat populations. Indeed, compared to recent fur harvests, the ADC's entire take of the animals, reported and otherwise, is a drop in the bucket. But ADC's vulnerability to the kind of bad publicity it received when Andrew Allen was convicted ought to give the agency one more excuse for doing what it should have done some time ago, namely, get out of the bobcat business altogether.

During my conversations with ranchers, I noticed that the bobcat scarcely figured in their complaints about predators. There is good reason for this. Even in areas where bobcats are permanent residents in sheep pastures they do not usually cause trouble. Most of the research studies already mentioned in connection with coyote and eagle predation report little if any bobcat predation. In questionnaire surveys, ranchers list the bobcat as even less bothersome than the eagle wherever the two species coexist, and both, of course, trail far behind the coyote in the unpopularity polls. Indeed, the bobcat is so lightly built, so poorly designed to tackle any sizeable prey animal, that a lamb is usually safe from it by the time it is a few weeks old. This is not to say that an adult bobcat does not occasionally make a real nuisance of itself. However, such animals can be easily caught by the sheepmen themselves if they want to make the effort. Bobcats never do get the hang of traps.

The bobcat's low rating as a sheep-killer, plus the very real possibility of skullduggery on the part of some government trappers, should be reason enough for the ADC to quit its one-sided relationship with this reclusive little beast. Even corrective control is not justified, much less the kind of preventive killing that still inexcusably goes on. If the ADC did back off, most sheepmen would not even notice since only a few count on the government to control bobcats for them anyway. On the other hand, the change in policy would eliminate a possible source of scandal; it would make life a little easier for a couple of thousand bobcats; and it might even improve the ADC's somewhat battered public image.

The bobcat is often linked with the coyote—as varmint, rodent catcher, and recently as fur bearer. But that connection should not apply in management. The bobcat is by far the more vulnerable species. The fact that there are still a lot of them left in relatively inaccessible areas does not quite justify the relaxed attitude of most of the wildlife people at the recent Bobcat Symposium. Too often, the professionals classify the majority of wildlife species in a not-to-worry limbo where, as long as they are still in reasonable supply. they are said to be doing fine. One explanation is that the managers have enough to worry about dealing with animals like the still plentiful, heavily exploited mule deer or the all-but-extinct black-footed ferret, without trying to cope with the in-betweens. Fair enough. But I also suspect their attitude has something to do with the old-line managers' traditional alliances and the unstated assumption that wildlife does not pay for itself until it is dead. Dead bobcats have now become, in a modest way, a cash crop; that, plus the environmentalists' expressions of concern, has earned the animals a bit of attention. But many professionals still do not quite grasp the real basis of general concern about the species' status. It is not good enough for them to decide (rightly) that the bobcat is still in fair supply—even though their decision may resolve (probably wrongly) the issue of whether its fur should be shipped overseas. The point they need to register is that the bobcat, whether threatened or not, deserves to exist at maximum population levels throughout its range, including those areas where it is most accessible to optimum harvesting.

Having unburdened myself of all that theory, I should add that the bobcat's uninvited popularity with the furriers may work to its advantage in the long run. During the last year or two all but a handful of counties in the U.S. have stopped paying bounties on its brindled hide; some research projects, including telemetry studies, are underway; and several states (notably Idaho and Montana) in which the animal has always been up for grabs have now limited trapping seasons. Better late, as they say, than too late.

MOUNTAIN LIONS

No large wild animal in the West is more difficult to get to know than the mountain lion. Much of its ecology and behavior is still a mystery, and it is an oft-repeated truth that even people who spend a lifetime hunting it hardly ever glimpse it without benefit of a pack of hounds. And yet it is not some sort of wraith. When researchers track cats fitted with telemetric collars they sometimes come upon them indolently stretched out along a high rocky shelf, looking for all the world like backyard tabbies, so oblivious to any human presence that their visitors could clip them with a stone. It is their relative scarcity, their inability to stay put, above all the vertical immensity of their necessary habitat, that accounts, more than their wariness, for their being hard to see.

The same circumstances also explain why the lion has managed to survive in the remote high country of the West against terrific odds. Because of its lamentable tendency to kill sheep (sometimes in batches), as well as the occasional calf, it has been pursued implacably by ranchers,

Incident at Eagle Ranch

government hunters, and sportsmen, in all seasons, with extermination the only perceivable management goal, right up until the last dozen years. Its reputation as a deer killer has not helped either, with the result that even in the national parks it was not safe until the fifties. In films it was repeatedly presented—sometimes still is—as possessing an insatiable lust for the tender flesh of young pioneer children and thoroughbred horses. The belief that lions have a peculiar predilection for horse meat is still very popular even in areas where both horses and lions coexist. Several Westerners I met in my travels had a repertoire of stories, usually received at second or third hand, about ranchers whose horses had returned to the stable with long wounds on their backs. For all I know some of the tales are true. During earlier generations, tens of thousands of feral horses roamed the West and it seems likely that lions became used to them as another type of ungulate prey. Horses must certainly have looked easier to tackle than bulky cows. However, confirmed kills of horses and colts by mountain lions—the sort of loss that ranchers would be most likely to report—are surprisingly scant according to ADC records—seven kills in 1975, and only one or two in each year thereafter. But then, there are not as many horses around as there used to be either.

In spite of the bad press it has received, or maybe because of it, the mountain lion works a strong magic in the imaginations of many Americans. It is the ultimate loner, a renegade presence in the wildest canyons and the wildest mountains, the sign of everything that is remote from us, everything that we have not spoiled.

During the last ten years the big cat has been left more alone than at any time in the preceding century. Although neither lion nor man has reason to feel smug or secure about this detente, there is some indication that in much (though not all) of its remaining range it is better off than it has been in a long time, which is saying a lot for a large carnivore roaming an increasingly crowded world. Roy McBride ascribes this altered state of affairs to the diminishing numbers of sheep on the Western range. Don Balsar at Denver Wildlife Research Center believes the shift in attitude is due to the lion's new status as a game animal. Frank Smith, a lion hunter in western New Mexico, attributes it to the dying-out of the old time lion hunters and the failure of their sons, like the sons of the sheepmen, to follow in their fathers' footsteps. Harley Shaw, a research biologist with Arizona Game and Fish, thinks the lion is more adaptable than most people realize. Environmental leaders believe that more tolerant public attitudes towards predators have a lot to do with the change. All of them are right. There is even another reason: the influx of the New People. If they have been displacing the lion in some of its last remaining habitat, it is also true that they have been displacing anti-lion ranchers in the legislatures of Western states, a circumstance that has worked in the lion's favor.

In Texas, which supports twenty percent of the remaining sheep in the West, and where lions and sheep still encounter each other to their mutual misfortune, lions continue to be varmints that can be killed by anyone, anytime. Yet even here the pressure on lions has let up now that sheep have almost cleared-out of the Trans Pecos. In other Western states, the reports indicate that lion populations have remained stable or are moderately increasing. State officials are only guessing, of course; but in this case the fault is not theirs. There is no convenient way of keeping tabs of an animal that may cover 50 or 100 miles in a couple of nights.

Nevertheless a few important telemetry studies have been conducted in the last decade—Dr. Maurice Hornocker's remarkable study in the wilds of Idaho was the breakthrough project in this respect[30]—which for the first time have provided some insights into the mountain lion's secretive private life. There is considerable evidence, for example, that under wilderness conditions the creatures are territorial, and that their ranges may not be as vast as was once supposed. Frank Smith, the "lion man" with New Mexico's Department of Game and Fish, found that territorial males in the Burro Mountains had ranges of a mere 100–150 miles, and the females about half that. The cats in Hornocker's winter studies were even more stay-at-home, a fact most obviously explained by the geography of his study area, a mountain valley system, and the heavy winter concentrations of prey animals. In both cases, the females were more socially tolerant than the males, with ranges that often overlapped. (On one day, Smith found three of his collared female lions within a mile of each other.) The movements of these settled adults must, however, be weighed against the distribution of prey animals as well as the peregrinations of surplus males and evicted younger animals which are obliged to wander, often for hundreds of miles and for considerable periods of time, until they are eventually killed or find a territory of their own. (One of Smith's young New Mexico females moved to Arizona when her mother eventually drove her off.)

Incident at Eagle Ranch

It should be noted that Roy McBride disputes this territorial concept, at least in his part of the world. During a telemetry study in the Big Bend area, his collared lions travelled widely. "If they have territories," he says, "they're too large to defend. Even the National Park isn't big enough." Topography, he admits, may have something to do with it, since "lion habitat in west Texas is in long, narrow strings of mountains, whereas if it was a circular situation, if they could move in all directions, it might be different." Harley Shaw's collared lions in central Arizona seem unable to make up their minds whether they are territorial or not. Three adult females did have established ranges, averaging fifty square miles, but the rest of the population, including all the toms, wandered at will. Shaw suspects that both human hunting pressure and the wide distribution of prey may account for some of the inconsistencies.[31]

The studies also suggest that population densities of lions can be somewhat greater than had hitherto been thought. Still, the animals are nowhere abundant in any ordinary sense of the word. Hornocker's large, almost inaccessible wilderness contained only about a dozen lions among its permanent residents. In New Mexico's Burro Mountains, Smith estimated that an area of 1,500 square miles supported not more than twenty or twenty-five of the big cats. Shaw figured nine or ten of the animals in a 150 square mile tract of Arizona rangeland, but only thirty in the 1,200 square miles of the Kaibab Plateau north of the Grand Canyon.

Along with the degree of human predation, and the matter of territoriality, a critical factor in the relative abundance of lions is the abundance of their prey. In that Idaho valley, elk and deer were numerous; in Smith's study area, the deer herd "was not at a high density, but stable." But as we have seen, the mule deer herd in most areas of the West has not been very stable of late, and, along with coyotes, lions are increasingly blamed for the decline. Mountain lions, particularly the males, are incredibly powerful animals. (I remember my amazement when I examined two recently killed specimens in a commercial freezer locker at Alpine; they were far more powerful than the soft, loose-skinned creatures one sees in zoos.) They will eat anything from jack-rabbits to porcupines if they have to, but their preferred prey are deer and, when available, elk. Unlike the foolish sheep, these animals do not mill about and wait to be slaughtered; the best available evidence suggests that lions get by very comfortably killing one deer every week or ten days. Hunting deer and elk is arduous and dangerous work; and for all their restlessness, mountain lions, like all cats, adore leisure. They return frequently to their old kills before they seriously try for a new one. "All the same," Frank Smith points out, "you figure what a dozen lions eat in a year, at a rate of one deer a week. That's a lot of deer."[32] In the Trans Pecos, Roy McBride, like that other Texas lion hunter, Jim Espy, Jr., believes that the recent increase in lions and the decrease in mule deer is more than a coincidence. Most ominous of all are the published opinions of Harley Shaw which suggest strongly that lions are holding down deer populations on one study area in Arizona.[33] It should be noted, however, that during recent telephone conversations with him, Shaw sounded more cautious about his current research findings on the Kaibab. There, because of heavy hunting pressure and the scarcity of deer, the number of cats has been halved in the last three years; yet the deer herd, which he had suspected the lions of depressing, refuses to "erupt" on schedule. Shaw now has his eye on coyotes.

In contrast to the above theories, Hornocker's ten-year study—the only one to measure the effects of lion predation—confirms that lions are not limiting populations of mule deer in a wilderness environment in central Idaho. Indeed, his address on that subject at the Logan mule deer conference has a logic that is hard to argue.[34] He points out that the mule deer and lion evolved together in the West and "both have survived, often flourished" in a "straightline" predator-prey relationship. Mule deer populations began their present decline during a period when lions were still being hunted as vermin; and the decline has continued both in areas where mountain lions are and are not present. Finally, Western white-tailed deer have not experienced a similar decline in area where they are preyed upon by lions. Hornocker does concede that "lion predation, like any other predation, *may* (his italics) under certain conditions act to limit prey populations. When a prey population is lowered drastically by whatever factor, then any depressing factor gains more importance. In this situation, predator control may help, but usually doesn't solve the problem."

Granting Hornocker's premise about "any" predation having a limiting effect on prey populations, one can only wonder whether some of his listening colleagues may have drawn the obvious inference that the most effective way to cut down on predation would be to further reduce the bag limits and seasons on mule deer rather than to increase them on lions. In any case, Hornocker's concluding remarks have got to be, in terms of enlightened wildlife management, the penultimate word: "Lion predation, like any other predation, normally is ineffective in drastically reducing numbers of prey species when the prey species has suitable habitat . . . but if suitable habitat is not available for a prey species, then no amount of predator control will bring about flourishing populations of that prey species."

Hornocker's word is not quite the final one because, like so many of his colleagues, he seems unwilling to state the ultimate managerial fact that man, alone among predators, is perfectly capable of drastically reducing prey species—which in his case includes all wildlife species— whether there is enough suitable habitat available or not. The mountain lion, like the eagle and even the bobcat, is a useful reminder of this simple truth. The great cat has never lacked suitable habitat, yet during the last century his numbers have certainly been drastically reduced. The reason, of course, is that a new symbiosis has envolved, quite un- naturally, in which this natural predator has become the prey.

If the deer herd continues to decline, there may be other problems ahead for the mountain lion which concern its relationship with cattle, not deer. Wherever I travelled in the lion country of the West, I was struck by the fact that none of the cattlemen I spoke with regarded the animal as a threat. Some of them actually liked the idea of "having a lion or two around." One rancher, having discovered a dead calf that might have been killed by a lion (it apparently was not; at any rate, there was no recurrence) was mainly worried that neighboring sheepmen would get wind of the incident and relish his discomfiture. Frank Smith, who is responsible for all lion control work in the southern half of New Mex- ico, gets an average of fifteen confirmed complaints about lions killing cattle, almost always calves, a year. His figures are not inclusive, how- ever, since in the southwestern part of the state a few ranchers still keep dogs and take care of their own problems. Even so, the average annual loss of cattle to lions in southern New Mexico probably never exceeds thirty or forty head.

As for west Texas, Roy McBride reports that the expanding lion population and the omnipresent cattle industry are coexisting thus far without friction. In Western states further north, the likelihood of con- flict is even less, since calving usually occurs when the cattle are not in the high lion country.

The exception to the general truce is Arizona, a state that has al- ways had more than its share of lion troubles, in part because it has more than its share of the intransigently rough rimrock country that lions love. The fact that in Arizona cattle management practices differ from those in most other parts of the West seems to have a lot to do with the problem, too. So does the decline of the Arizona deer herd.[35] At any rate, on the two ranches encompassed by Shaw's study area northwest of Prescott, the local cats were taking somewhere between three and nine percent of the calf crop (they virtually never attack grown cows). In the Kaibab, where deer are somewhat more abundant, and cattle and lions scarce, predation on calves does not amount to much.

But a few lion men speculate that Arizona's problems might eventually be catching. If deer numbers continue their decline, the lions may be tempted to substitute veal for venison, and the habit, once established, might be hard to break. Still, there is no evidence to suggest that this has happened yet.

Wildlife agencies in at least seven of the Western states believe that they each have between one and two thousand lions within their borders. California's generous guess is twenty-four hundred; and there is an ongoing battle in that state about whether the lion should remain on the protected list or not. Arizona's claim that it has fifteen hundred to two thousand, thereby justifying the sale of a lot of cheap hunting licenses and a year long hunting season, has miffed some environmentalists. They point out that the state's estimate of its deer population does not match up with its lion estimate—given the tentative evidence that mountain lions exist in a ratio of one lion to about four or five hundred deer.[36]

The truth is that no one can be certain how many lions survive in the West; the figures are guessing games with no evidence except two or three studies like Hornocker's and Shaw's to back them up. The one certainty is that the total population can not be very large, given what is known of the animal's habits and ecology. Vagrant cats show up from time to time in many areas of the West, but enormous tracts of singularly rough terrain, adequately furnished with deer and devoid of domestic sheep, are required to maintain a safe breeding stock of lions. Even some wilderness areas, Yellowstone National Park for example, do not meet the animal's specifications very well for one obscure feline reason or another. After figuring in all the ifs-and-buts, what one ends up with is the suspicion that there may be a breeding population of between six and ten thousand adult mountain lions in the Western states, plus an

Incident at Eagle Ranch

annual average of about one fourth that many footloose, often ill-starred offspring.

In spite of all the vagaries, these splendid beasts can be managed. There is still enough of the necessary habitat available, most of it on public lands, to ensure that a goodly number of the big cats make it into the next century, provided they are not literally hounded to death or trapped within constricting networks of roads. More studies of the sort undertaken by Hornocker are needed to determine the influence of lions on prey populations, but such projects require a lot of time and money. Meanwhile, by working closely with resident lion hunters and state conservation officers, the professionals should eventually be able to map out pretty accurately those areas of a state that constitute optimum lion country. In some of these areas, the lion ought to be left alone. At the very least, the idea of "rotating" hunting areas—a proposal already suggested by some biologists—should be put into effect.

In addition, wildlife managers might consider deliberate campaigns to popularize no-kill lion hunts. Most articulate hunters, discussing the mystique of their sport, repeatedly emphasize that the thrill is in the chase, not the kill. Out in the boondocks, of course, millions of their fellows, hell-bent on getting their buck, would privately disagree. But even those who normally stress the blood in bloodsports are apt to admit that in the case of a lion hunt the kill has got to be an anticlimax. There is bound to be something disconcerting, even repellent, about shooting any animal that is hopelessly cornered in a tree or on a ledge. And this feeling must intensify when the cornered animal is both uncommon and uncommonly beautiful, and has given one a lordly run into the bargain. Whereas—how brave, how sanely dashing!—if one were to whip out a camera instead of a gun, and pose (quite safely) within two or three yards of your snarling quarry while the professional hunter filmed the scene. Just once, the neighbors might stay awake while you showed home movies. Moreover, the professional hound men would prosper. And the lion, not incidentally, would keep its skin—which does not make a very handsome or long-lasting trophy anyway. On the other hand, if a hunter must have the hide, he should pay three or four times as much for a license as the sportsman who lets the lion go. He should also admit to himself the real reason why he likes to hunt.

The idea behind such strategems is to ensure that the lion will not only survive into the indefinite future, but that at least in some parts of its range it will be permitted to exist under reasonably natural conditions at those optimum population densities about which I have already said enough in the preceding discussion of the bobcat.

"Which is neater," Roy McBride asked me, "the lion or the deer?" The lion, of course. It is the more majestic, less common, more uncompromising of the two animals. Furthermore, in a human scale of values we are obliged to admit that the predator is always neater than its prey if we are to justify our cheerful certainty that *we* are the neatest thing on earth. That consideration should enter powerfully into managerial decisions concerning the influence of lions on the West's deer herds. Among the factors that the biologist Guy Connolly weighed while discussing predator control as a tool in game management was the important question of whether the wildlife to be saved was more valuable than the predator to be destroyed. In that balance, any mountain lion is worth as many deer as it must kill to stay alive.

13. The New People

THE PRECEDING CHAPTERS have been concerned with the ranchers, trappers, and managers who deal directly with predators in one way or another. But frequently in these pages another much larger category of Western humanity has made its presence known. I refer to the New People, a classification that is meant to be as encompassing as it sounds. It includes almost everybody who lives in the West, not only that majority of the region's adult citizens who were born somewhere else, but also those longtime natives whose occupations and lifestyles have become more or less indistinguishable from those of their countrymen in other parts of the United States. Though reluctant to narrow that definition further, I might grant that the most representative of the New People are the ones who have consciously sought out what was most western in the West as a desirable background to their lives, the people who have been stirred by the region's stupendous geography, its half-kept promise of a world that is free and unspoiled. These are the people who, like Willard Phillips of Leakey, move further and further out into the almost infinite suburbs of Western cities and then finally colonize the hinterlands beyond, restlessly trying to get nearer to the reality of the "real" West, which, like Ulysses' untravel'd world, fades forever as they move.

The New People are as unclassifiable in their relation to wildlife, including predators, as in other respects. Some are card carrying environmentalists, or conscientious sportsmen; some wear fun furs, and others—occasionally the same ones—oppose leg-hold traps; some search for a wilderness experience; some would not recognize a coyote if they saw one; some take pot shots at antelope in the shale fields where they work. In the present context, however, these differences are less significant than the one characteristic which all New People share, namely their superabundant presence which inevitably displaces everything that is traditionally western about the West.

Among the displaced, the predators are preeminent. The people who celebrate the survival of coyotes in the suburbs of Denver or Los Angeles somewhat miss the point. Such animals, living in expressway interchanges and on hillsides too steep for building, where they devour garbage and car-hit dogs, are the hangers-on, the Ishis of a once diverse wildlife community. Only a couple of generations ago they occupied hundreds of thousands of square miles of the Rockies' front range, the Pacific northwest, the hills and desert valleys of Southern California. Nor is it just the New People's cities that have consumed their space. To provide housing, jobs, food and water, transportation and recreation for new people, the New People must grid the fertile valleys with irrigation projects, drain and dam the dying rivers, strip mine the high plains, run interstates across the deserts, ram logging roads deeper into the mountains, always building more retirement villages, ski slopes, and trailer camps along the way. Meaning no harm, they expel the last lion or grizzly from the clear-cut mountain top, or extinguish obscure tortoises and kit foxes while exercising their ORVs.

The changes imposed by the New People have happened with stunning swiftness—within the lifetime of every middle-aged American. Nowhere, not ever, has that kind of epic tranformation occurred in so short a time. The remarkable thing is that there is anything left to the West-with-a-capital-"W" at all. There *is* a lot left, of course. The West is the only large area of the nation that has retained much of its regional identity. The East, Middle West, even the South in recent years, have become part of the Great American Everywhere; only their accents, climates and topographies remain their own; for the rest, you must wait in line at parks, museums, or dollar-a-tour plantations to savour what once made them distinctive. In the West this has not altogether happened. There are still cowboys and the lone prairie; there are still Stinebaughs, Aulds, and McBrides. The purple mountain's majesty continues to rise above the subdivided plain in spite of all the opulence and the

Incident at Eagle Ranch

limitless tawdriness that prevails. The West of Muir's transcendental prose and the hokey cowboy songs is still out there, about half of it anyway, still open, wild, and free.

The question is, how much of that remaining half do the New People want to keep for the next century? Where will they stop, in the less affluent but perhaps more rapacious decades that are coming up, before most of the Western inheritance is replaced by alternating vistas of Las Vegas and Bangladesh?

The answer is that if they want to keep any of it, they will have to stop pretty soon. No doubt a section pasture looks like wide open space to a retiree from Hoboken or Cincinnati, and a glimpse of a few mule deer constitutes a lot of wildlife viewing. But the West with a capital "W" depends on its immensity for its definition, on the kinds of every-day distance in which you can travel for fifty miles even on a four lane highway without seeing a house. And on the kind of consciousness that goes with the perception of that kind of space. When it comes to pre-serving *that,* the parks and preserves can never be enough, simply be-cause they are parks and preserves. Nor are the National Forests and BLM lands a protective guarantee. The New People are gradually win-ning their battle to make these vast areas truly multi-purpose, but their victory is not without its ironies. The high country hosts somewhat fewer sheep and cattle than in days of yore, but the roar of the chain saw and the bulldozer is heard more than ever, trying to keep up with the New People's demand for housing and fuel. And recreation: Millions of New People now hunt, camp, hike, trap, rev-up their dune buggies and land rovers, feel exalted (or a little bored) in places where nary a soul could be seen twenty years ago. There is even a "sagebrush rebel-lion" in the works, which, if it succeeds, would permit the states to claim —and exploit—much of the public lands for themselves.

Some of the New People worry about these developments, this over-winning and over-running of the West. They join organizations and write letters. Other New People seem consciously to relish the tra-ditional West's demise: the poachers, the litterers and vandals, the honky-tonk builders who hasten it along with an almost pathological aptitude for making squalid everything they touch. But most of the New People are too preoccupied with the payments on their split levels and Winnebagos, and with generally trying to keep up, to be actively concerned about the taming of the West. And yet they want it to survive; they feel fleetingly guilty when they become aware of its domestication.

The New People

The New People, like all of us, are intrinsically self-interested. We deplore the better throw-away bottle and the more energetic snow-mobile even as we use them; we praise the wilderness while demanding that Glacier Park officials kill off the grizzly bears so we can hike in it more safely; we pity bobcats when they are trapped but not when we build ranchettes above their dens. It is obvious—even if there had not been the will-o-the-wisp sixties to remind us—that our good intentions and consciousness–raisings are not enough. The New People must sub-mit to laws that protect the West not just from ranchers, trappers, hunt-ers, and the like, but from themselves. It is a curious but by no means unique paradox that we must now pass more laws and restrictions if we are to save ourselves and the West from becoming less free: laws that restrict the expansion of Western cities and second home develop-ments; that discourage further immigration; that encourage ranch-ers not to sell their lands; that impose special use taxes for the "non-consuming" use of wildlife; that more strictly ration water and fuel; that keep off-the-road vehicles on the roads; that stop the prolifera-tion of back roads and ski resorts.

Some of these management programs are already underway, though they are more often the result of inflation and sudden shortages than of enlightened planning. Meanwhile human population continues to expand; and out in Montana, Colorado, and Wyoming the strip miners are only just beginning to get to work. It is of course conceivable that economic austerity may in some ways complement efforts to save what is intrinsically western about the West. It is equally possible that the New People, their lives less comfortable and secure, their lifestyles more escapist, may end by crowding the Western inheritance right off the map.

What is certain is that the New People do not want that to happen. Surveys and polls demonstrate that by quite overwhelming majorities they wish to defend what they destroy—the natural environment, wild-life, the West—even at the expense of housing, jobs, development proj-ects. Not their own jobs, housing, projects, naturally. But still, the collective wish is there, waiting to be shown the way.

The fate of the predators has eveything to do with that wish. Like the West itself, it will not be too hard to save these difficult crea-tures in relict bits and pieces: a scattering of bobcats and, certainly, coyotes; a few eagles and lions in wilderness areas here and there. And we will always be able to see them in zoos—which is where, it will be remembered, Dan Auld's secretary said they belonged. The question that really matters is, how many of them do we want to save? Or to put it another way, how much of the West do we want to keep?

If there is anything that we have learned about the Western predators, it is that their economic importance does not amount to much. They do not kill nearly the amount of livestock they are blamed for killing; although the coyote, at least, does kill a lot of sheep. Their value as rodent controllers will be debated for a long time to come. Their importance as fur bearers is already evanescing. Their potential as game species will always be limited either because they are too uncommon (lions) or too varminty (coyotes) or secretive (bobcats) or off-limits (eagles) to lend themselves to that kind of use. If we are to decide we want them as a pervasive rather than a token presence in the West, it will probably have to be because we want to save the West itself.

The connection between the predators and the West is not a symbolic one. Truth is, all the talk about coyotes or eagles being incarnations of the Old West has never gotten them or us very far. Thousands of ranch and suburban living rooms are furnished with reproductions of yodeling coyotes, while the real article is being trapped, shot, or otherwise displaced on the other side of the picture window. Besides, it has always struck me as unfair to saddle wild animals with abstract significance; they have it tough enough just being themselves. A rose is a rose is a rose; and an eagle is an eagle. For that matter, the same is true of that West we have been speaking of. It is a place in time, not an abstract idea or a state of mind. It does not exist, even metaphysically, in Western parking lots and shopping centers.

No, the connection between the West and the predators is as literal as it can be. The West is wherever they are. You can have some of the predators, of course, without the West—the bobcat and the coyote have ranges in the East—but you can not have the West without them. It may survive only in broken hints and patches—where the coyote can scrounge a living from overgrazed pastures and ranchette garbage dumps. Or it may exist pure and unalloyed—the solid gold coin—wherever the eagle and the lion have their place. But the West must have something of them or it has nothing of itself.

The predators are our test. Finally, the issue is not so much how we should manage them—as how we should manage ourselves.

The New People

Epilogue

TIME HAS DEALT VARIOUSLY with the principals in the eagle case. For two of the three defendants in the San Antonio trial, Buddy Pape and Lanny Leinweber, life has not notably changed. Both ranchers retain their former positions in the community, Leinweber a county commissioner, Pape a member of the school board. Yet for Pape, at least, the jury's verdict took some getting used to. Months later, when calling on acquaintances in Uvalde, he would only half jokingly ask if it was all right for "an old outlaw" like himself to come visiting.

Andrew Allen, the third defendant, has been more seriously affected by the outcome of the case. His conviction meant the end of his job as a government trapper. For a time he worked for South Texas Helicopter Service while awaiting trial for perjuring his grand jury testimony during the course of the investigation. However, that trial never took place. At the last minute, Al Barnes, one-time president of the helicopter service, pled himself and the company guilty to complicity in the killing of eagles, but only on the condition that no further action would be taken against Allen or anyone else involved in the case. Allen now works as a cowboy and trapper on a west Texas ranch. He has never said who the "big ones" were who got away.

Allen's boss at ADC, Milton Caroline, has also become a casualty of the eagle case. When Bill Nelson, the regional director of U.S. Fish and Wildlife, offered him a choice of accepting a transfer to the Albuquerque office or retiring, he chose the latter. He now heads a private organization in Texas dedicated to the control of predators.

The judge who presided at the trial, John Wood, Jr. has been murdered, apparently in retaliation for the stiff sentences he was wont to mete out to underworld figures in Texas. His killers are still at large.

As for Al Barnes, after admitting his involvement in the eagle killings, he left Uvalde for a year. Recently, however, he has returned and opened up shop again as an employee of the Uvalde Helicopter Service. Local advertisements announce his availability for aerial cattle round-ups and predator hunts. He avoided the necessity of acquiring a new aerial hunting permit by the simple expedient of going into business with someone who already had one. His former partner, Clay Hunt, had no trouble at all reacquiring a permit. However, Hunt's legal efforts to regain the helicopter that Stinebaugh confiscated, along with its rig and truck, have been unsuccessful. Among Hunt's current enterprises is a newly formed company, CHR (Clay Hunt Ranchers) Helicopter Service.

Barnes' and Hunt's one-time employee, later mortal enemy, Jerry Heintzelman, has been grounded for good. In the months following the trial, the federal government found him a job as a pilot with a helicopter company in Colorado. By then, however, the young man's never-very-stable life was in greater disarray than ever. He was estranged from his common-law wife, dissatisfied with the prospect of the new job, discontent with himself. He returned to Uvalde in connection with a legal matter (unrelated to the eagle case), and in that unhappily familiar setting tried to kill himself with the help of a .243 rifle. An invalid now, he lives a secluded life in south Texas in the care of his mother.

Young Cecil Zimmerman also leads a reclusive life. He has taken the place of his murdered father as manager of the Eagle Ranch. Partly because he makes himself scarce when federal agents try to contact him, but chiefly through government inertia, he has never been paid the reward in the eagle case, which, in lieu of his father, he should rightfully receive. His mother, Alyn, was sentenced to a ten-year term for the killing of Alfred Zimmerman, but her attorney has won her a new trial and she is presently at liberty.

In Leakey the political season has changed. During the last election, Real County's citizens ended the long reign of Judge Sansom. According to one observer, "Folks used to be afraid that if they didn't vote for him their roads wouldn't get graded." But during the course of the eagle investigation and the confrontation with Sheriff John Elliott, this perception changed. "People saw he wasn't invulnerable. They started realizing they were tired of him." Sansom is retired now and reportedly in poor health. But he may take some grim satisfaction in the thought that his political rival, Elliott, has not fared much better than he. The sheriff, never cut out to be a controversial figure, has called it quits. The polarized political climate in Leakey had begun to affect his family's morale as well as his own. Moreover, he concluded that he would never win a liveable wage as long as men like Lanny Leinweber controlled the Commissioners' Court. In 1979 he resigned and moved back to east Texas, to Victoria, where he works for an oil company.

Victoria is also the home of the federal agent, Joe Matlock. Although he is retired, the regional office of U.S. Fish and Wildlife sometimes asks him to take part in an investigation as an advisor. Most recently he has been assisting his friend and partner, Jim Stinebaugh, in a case that has brought the two men back to a familiar scene, the Auld Ranch. One of the captive eagles that Sam Crowe was using in his live-trapping operations on the ranch had been killed by a person or persons unknown while it was helplessly staked out in a pasture as a decoy. So far there are no leads. But it is mildly ironic that Buddy Pape, eager that the live-trapping should continue, is now cooperating with the same investigators who, not so long ago, were investigating him.

Jim Stinebaugh is glad to be back in Texas. He has been promoted to the rank of senior resident agent, and he and his family live on the out-skirts of Fort Worth. His main complaint is that the federal government, in its efforts to conserve one natural resource, oil, has drastically cut his gasoline allowance and his mobility, thereby limiting his efforts on behalf of that other resource, wildlife, which he is committed to protect.

Meanwhile, the ADC's live-trapping and deportation project in Real County continues. If it goes on for a few more years, it may accomplish what even aerial gunning could not achieve: the elimination of perhaps the largest annual wintering concentration of golden eagles in the world. Dan Auld is said to be very pleased.

Notes

CHAPTER 2

[1] This account of the investigation is based chiefly on extended interviews with Jim Stinebaugh, Joe Matlock, and Jerry Heintzelman, and on the testimony at the San Antonio trial. However, much incidental information was acquired, and a great deal of cross-checking accomplished, by means of interviews with almost all the principals involved in the case.

CHAPTER 4

[1] *Golden Eagle Population Studies,* Wildlife Research Center *Annual Progress Reports,* U.S. Fish and Wildlife Service (Denver, 1978), p. 40.

[2] *Predator Damage in the West: A Study of Coyote Management Alternatives* U.S. Fish and Wildlife Service, December 1978, pp. 5–6.

[3] Cf. for example, V. W. Lehmann, *Forgotten Legions: Sheep in the Rio Grande Plain of Texas,* El Paso: Texas Western Press, 1969.

[4] C. Kerry Gee, Richard S. Magleby, Warren R. Bailey, Russell L. Gum, and Louise M. Arthur, *Sheep and Lamb Losses to Predators and other Causes in the Western United States,* Economic Research Service, Agricultural Economic Report No. 369, Washington, D.C., U.S. Department of Agriculture, April 1977.

[5] Volbey W. Howard, Jr., and Richard E. Shaw, *Preliminary Assessment of Predator Damage to the Sheep Industry in Southeastern New Mexico, Agricultural Experiment Station, Research Report No. 356,* New Mexico State University, February 1978.

[6] Gee, et al. *Sheep and Lamb Losses,* p. 20. According to figures collected from the Statistical Reporting Services for several Western states over periods of from three to nine years, the variation in reported predator losses almost never exceeds more than one percent from one year to the next, and is usually much less. Also note Howard and Shaw's *Preliminary Assessment,* cited above, in which there is virtually no change in claimed predator losses between 1972 and 1973.

[7] *Predator Damage,* p. 26.

[8] Donald G. DeLorenzo and V. W. Howard, Jr., *Evaluation of Sheep Losses on a Range Lambing Operation in Southeastern New Mexico,* Agricultural Experiment Station, Research Report No. 341, New Mexico State University, June 1977.

[9] M. Shelton, "Predator Losses in One Flock of Sheep and Goats," *National Woolgrower,* 62 (1972); D. A. Klebenow and K. McAdoo, "Predation On Domestic Sheep in Northwestern Nevada," *Journal of Range Management,* 29 (1976); R. D. Nass, "Mortality Associated With Sheep Operations In Idaho," *Journal of Range Management,* 30 (1977); J. R. Tigner and G. E. Larson, "Sheep Losses on Selected Ranches in Southern Wyoming," *Journal of Range Management* 30 (1977)

[10] For a useful summary of these surveys, see *Predator Damage,* pp. 20–30.

CHAPTER 5

[1] Walter R. Spofford, "The Golden Eagle in the Trans-Pecos and Edwards Plateau of Texas," Audubon Conservation Report No. 1, November 1964.

[2] *Predator Damage in the West,* p. 76.

[3] Robert D. Roughton and Mark W. Sweeny, coords., *Indices of Predator Abundance in the Western United States, 1978,* U.S. Fish and Wildlife Service, Wildlife Research Center, U.S. Government Printing Office, #679-496/413, 1979, p. 5.

[4] Fred A. Glover and Leo Heugly, "Final Report: Golden Eagle Ecology In West Texas," submitted to the National Audubon Society by the Colorado Cooperative Wildlife Research Unit. Fort Collins: Colorado State University, October 1970.

[5] Glover, "Final Report," pp. 37–38.

CHAPTER 6

[1] *Predator Damage,* p. 13, 17.

[2] Department of Agriculture figures on the number of producers were not com-

piled during the 1940s. The figure suggested is the minimum to be inferred from later recorded rations of producers to numbers of sheep.

[3] *Predator Damage,* p. 19.

[4] Concerning selective predation in coyotes, cf. E. A. Gluesing, "Sheep Behavior and Vulnerability to Coyote Predation," PhD Diss., Utah State University, 1977. Also, *Predator Damage,* p. 75.

[5] Cf. C. Kerry Gee, Richard S. Magleby, Darwin B. Nielsen, Delwin M. Stevens, *Factors in the Decline of the Western Sheep Industry,* U.S. Department of Agriculture, Research Service Economic Report No. 397 (1977). Former sheep raisers in the four western states of Colorado, Texas, Utah, and Wyoming, particularly the latter two, ranked predation losses as a major reason for going out of business, along with the labor shortage. Yet a personal survey in Utah (D. B. Nielson and D. Curle, *Predator Costs to Utah's Range Sheep Industry,* Logan: Utah State University, 1970) indicated that four fifths of the ranchers there sustained a 2.5 percent or less predator loss. Gee et al. (p. 19) correctly conclude that "in many instances it was hard or impossible to disentangle the causal factors," and "General discouragement caused by the situation and outlook . . . along with increased attractiveness of other occupations and enterprises" caused the exodus from sheep raising.

CHAPTER 7

[1] *Review of the Animal Damage Control Program.* U.S. Department of the Interior, Office of Audit and Investigation, November 1978.

CHAPTER 8

[1] Frederic H. Wagner, "Coyotes and Sheep: Some Thoughts on Ecology, Economics, and Ethics" Forty-Fourth Honor Lecture delivered at Utah State University, Logan, Utah, Winter 1972, p. 46.

[2] Cf., for example, Francoise Leydet's chapter, "Days of Whines and Poisons," in *The Coyote, Defiant Songdog of the West,* San Francisco: Chronicle Books, 1977.

[3] *Predator Damage,* p. 78

[4] *ADC Environmental Impact Statement,* p. 97.

[5] Ibid.

[6] Fred S. Guthery and Samuel L. Beasom, "Effectiveness and Selectivity of Neck Snares in Predator Control," *Journal of Wildlife Management,* 42 (April 1978): 457–59.

[7] Aerial transect surveys of wintering eagles in Kilgo's district have averaged between six and nine birds per one hundred square miles during the last six years. *Golden Eagle Population Studies*, p. 40.

CHAPTER 10

[1] *Predator Damage*, pp. 3–4, for a useful review of previous policies.

[2] News release, Connor/Deerhorn. Department of the Interior, Nov 9, 1979.

[3] *Review of the Animal Damage Control Program*. U.S. Department of the Interior; Office of Audit & Investigation. November 1978.

[4] *ADC Final Environmental Impact Statement*, U.S. Fish and Wildlife Service, FES 79 25, 1979.

[5] *Predator Damage*.

[6] In its *Environmental Impact Statement*, ADC notes (p. 153): "field experience and unpublished research data indicate that more than fifty percent of the local coyote populations may be responsible for the losses." ADC does not further identify its sources; and with the possible exception of the report mentioned in the following note I have been unable to discover what they are. However, there *is* some published data indicating that high population densities of coyotes do sometimes coexist with sheep and goats without correspondingly high predation. See S. L. Beasom and D. R. Gober, "The Effectiveness of the M-44 as a Tool to Curtail Sheep Losses to Predation," U.S. Environmental Protection Agency Annual Report (1975). Also note G. E. Connolly et. al., "Sheep Killing Behavior of Captive Coyotes," *Journal of Wildlife Management*, 40 (1976): pp. 400–7. In this study, thirty percent of a group of captive wild coyotes refused to kill sheep even after several days without food.

[7] Surprisingly, no published data is available on this vital question (See the excellent discussion in Wagner's *Coyotes and Sheep*, pp. 36–37). However, a single unpublished study (Lee Stream, "Final Report to Washington State Game Department on 1976 Lithium Chloride Coyote Aversion Experiment in Whitman County, Washington," Washington State Department of Game, Region 1) does seem to demonstrate, as an aside to the main purpose of the study, that during a seven-year period on a Washington ranch there was an inverse relationship between the number of sheep lost to predators and the number of predators (coyotes) killed.

[8] ADC's EIS glossary definition clearly suggests that corrective control applies only to offending animals. However, a notably different definition crops up when corrective control is mentioned as a component under "Alternatives to the proposed Program," p. 153. Here, "corrective measures"

means that "all individuals of the offending species in the general loss area are targeted until the losses cease." Since sporadic predation occurs on much of the sheep range in the west, there can be no distinction between that kind of "corrective" measure and preventive control.

[9] *ADC Environmental Impact Statement*, p. 37.

[10] As this book goes to press Secretary Andrus announced that he had agreed to relax his ban on 1080 research enough to permit further experimentation at Texas A&M University.

[11] ADC's EIS, p. 37.

CHAPTER 11

[1] In this essay on wildlife management, terms such as "the professionals," and "wildlife managers" are used in a general sense that includes not only state and federal managers at the decision–making levels, but, where appropriate, government researchers, academic consultants and others who influence and direct wildlife-management decisions on policy and funding.

[2] For transcripts of the papers presented, see Gar W. Workman and Jessop B. Low, eds., *Mule Deer Decline in the West: A Symposium*, Utah State University Collge of Natural Resources, April 1976.

[3] In some areas, the decrease has occurred where hunting pressure was light.

[4] Daniel A. Poole, "An Overview of Big Game Management" (p. 68), and R. B. Gill, "Mule Deer Management Myths and the Mule Deer Population Decline" (p. 100), in Workman *Mule Deer Decline*.

[5] Cf. The commentary by L. L. Eberhardt in "Appraising Variability in Population Studies," *Journal of Wildlife Management*, 42 (April 1978): 209.

CHAPTER 12

[1] *Golden Eagle Population Studies*, p. 40.

[2] As reported by Bart O'Gara in "Sheep Depredation by Golden Eagles in Montana," *Proceedings of the Eighth Vertebrate Pest Conference*, W. E. Howard and R. E. Marsh, eds., Sacramento, California, 1978.

[3] "Sheep Losses on Selected Ranches in Southern Wyoming."

[4] "Sheep Depredation by Golden Eagles," p. 206.

[5] Ibid., p. 210.

[6] Carter Niemeyer, "Montana Golden Eagle Removal and Translocation Project" in *Final Reports, 1977 and 1978*, (submitted to U.S. Fish and

Wildlife Service Billings, Montana Area Office.) p. 21 (1977) and pp. 8–9 (1978).

[7] Personal communication.

[8] *Golden Eagle Management: A Conceptual Plan,* U.S. Fish and Wildlife Service September 1978 (unpublished) p. 5.

[9] For example, Dr. Philip L. Schultz, noted for his efforts to rehabilitate wounded golden eagles, believes that in Northern New Mexico "our breeding population has declined by perhaps twenty five percent . . . these impressions are based on personal observations, and the reported observations of [biologists] Tom Smylie and John Hubbard" (Personal communication).

[10] The Denver Wildlife Research Center is currently undertaking a study of the effects of strip mining on breeding pairs of golden eagles. Worthwhile as this effort is, note that, all too typically, the study was funded because strip mining is now a "hot" environmental issue, not because of the project's relative importance in an overall plan to study and manage the golden eagle. In terms of priorities, there can be little doubt that the hundreds of thousands of dollars appropriated would be better used to more accurately determine the overall status of the species.

[11] In its *Environmental Impact Statement,* ADC offhandedly notes that its efforts to investigate "some common parameters" for areas in which predation loss is high have been hampered because "this research, begun in 1978, was slowed by a shortage of high loss study areas" (p. 37). Efforts to test the toxic collar in Montana have been held up for the same reason. And in a recent telephone conversation, Don Balsar at the Denver Wildlife Research Center also informed me that his sources indicate there has been a general decline in predation losses in the West during 1979–80. Many observers believe this development is tied to an upswing in the jackrabbit population cycle, as well as pressure from the fur industry.

[12] Lamar Windberg, biologist, U.S. Fish and Wildlife Research Station, Laredo, Texas. (Personal communication)

[13] L. C. Stoddart, "Population Dynamics, Movement and Home Range of Black-tailed Jackrabbits in Curlew Valley, Northern Utah." U.S. Energy Reserve Development Administration, Annual Progress Report, Contract No. E (11-1)-1329, 1977.

[14] W. L. Robinette, N. V. Hancock and D. A. Jones, "The Oak Creek Mule Deer Herd in Utah," Utah Division of Wildlife Publication No. 77–15, (1977); D. D. Austin, P. J. Urness, and M. L. Wolfe, "The Influence of Predator Control on Two Adjacent Wintering Deer Herds," *Great Basin Naturalist,* 37 (1977); R. J. Smith and A. LeCount, "Factors Affecting Survival of

Mule Deer Fawns," Arizona Game and Fish Department, Federal Aid Project, Final Report W-78-R, Work Plan 2, Job 4. (1976); N. J. Papez, "The Ruby-Butte Deer Herd," Nevada Department of Fish and Game, Biology Bulletin No. 5, (1976).

[15] Cf. *Predator Damage,* p. 83.

[16] F. F. Knowlton, C. J. Carley, R. T. McBride, "Mammal Damage Control Research—Predators and Predator-Prey," Denver Wildlife Research Center, Annual Progress Report, 1970–71, Work Unit DF-103.9, U.S. Fish and Wildlife Service (1971).

[17] "Antelope Respond to Coyote Control," Oregon State Game Commission Bulletin, 27 (1972).

[18] In areas where antelope are abundant and widely distributed, e.g., Wyoming and Montana, coyote predation is not a serious problem.

[19] Cf. the summary of evidence in *Predator Damage,* pp. 78–79.

[20] According to one current theory, coyotes may cause problems in some areas not because they prey on mule deer but because, ironically, they distribute a muscular parasite, *Sarcocystis,* through their feces, which severely debilitates mule deer.

[21] Peter Escherich, staff zoologist, ESSA. (Personal communication)

[22] As reported by Fred F. Knowlton, U.S. Fish and Wildlife Service staff biologist. (Personal communication)

[23] Defenders takes a more optimistic view, arguing, with much justice, that it compelled the Department of Interior to take stock of the situation. By winning a ban on exports from several states shipping bobcat pelts overseas, Defenders reduced overall exports significantly.

[24] As reported in *Louisiana Out-Of-Doors; The Official Publication of the Louisiana Wildlife Federation,* 7 (April 1979): p. 2.

[25] The closer a species is to the top of the food chain, the more true the principle, providing there is no significant human predation. The rule even operates among some quite humble species. For example, squirrels in an unhunted population have been found to be more numerous and long-lived than those in an exploited population in comparable habitat.

[26] S. H. Fritts and J. A. Sealander, "Reproductive Biology and Population Characteristics of Bobcats in Arkansas," *Journal of Mammalogy,* 59 (1978): pp. 418–22; D. M. Crowe, "A Model for Exploited Bobcat Populations in Wyoming," *Journal of Wildlife Management,* 39 (1975): 408–15.

[27] For all its renowned cleverness, the coyote does not fare much better than the bobcat in terms of life expectancy. Several studies of coyote survival indicate that almost fifty percent of the adult coyote population dies annually. Eighty five or ninety percent of these deaths are caused by man—even in areas (such as Jackson Hole, Wyoming), where one would expect the human toll to be relatively light. Immature coyotes have an even higher death rate, about fifty seven percent. *ADC Environmental Impact Statement,* p. 69.

[28] *ADC Environmental Impact Statement,* p. 112.

[29] Vernon Cunningham. (Personal correspondence)

[30] Maurice G. Hornocker, "Winter Territoriality in Mountain Lions," *Journal of Wildlife Management,* 33 (July 1969): 457–64.

[31] Harley G. Shaw, Arizona Game and Fish Department. (Personal communication)

[32] Frank Smith, New Mexico Department of Game and Fish. (Personal communication)

[33] Harley Shaw, "Impact of Mountain Lion on Mule Deer and Cattle in Northwestern Arizona," Proceedings of the 1975 Predator Symposium, ed. Robert L. Phillips and Charles Jonkel, Montana Forest and Conservation Experiment Station (Missoula, Mont.: University of Montana, 1977): pp. 17–32.

[34] Hornocker, *Mule Deer Decine,* p. 109.

[35] Harley Shaw theorizes that, because Arizona's peak calving season occurs in mid-March, when the deer herd is at its lowest ebb, mountain lions are able to sustain a high population by preying on calves during a period of the year when some lions might otherwise starve. In the Kaibab, however, where deer are more common and cattle are relatively scarce, the number of lions is tied to the population cycles of the deer.

[36] Harley Shaw claims (personal communication) that the higher figure is "far-fetched but legitimate" based on the extrapolated densities of lion populations in his central Arizona study area.

Selected Bibliography

ADC Final Environmental Impact Statement. U.S. Fish and Wildlife Service, FES 74 25, June 1979.

Austin, D. D., P. J. Urness, and M. L. Wolfe. "The Influence of Predator Control on Two Adjacent Wintering Deer Herds." *Great Basin Naturalist 37*, 1 (1977).

Balsar, Donald S. "An Overview of Predator-Livestock Problems with Emphasis on Livestock Losses." In *Transactions of the Thirty-Ninth North American Wildlife and Natural Resources Conference.* Washington, D.C.: Wildlife Management Institute.

Beasom, S. L., and D. R. Gober. *The Effectiveness of the M-44 as a Tool to Curtail Sheep Losses to Predation.* U.S. Environmental Protection Agency Annual Report, 1975.

Bekoff, Marc, ed. *Coyotes: Biology, Behavior, and Management.* New York: Academic Press, 1978.

Bolen, Eric G. "Eagles and Sheep: A Viewpoint." *Journal of Range Management* 28 (January 1975): 11–17.

Brawley, Kimber C. *Domestic Sheep Mortality During and After Tests of Several Predator Control Methods.* Master's thesis, University of Montana, 1977.

Brown, William G., and David Fawcett. *Estimated Economic Losses by Oregon Sheep Growers Associated with Restricted Predator Control, 1965–1972: Some Preliminary Findings.* Oregon State University Agricultural Experiment Station, Special Report 418, Sept. 1974.

Connolly, G. E. "Predators and Predator Control." In *Big Game of North America: Ecology and Management,* ed. J. Schmidt and D. L. Gilbert. Washington, D.C.: Wildlife Management Institute, 1978.

Connolly, G. E., R. M. Timm, W. M. Longhurst. "Sheep Killing Behavior of Captive Coyotes." *Journal of Wildlife Management* 40 (1976): 400–7.

Connolly, Guy E., and William M. Longhurst. *The Effects of Control on Coyote Populations: A Simulation Model.* Division of Agricultural Sciences Bulletin 1872. Berkeley: University of California, August 1975.

Conover, Michael R., Joseph G. Francik, and Don E. Miller. "Aversive Conditioning in Coyotes: A Reply." *Journal of Wildlife Management* 43 (1979): 210–211.

Crowe, D. M. "A Model for Exploited Bobcat Populations in Wyoming." *Journal of Wildlife Management* 39 (1975): 408–15.

DeLorenzo, Donald G., and V. W. Howard, Jr. *Evaluation of Sheep Losses on a Range Lambing Operation in Southeastern New Mexico.* Agricultural Experiment Station, Research Report No. 341. Las Cruces: New Mexico State University, June 1977.

Dobie, J. Frank. *The Voice of the Coyote.* Lincoln: University of Nebraska Press, 1961.

Eberhardt, L. L. "Appraising Variability in Population Studies." *Journal of Wildlife Management* 42 (1978): 209.

Faulkner, E. K., and James R. Tigner. *Birth Rates of Sheep from Range Operations in Carbon County, Wyoming.* Agricultural Extension Service Report No. B-643. Laramie: University of Wyoming, May 1977.

Foster, H. Alan, and Robin E. Crisler. *Evaluation of Golden Eagle Predation on Domestic Sheep, Oregon, 1979.* Report to Oregon ADC Office, Fish and Wildlife Service.

Fritts, S. H., and J. A. Sealander. "Reproductive Biology and Population Characteristics of Bobcats on Arkansas." *Journal of Mammalogy* 59 (1978): 418–22.

Gee, C. Kerry, Richard S. Magleby, Darwin B. Nielson, and Delwin M. Stevens. *Factors in the Decline of the Western Sheep Industry.* U.S. Department of Agriculture, Research Service Economic Report No. 377, 1977.

Gee, C. Kerry, Richard S. Magleby, Warren R. Bailey, Russell L. Gum, and Louise M. Arthur. *Sheep and Lamb Losses to Predators and Other Causes in the Western United States.* U.S. Department of Agriculture, Agricultural Economic Report No. 369. Washington, D.C.: 1977.

Glover, Fred A., and Leo Heugly. *Final Report: Golden Eagle Ecology in West Texas*. Submitted to the National Audubon Society, Colorado Cooperative Wildlife Research Unit. Colorado State University, October, 1970.

Gluesing. E. A. *Sheep Behavior and Vulnerability to Coyote Predation*. PhD diss., Utah State University, 1977.

Gum, Russell L., Louise M. Arthur, and Richard S. Magleby. *Coyote Control: A Simulation Evaluation of Alternative Strategies*. U.S. Department of Agriculture, Economics, Statistics, and Cooperative Service, Report No. 408. Washington, D.C.: 1978.

Gustavson, Carl R. "An Experimental Evaluation of Aversive Conditioning for Controlling Coyote Predation: A Critique." *Journal of Wildlife Management,* 43 (1979): 208–10.

Guthery, Fred S., and Samuel L. Beasom. "Effectiveness and Selectivity of Neck Snares in Predator Control," *Journal of Wildlife Management,* 42 (1978): 457–59.

Henderson, F. Robert, Edward K. Boggess, and Bennett A. Brown. *Understanding the Coyote*. Cooperative Extension Service Report No. C-578. Kansas State University, August 1977.

Hornocker, Maurice. "Winter Territoriality in Mountain Lions." *Journal of Wildlife Management* 33 (1969): 457–64.

Howard, Volby W., and Richard E. Shaw. *Preliminary Assessment of Predator Damage to the Sheep Industry in Southeastern New Mexico*. Agricultural Experiment Station, Research Report No. 356. Las Cruces: New Mexico State University, Feb. 1978.

Howard, W. E., and R. E. Marsh, eds. *Sheep Depredation by Golden Eagles in Montana*. Proceedings of the Eighth Vertebrate Pest Conference. Sacramento, Calif., 1978.

Kalmbach, E. R., Ralph H. Imler, and Lee W. Arnold. *The American Eagles and Their Economic Status, 64*. U.S. Department of the Interior, Fish and Wildlife Service, Report No. GPO 856-224. N.d.

Klebenow, D. A., and K. McAdoo. "Predation on Domestic Sheep in Northwestern Nevada." *Journal of Range Management* 29, 2 (1976).

Knowlton, F. F., ed. *Coyote Research Newsletter,* Vols. 2, 3. Denver Wildlife Research Center, January 1975.

Knowlton, F. F., C. J. Carley, and R. T. McBride. *Mammal Damage Control Research—Predators and Predator-Prey*. U.S. Fish and Wildlife Service, Denver Wildlife Research Center, Annual Progress Report, 1970–71, Work Unit DF-103.9, 1971.

Lehmann, V. W. *Forgotten Legions: Sheep in the Rio Grande Plain of Texas.* El Paso: Texas Western Press, 1969.

Lehner, P. N., R. Krumm, and A. T. Cringan. "Tests of Olfactory Repellents for Coyotes and Dogs." *Journal of Wildlife Management* 40 (1976): 145–50.

Leydet, Francois. "Days of Whines and Poisons." In *The Coyote: Defiant Songdog of the West,* San Francisco: Chronicle Books, 1977.

Linhart, S. B., and W. B. Robinson. "Some Relative Carnivore Densities in Areas Under Sustained Coyote Control." *Journal of Mammalogy* 53 (1972): 880–884.

Louisiana Out-of-Doors: The Official Publication of the Louisiana Wildlife Federation 7 (1979): 2.

Nass, R. V. "Mortality Associated with Sheep Operations in Idaho." *Journal of Range Management* 30 (1977).

Nielson, D. B., and D. Curle. *Predator Costs to Utah's Range Sheep Industry.* Logan, Utah: Utah State University, 1970.

Niemeyer, Carter. *Montana Golden Eagle Removal and Translocation Project.* U.S. Fish and Wildlife Service, Area Office, Billings, Montana: Final Reports, 1977, 1978.

Oregon State Game Commission. *Antelope Respond to Coyote Control.* Bulletin 27 (1972)

Munoz, John R. *Causes of Sheep Mortality at the Cook Ranch, Florence, Montana, 1975–76.* Master's thesis, University of Montana, 1977.

Papez, N. J. *The Ruby-Butte Deer Herd.* Nevada Department of Fish and Game, Biology Bulletin No. 5, 1976.

Robinette, W. L., N. V. Hancock, and D. A. Jones. *The Oak Creek Mule Deer Herd in Utah.* Utah Division Wildlife Publication No. 77–15, 1977.

Roughton, Robert D., and Mark W. Sweeny, coords. *Indices of Predator Abundance in the Western United States, 1978.* U.S. Fish and Wildlife Service, Wildlife Research Center. U.S. Government Printing Office No. 679-496/413, 1979.

Russell, Kenneth R. "The Mountain Lion." In *Big Game of North America: Ecology and Management.* Ed. J. Schmidt and D. L. Gilbert. Washington, D.C.: Wildlife Management Institute, 1978.

Shaw, Harley. "Impact of Mountain Lion on Mule Deer and Cattle in Northwestern Arizona." In *Proceedings of the 1975 Predator Symposium,* ed.

Robert L. Phillips and Charles Jonkel. Montana Forest and Conservation Experiment Station. Missoula: University of Montana, 1977.

Shelton, M. "Predator Losses in One Flock of Sheep and Goats," *National Woolgrower* 62 (1972).

Smith, R. J., and A. LeCount. *Factors Affecting Survival of Mule Deer Fawns.* Arizona Game and Fish Department Final Report, Federal Aid Project W-78-R, Work Plan 2, Job, 4, 1976.

Spofford, Walter K. *The Golden Eagle in the Trans-Pecos and Edwards Plateau of Texas.* Audubon Conservation Report No. 1. November 1964.

Stoddard, L. C. *Population Dynamics, Movement and Home Range of Black-Tailed Jackrabbits in Curlew Valley, Northern Utah.* U.S. Energy Reserve Development Administration Annual Progress Report, Contract No. E (11-1)-1329, 1977.

Stream, Lee. *Final Report to Washington State Game Department on 1976 Lithium Chloride Coyote Aversion Experiment in Whitman County, Washington.* Washington State Department of Game, Region 1.

Stuby, Richard G., Edwin H. Carpenter, and Louise M. Arthur. *Public Attitudes Toward Coyote Control.* U.S. Department of Agriculture, Economics, Statistics and Cooperatives Service Report No. ESCS-54. Washington, D.C.: May 1979.

Tigner, J. R., and G. E. Larson. "Sheep Losses on Selected Ranches in Southern Wyoming." *Journal of Range Management* 30 (1977).

U.S. Fish and Wildlife Service. *Golden Eagle Population Studies.* Wildlife Research Center Annual Progress Reports. Denver: 1978.

U.S. Fish and Wildlife Service. *Predator Damage in the West: A Study of Coyote Management Alternatives.* December 1978.

U.S. Fish and Wildlife Service. *A Review of Predator Research Conducted by the U.S. Fish and Wildlife Service.* Denver Wildlife Research Center, May 1977.

Wagner, Frederic H., "Coyotes and Sheep: Some Thoughts on Ecology, Economics, and Ethics." Forty-Fourth Honor Lecture delivered at Utah State University, Winter 1972.

Wagner, Frederic H., and L. Charles Stoddard. "The Influence of Jackrabbit Density on Black-Tailed Jackrabbit Populations in Utah." *Journal of Wildlife Management* 36 (1972): 329–342.

290   Workman, Gar W., and Jessop B. Low, eds. *Mule Deer Decline in the West: A Symposium.* Logan: Utah State University College of Natural Resources April 1976.

Young, S. P., and H. H. T. Jackson. *The Clever Coyote.* Harrisburg, Penn.: The Stackpole Co., 1951.

Incident at Eagle Ranch

Index

*Incident at Eagle
Ranch* was designed
by Jon Goodchild. The
text was photo-composed in
Sabon by Community Type & Design,
Fairfax, California. The book was printed and
bound by Haddon Craftsmen, Scranton, Pennsylvania.